Expel the Pretender

Lauer Series in Rhetoric and Composition
Editors: Catherine Hobbs, Patricia Sullivan, Thomas Rickert, & Jennifer Bay

The Lauer Series in Rhetoric and Composition honors the contributions Janice Lauer has made to the emergence of Rhetoric and Composition as a disciplinary study. It publishes scholarship that carries on Professor Lauer's varied work in the history of written rhetoric, disciplinarity in composition studies, contemporary pedagogical theory, and written literacy theory and research.

Books in the Series

Expel the Pretender (Wiederhold, 2015)
First-Year Composition: From Theory to Practice (Coxwell-Teague & Lunsford, 2014)
Contingency, Immanence, and the Subject of Rhetoric (Richardson, 2013)
Rewriting Success in Rhetoric and Composition Careers (Goodburn, LeCourt, Leverenz, 2012)
Writing a Progressive Past: Women Teaching and Writing in the Progressive Era (Mastrangelo, 2012)
Greek Rhetoric Before Aristotle, 2e, Rev. and Exp. Ed. (Enos, 2012)
Rhetoric's Earthly Realm: Heidegger, Sophistry, and the Gorgian Kairos (Miller)
    *Winner of the Olson Award for Best Book in Rhetorical Theory 2011
Techne, from Neoclassicism to Postmodernism: Understanding Writing as a Useful, Teachable Art (Pender, 2011)
Walking and Talking Feminist Rhetorics: Landmark Essays and Controversies (Buchanan and Ryan, 2010)
Transforming English Studies: New Voices in an Emerging Genre (Ostergaard, Ludwig, and Nugent, 2009)
Ancient Non-Greek Rhetorics (Lipson and Binkley, 2009)
Roman Rhetoric: Revolution and the Greek Influence, Rev. and Exp Ed. (Enos, 2008)
Stories of Mentoring: Theory and Praxis (Eble and Gaillet, 2008)
Writers Without Borders: Writing and Teaching in Troubled Times (Bloom, 2008)
1977: A Cultural Moment in Composition (Henze, Selzer, and Sharer, 2008)
*The Promise and Perils of Writing Program Administration (*Enos and Borrowman, 2008)
Untenured Faculty as Writing Program Administrators: Institutional Practices and Politics, (Dew and Horning, 2007)
Networked Process: Dissolving Boundaries of Process and Post-Process (Foster, 2007)
Composing a Community: A History of Writing Across the Curriculum (McLeod and Soven, 2006)
Historical Studies of Writing Program Administration: Individuals, Communities, and the Formation of a Discipline (L'Eplattenier and Mastrangelo, 2004). Winner of the WPA Best Book Award for 2004–2005.
Rhetorics, Poetics, and Cultures: Refiguring College English Studies Exp. Ed. (Berlin, 2003)

EXPEL THE PRETENDER

Rhetoric Renounced and
the Politics of Style

Eve Wiederhold

Parlor Press
Anderson, South Carolina
www.parlorpress.com

Parlor Press LLC, Anderson, South Carolina, USA

© 2015 by Parlor Press
All rights reserved.
Printed in the United States of America

SAN: 254-8879

Library of Congress Cataloging-in-Publication Data

Wiederhold, Eve, 1961-
  Expel the pretender : rhetoric renounced and the politics of style / Eve Wiederhold.
      pages cm. -- (Lauer series in rhetoric and composition)
  Includes bibliographical references and index.
   ISBN 978-1-60235-562-0 (pbk. : acid-free paper) -- ISBN 978-1-60235-563-7 (hardcover : acid-free paper)
  1. English language--Political aspects--United States. 2. Persuasion (Rhetoric)--Political aspects--United States. 3. Mass media--United States--Language. 4. Freedom of speech--Social aspects. I. Title.
  PE2809.W54 2015
  306.44'0973--dc23
                      2015006817

1 2 3 4 5

Lauer Series in Rhetoric and Composition
Editors: Catherine Hobbs, Patricia Sullivan, Thomas Rickert, & Jennifer Bay

Cover design by Scott Warren.
Cover image by Lee Scott. From Unsplash. Used by Permission.
Printed on acid-free paper.

Parlor Press, LLC is an independent publisher of scholarly and trade titles in print and multimedia formats. This book is available in paper, cloth and eBook formats from Parlor Press on the World Wide Web at http://www.parlorpress.com or through online and brick-and-mortar bookstores. For submission information or to find out about Parlor Press publications, write to Parlor Press, 3015 Brackenberry Drive, Anderson, South Carolina, 29621, or email editor@parlorpress.com.

Contents

Acknowledgments   ix
Introduction   3

1 Authenticating the Liar   20
2 The Force of the Fit   75
3 The Politics of Ethos   136
4 Inhabiting the Call to Change   187
5 Conclusion: Passionate Linkages   234

Notes   247
Works Cited   265
Index   275
About the Author   283

*To my idiosyncratic and lovely family . . .
with a shout out to Mr. Ko*

Acknowledgments

Without the help of generous and thoughtful readers, this book would have remained stuck in the realm of fantasy. I am profoundly grateful to E. Shelley Reid and Deborah Kaplan, who wrestled with an early draft and did not declare it nonsense, but instead offered patient advice and generative feedback about how to focus and revise. Other generous colleagues who helped with editorial support and/or stimulating conversations include Robert Matz, Terry Zawicki, Tamara Harvey, Keith Clark, Stefan Wheelock, Barbara Gomperts, Richard Todd Stafford, Byron Hawk, Hephzibah Roskelley, Elizabeth Chiseri-Strater, Stephen Yarbrough, Nancy Myers, Wendy Sharer, Bruce Southard, Sara Littlejohn, Abby Arnold, and Brandy Grabow. I am especially grateful to Laura Micciche for demonstrating that academic writing can be both lively and meaningful. I owe a debt of gratitude (after all these years) to the creative faculty I was fortunate to work with at UIC, including Clark Hulse, Chris Messenger, Margherita Pieracci Harwell, Virginia Wexman, Michael Lieb, Gene Ruoff, William Covino, David Jolliffe, and especially James Sosnoski and Patricia Harkin. My sincere thanks to Publisher David Blakesley for seeing potential in the manuscript and to copyeditor Heather Christiansen for meticulous editorial assistance. Friends who have energized my spirit with wisdom, humor, aplomb, and encouragement include Annette Van, Jeanne Follansbee, Alexandra Schultheis Moore, Beth Franken, Jeanne Herrick, Cathy Colton, Consolato Gattuso (and Melissa, Tess, Dominick, and Jen), and Joe Rubino. I would also like to honor the memory of those who continue to matter, even if no longer here, including Antonetta Deddo, Helen Wiederhold, Charles Winslow Dulles Gayley, Michele Ciavarella Martinelli, Stephen Stallcup, Ryan Jenson Plachy, and Loran Dale Wiederhold. For evenings of merriment and camaraderie, I am most beholden to Denise Gayley, Joe Stack, Hope Nightingale, David Ellis, John and Margie Gayley, Anne Gabbert, Madi Ellis, and Iain Gayley. And above all, for support and inspiration (and pens, paper, eyedrops, and Italian sausage) I thank my family: Micki Deddo, Lou Armidano, Toni and Derrick Saunders, Brenda Leigh, Jeff Opie, Mark Wiederhold, and, especially, Jim Gayley, who sees between the leaves, hears what is unspoken, and understands my ideas before I do.

EXPEL THE PRETENDER

Introduction

People in the United States are expected to cherish the idea of free speech, but not all speech acts are welcome within public venues. The responsible citizen is expected to guard against the false claims and manufactured "talking points" of politicians whose rhetorical flourishes give cover to an unsavory lust for power. Political candidates tend to be commended when they speak with a blunt candor that seems to get to the facts and avoid verbal complexities. John McCain made an explicit promise when campaigning for president in 2008 to board the "straight talk express" in an effort to present himself as the people's humble servant committed to a forthright style, as if making this pledge was unquestionably commendable and distinctive. The idea that honesty in speech means advancing past any distractions contrived by rhetoric has a long history in U.S. political discourse, its potency retained in part because of the undertheorized yet durable metaphor that crafts a conceptual linkage between linearity and discursive integrity.

This metaphorical cluster encodes a seemingly basic premise: methods exist for ascertaining how and what words mean. A promise to "speak straight" seems obtainable if language is imbued with a power to convey who signifies with probity and if citizens believe in their own integrity (i.e., honest citizens will know an honest representation when they see one and may justifiably castigate any speaker who puts forth anything but). Such beliefs create expectations about how language should be stylized, namely, that styles should be transparent so that rhetors may convey ideas that exist independently of the languages used to represent them. By channeling ideas and logic through figurative forms that do not obstruct the clarity of meaning, the plain style seems to fulfill this expectation.

One can hear echoes of the same idea in books such as the impatiently titled *On Bullshit* that found a publisher in 2005 as well as a receptive audience. Or in a 2008 advertisement for a local Chicago news station:

"No bull. Truth in politics with Mike Flannery."[1] It underwrites the endeavors of cable news hosts such as Anderson Cooper who devotes a portion of his nightly program on CNN to "keeping them honest" by comparing a given politician's statements to "the facts." And it is an element in every media commentary that praises frankness and clarity in political speech when speculating on how a given statement has been interpreted by "America." Such commentaries call upon audiences to trust those representations that deploy a positivistic logic that seems to bypass the arts of rhetoric by actively refusing the politicized, the false, the desirous and the mercenary. Audiences, meanwhile, are expected to appreciate representations that are factual, reasonable, and compelling to a majority, and to feel like virtuous citizens for ferreting out any attempted manipulation.

This book takes a closer look at how discourses of nationalism are encoded within the appeal of an "innocent rhetoric" that implicates public expectations about how language should be used and credibility judged. We are encouraged to find words that grab onto a quality of "apolitical authenticity" and turn it into a representational real. But the persistent need to proclaim that one is using language honestly and sincerely also expresses anxiety about the possibility of doing so. Contemporary language theories have fed that anxiety by challenging commonplace assumptions about how persuasive power works to achieve effects. They alert us to the ways in which attempts to clarify how to judge the genuine also obscure by concealing irresolvable ambiguities that inhere within the interpretive technologies used to evaluate who and what is credible. Indeed, the conceptual underpinnings of discursive practices that seem to disseminate representations that are straight, honest, and logical are tied neither to logic nor to a structural grammar but to narrative. We tell stories about a nation committed to discursive integrity, peopled by citizens who speak freely and invoke innate wisdom when distinguishing the reliable speaker from the political hack. A closer look at the storytelling elements of our conceptual frameworks raises an analytical problem about how to validate the interpretive apparatus that would steer evaluations of which language uses should make us wary.

That problem is made even more complicated by the question of how to regard style's role within judgments of who to believe. Rhetorical style presents a particularly vexed topic because its status as an object of inquiry is paradoxically and simultaneously material and insubstantial. Style, one of the five canons of classical rhetoric, is most commonly described as the artful expression of ideas. But in contemporary life, the word *style* signifies multiple meanings that range from the demonstration of basic grammatical competence to a repertoire of protocols to aid communication to thoughtfully arranged word choices that convey a quality that is noticeable, idiosyncratic (Edward Corbett's word), potentially provocative, and also indescribable. While rhetorical style is considered to be basic and elemental, exactly *how* style acts to influence the exchange of ideas remains undertheorized. Literary traditions have belittled rhetorical style, depicting it as a bureaucratic tool, its purview merely practical and detached from the honorable sublimity of the poetic. In political venues, style is treated with overt suspicion, envisioned as an impediment to the authentic presentation of heartfelt political points of view. Both of these stances call for further review.

It is my contention that rhetorical style plays a crucial role in establishing a democratic aesthetic, to borrow a phrase from Thomas Docherty, who portrays aesthetics as a "founding condition" for "establishing social and political democracy" (back cover). *Aesthetics*, like rhetorical style, is a term that conveys multiple meanings that range from the sensual appreciation of signs of beauty to formalized conceptions of representational action that have become too rigid. Acknowledging an aesthetic dimension to political discourse reminds us that illusory elements inhere within endeavors to certify methods of political adjudication. Docherty takes note of a formalizing impulse commandeering theoretical frameworks that repeat precepts about how we make meaning, an impulse able to render the stories told about how to judge the good man speaking well into ritualized performances rather than authentic experiences of critical inquiry. He then proposes a democratic aesthetic that countermands the formalizing dynamic by highlighting the narrative origins of routine conceptions of what we do with words. This approach incorporates a Lyotardian framework that aims to keep open the question of judgment and avoid the trap of conflating textual depictions of interpretive action with interpretive mastery. We may be reminded of their differences whenever we take recourse in explanations of how persuasive processes work to instigate audience adherence. When we acknowledge that we tell stories about who we are as citizens who judge, we interrupt the automatic reproduction of taken-for-granted commonplaces that describe how discourses organize a majority view of what has meaning and significance. Plain speech offers a case in point. It denotes a ritualized mode of expression that promises truth's unadorned delivery. What audiences procure through its invocation may be something else entirely.

This book applies Docherty's conception of a democratic aesthetic to commonplace conceptions of rhetorical style. Most studies of style offer advice about how to correlate language with civics when conceiving of the formation of, for example, "the national community." I instead am concerned with the means by which people are kicked out—symbolically disqualified for failing to adhere to the stylistic protocols that appear to demarcate a representational integrity read as emblematic of a national character. Indeed, I am especially interested in those utterances that seem to provoke strong negative responses of consternation, resentment, and even anger.

Often, such responses are treated as if self-explanatory, especially within media narratives that report on public responses to stylized deliveries. I am less interested in examining the style of news reports themselves (although this does come up throughout my analysis) but in considering how such reports rely upon conventional conceptions of style's role in political judgment. I argue that rather than act to aid or obstruct the delivery of meaning, signifiers of style can be examined to excavate the multiple points of tension within conceptions of language use and democratic access. Styles are provocations and integral to the judgments audiences make about who to believe and who to ostracize. Within the stories that we tell about what styles should *do*, we may locate cultural narratives that have staked out conceptions of how persuasive power works to achieve its effects. A study of style draws attention to the ways in which narrative constructions of persuasive action get treated as factual and evidentiary and then referenced as if automatically legitimate resources aiding public evaluations about who to believe, who to dismiss, and who to revere for speaking in ways that benefit the nation.

Expel the Pretender: Rhetoric Renounced and the Politics of Style addresses examples of discredited political speech and the cultural logics that endorse their dismissal. Specifically, this book analyzes well-known public speeches that not only failed to enact community but also triggered collective public ridicule, including arguments in 1998 proposing a presidential impeachment, President Bill Clinton's responses to those arguments, his national apology after admitting that he had an affair with a White House intern, Linda Tripp's first public statement in defense of her actions that launched the impeachment drive, and the 2008 press appearances of the Reverend Jeremiah Wright, President Barack Obama's former pastor who was subsequently ostracized by the Obama campaign. In each representative example, I demonstrate how rhetorical style was at the center of public concerns about whose speech could be trusted. Not only was style central to assessments of each speaker's credibility, its significance was only noticeable when speakers failed to meet cultural expectations about what kind of speech is permissible on the occasion of its delivery.

Judgments of dismissal were fortified by the simplistic binary that depicts political truth-telling as opposite to the practice of deception. Style's study challenges the validity of that binary and its rendering of an interpretive process that oversees how to discern differences between words that are trustworthy and those that lead citizens *astray*.

Style and Expulsion

Expel the Pretender gets its title from Scott Durham's *Phantom Communities*, which questions whether the theoretical concept of simulation (simulacra) should be deemed an impediment to social justice. Conventionally, simulation is aligned with representational deception—when, for example, the act of voting for a reality television show is depicted as an authentic experience of political struggle or when consumer choice masquerades as democratic access. Simulacra empty representational signs of their reality and reduce them to mere appearances, a shell of what they promise to be. Durham points to a history of thought that has expressed anxiety about the inability to tell the difference between the real and the fake, and he explores those interpretive methodologies that promise to enable citizens to discern disparities and justify the practice of expelling anyone who "fakes it" by trying to pass off the inauthentic expression as truth's representative. I will have more to say about Durham's argument in the first chapter. (Ultimately, Durham rehabilitates simulacra with reference to postmodern theories that muddy the conceptual frameworks that enable distinctions between "the real" and "the simulated" to be made.) At the moment, however, it is possible to note that both the anxiety about the inauthentic expression and the proposed method of relief remain pertinent to U.S. political culture where, arguably, the dynamic of expulsion endures as a viable option when publics discern discursive threats.

When the political "gaffe," for example, is invoked as a newsworthy event, it functions as way of shaming and then silencing whoever delivered a statement that raised eyebrows. Countless websites are devoted to tracking this phenomenon: "The Top Ten Campaign-Ending Political Gaffes in Modern U.S. History." "They Said WHAT?! Politicians Most Notorious Science Flubs." "The Nine Worst Political Gaffes of 2012."[2] At first glance, this kind of exposure seems to be useful and necessary. It draws upon the idea that speakers bear social responsibilities and that it is incumbent upon audiences to make sure that all people, especially politicians, are held accountable for what they say. But a closer look at what the act of shaming is supposed to accomplish helps to illustrate the difficulty of distinguishing simulacra from genuine democratic actions. Presumably, pointing out instances of bad speech performs important political work, revealing, for example, something true about the person whose language use prompted ridicule, especially those objectionable flaws that, as put by one ardent truth-seeking blogger, "cannot be washed aside by the world's greatest spin masters."[3] The exposure of misleading attempts to escape accountability is presented as an ethical act itself, undertaken, presumably to enable citizens to determine who does not deserve their support. Confidence in this methodology may begin to waver, however, once we begin to question what, exactly, is revealed and then accomplished through the kind of self-righteous scrutiny that converts a gaffe into a spectacle. My point is not to discount the act of calling out the ridiculous things that politicians say. But it is important to note that the act of publicizing gaffes carries an implicit and vague demand for linguistic correctness—as if being correct should confirm a speaker's credibility and as if the point of analysis is to take note of the gaffe itself. Meanwhile, giving exposure to "the gaffe" implicitly treats all gaffes as equal, leaving open the question of how audiences are expected to weigh the significance of whatever flawed statement makes its way to the headlines.

When undertaking a study of style's significance to judgment, we will quickly discover the inadequacies of those cultural narratives that treat acts of revelation as expressions of an authenticating interpretive methodology necessary to the functioning of the democratic state. Too often the methodologies that we rely upon provoke habitualized judgments of what has validity. This is all the more significant given that rhetorical style itself is generally read as the agent of pretense and fakery and hence an obstacle to the endeavor to speak straight and insure that one's audience can distinguish the hollow political platitude from the sincere utterance of conviction. Culturally sanctioned stylistic protocols are presented as positive markers that signify not only ethical representational action but also the desirable qualities of the people who use them. Indeed, when speakers and writers use styles that have earned cultural regard, we are expected to classify them as the kind of people who think and speak reasonably, who aim to communicate ethically, and who then are deserving of whatever accolades their speeches (texts) might generate. In political venues, candidates who highlight a commitment to straight talk imply that such talk may be positioned as the personification of the candidate's moral character—a premise that conflates the qualities of seeming and being by suggesting that one's regard for discursive protocol offers a demonstration of one's commitment to *being* moral.

The question is whether the absence of culturally preferred stylistic markers necessarily indicates an absence of those qualities that have earned cultural regard (reason, common sense, good will, etc.) We might quickly downplay such a conclusion and maintain that when we judge, we weigh propositional content—the reasonableness of whatever political perspective is put up for review. Yet as my examples show, it is often the case that when valorized stylistic markers are absent, permission is given to audiences to deliver seemingly justifiable derisive judgments of whoever failed to follow the mandated methodology. When political speakers fail to follow discursive conventions, or worse, when they seem to purposely defy them, the styles associated with their noncompliance tend to be read as marking an absence of qualities that should be put on display. In effect, socially constituted, aestheticized discursive practices get conflated with real linguistic obligations.

My analysis of the politics of expulsion demonstrates that questions about style function as directives about how to participate with language. I use the word *participate* in the sense offered by Bill Readings, one that extends conceptions of language beyond that of communication. To communicate is to consider purpose and message, and to be concerned with protocols that assist the conveyance of one's message. Participation broadens those concerns by attending to the intertextual dynamics that play out when cultural conceptions of what language is and does influences conceptions of what language should do within specific occasions of its use. It is my contention that commonplace narratives about rhetorical style put constraints upon judgments of how and which language uses enact virtuous political participation. Indeed, this book encourages scholars in rhetoric and composition to discard the idea that style's main purpose is to further effective communication. As part of a democratic aesthetic, narratives about style can instead be refashioned to highlight the storytelling elements of political life that influence perceptions of how ethics and language meet. Indeed, when we restrict our understanding of style's purposes, we also restrict conceptions of rhetoric's significance to political life.

The idea that style should aid communication helps to sustain the convention that valorizes plain speech as a sign of a speaker's integrity and suppresses consideration of how rhetorical indeterminacy is featured within political judgment. Discourses about style are always about more than mere style, marking instead a complex space at which embodiment, text, and ideology converge. Styles are public expressions that provoke private responses to representational power. In this sense, style signifies the felt experience of interpretation—an experience that cannot necessarily be translated into a narrative chronicling what happens as we contend with words. Style, then, marks a happening that is itself not fully representable but nonetheless noteworthy. To consider style's significance to political judgment is to mull over commonplace visions of discursive participation, variously expressed in terms of how form relates to content, how narrative connects to lived experiences, how we endeavor to incorporate cognition, affect, and somatic responses into conceptions of deliberation that we would like to call democratic.

Rhetorical Interventions

Narratives about rhetorical style can be characterized as meditations about political access. Teach rhetors how to speak well and you give them tools for successful participation in social life. Such instruction need not be mercenary. Following Aristotle, style in rhetoric may be depicted as poetic's pragmatic counterpart—a socially productive facilitator of civic-minded goals such as fostering mutual understanding and building consensus. The idea that people should be taught to use language to compel assent and then build community is taken for granted within rhetorical traditions, which helps to explain why, for example, eloquence, at least since the writings of Cicero, has been championed as a primary instigator of audience identification and approval. Rather than regard style as a discursive "extra," as a superficial site of ornamentation inferior to poetic aesthetics and less significant than propositional content, rhetoricians historically have treated style as intrinsic to any concern with public welfare. For classical rhetoricians, style was central to the endeavor to persuade.

The recent return to style within composition studies pursues this trajectory by encouraging writing teachers to become more cognizant of style's relationship to pragmatic approaches to language study. Hence, for example, Elizabeth Rankin's important contribution from the 1980's that reintroduced the idea that style involves more than attention to the surface features of language; style is a component within processes of invention wherein writers make choices about how to represent themselves on the page to audiences who will have their own preferences about which styles are suited to a rhetorical occasion. Learning about style gives writers and speakers the chance to harness persuasive power by incorporating models of effective communication into their own texts. More recently, Paul Butler calls upon compositionists to reinvigorate studies in style so that they may join public conversations about why the study of composing processes should be of general public concern. Like other compositionists, Butler endeavors to invalidate an epistemological tradition that has vilified rhetoric by characterizing persuasion as a force that manipulates audiences into assenting to ideas that serve nefarious interests. Butler argues for style's importance to the work of interpretive collaboration, maintaining that it is through style that partnerships between rhetors and audiences get established. The thoughtful rhetor chooses styles that will produce favorable audience reactions, and in making such choices, he or she will be participating with language in socially redeemable ways: settling controversies, easing perceptual dissonances, establishing a means of identification. Styles execute a critical social function when put in the service of crafting shared perspectives about what matters and why.

There is a democratizing impulse within these formulations that clarifies how rhetorical conceptions of style differ from the aesthetic tradition that venerates authorial geniuses who devise representations with no concern for audience reception. In a rhetorical framework, it is precisely the care one has for one's audience that indicates a rhetor's integrity. Indeed, style is regarded as a kind of equipment in Kenneth Burke's sense of the term—a technology that offers a way to both acknowledge interpretive complexities and understand that one can purposefully attempt to use language to further sociability. One studies style not for the sake of art (or truth) but to be pragmatic—to determine how to use language to nurture a political sphere in which all agree that argument should replace war as a means of settling disagreements. A non-violent means of settling disputes will only work if all agree that the power of words should surpass that of physical violence. This perspective is bound by consent. It is, then, infused with rhetorical inconstancy. We might call its status fragile, if not precarious. Words are effective when all agree to the idea that a call to good argument is more authoritative than a call to arms. It is all too possible for citizens to change their minds and embrace war over argument as the right solution to a perceived threat. Consequently, when we talk about style in relationship to political legitimacy, the stakes are huge.

The conundrum imposed by narrative appears to be resolved via rhetoric's pragmatic interest in getting things done—i.e., furthering robust debate, learning writing strategies that are stylistically effective. When style's significance in rhetorical and composition studies is construed to be pragmatic it is, by implication, knowable, and what we think we know is that when rhetors think about how to style statements, they will become better communicators and, presumably, that knowledge will benefit the collective. This suggests that the validity of the civic-oriented study of style is itself demonstrable by looking at actual linguistic practices to see whether they accomplish the stated goal of furthering everyone's chance to speak up and be heard. Democratic principles would seem to be actualized when all are invited to take part in life's grand conversational give-and-take and when everyone has the same chances to invoke and respond to whatever is publicly displayed and subject to judgment. When all participate, many ideas will compete for public attention. Studies in rhetoric can effectively teach rhetors how to navigate an inclusionary discursive terrain to insure that one's ideas will get noticed. Because debate is intrinsic to democratic culture, it is perfectly reasonable to teach people how to use styles effectively and avoid being cast out of the community to which one seeks to belong.

These premises will make sense if language is structured to allow everyone to access its force and knowingly channel it in civic-minded directions. If democratic equity infuses language's very structure, then presumably, it may be tapped to oversee judgments of which language uses act sociably and which are uncommunicative. We should be able to understand the contours of deliberatory judgment and to put into practice ways of seeing and interpreting that are progressive, fair, subtle enough to contend with variance, general enough to be representative of a collective.

At this point, however, the authentic/pretense problem returns. We must still grapple with the enigmatic question of whether descriptions of interpretive processes tell us more than stories about how representations should be evaluated. Staking out competence means devising narratives that identify sanctioned repertoires of style. Narratives that place a premium upon rhetorical competency reinstall a binary logic to determine when competency makes an appearance. When it is absent, persuasive failure presumably follows. Stylistic markers of competency get treated as actualizations of the qualities that they would re-present, and, once so regarded, they appear to be necessary to accomplish the social purpose of constituting a democratic representational order that all can share and use at will. While rhetoricians acknowledge that cultural ideologies will influence judgments of issues, there has been less attention paid in rhetoric's history to the ways in which intertextual histories of preferred styles will influence evaluations of which stylistic forms should be deemed legitimate agents for enacting community formation. Indeed, regard for the power of debate to flesh out "the best" claim does not necessarily address the particular ways in which issues come to be identified and then commonly recognized through discursive practices that may or may not be equitable. Rhetoric's idealistic story of access, inclusion, and judicious evaluation does not address how to determine which forms of style constitute the kind of participation deemed to be properly "civic." Nor does that story consider the ways in which prioritizing coded models of "sayability" affirms an exclusionary logic that dispenses punishments and rewards and ways of naturalizing those outcomes.

Postmodern Materialism

Rhetorical theories that attempt to reinvigorate studies in style to advance democratic inquiry effectively promote a singular goal for linguistic participation (i.e., the interpretive resolution). This is accomplished by installing standards of evaluation that effectively "correspond to a control over the processes of legitimation" (Panagia 9). Indeed, many language theorists habitually rely upon a restricted set of discursive norms to assess and validate the unstructured work of interpretive negotiation. Feminist theorists, on the other hand, have challenged the habit of invoking dominant narratives of legitimation when exploring how audiences are conditioned to accept their persuasive power. Susan Miller, for example, considers the ways in which audiences learn to trust discursive practices that correspond to already formulated "prescriptive networks" (2). Lynn Worsham explores how dominant ideologies are reproduced when audiences learn to identify emotionally and feel the validity of ideological perspectives. Kristie Fleckenstein outlines the contours of a materialist rhetoric that would explore "the complex processes of perception and articulation that persuade a community that a certain material reality, including the reality of the body, exists" (7). Each of these perspectives indicates how sociopolitical criteria for evaluating whether speech acts are powerful are construed in ways that entangle emotional receptivity with representational action.

This book builds upon these theories to consider how citizens are instructed emotionally to internalize preferences for those styles that have already earned cultural approval as they render judgments about whose words matter. Accordingly, a concern with style can be regarded as a paradoxical point of contact between culture and embodied experience, where the narratives that would describe preferred styles also shape audience preferences. Styles are acts of signification that have been positioned within a nexus of narratives that would explain, define, and establish what style means in relation to an epistemic conception of how language communicates meaning. Hence our grasp of any particular "failed" speech act is also produced by a "host of technologies" (Greene 52) that teach how to imagine and then recognize what constitutes a legitimate rhetorical formation. Judgments about who to expel make explicit the narratives that citizens are expected to internalize and reference to demonstrate that they are in accord with the social rules overseeing acts of linguistic comportment.

If style is a historical condition (see Huyssen 9-12) rather than an essential quality that conveys a self-sufficient force, then style demarcates a locus for mulling over the effects of cultural training on our assessments of whose language uses seem to be authoritative *because* powerful and compelling. When we acknowledge the significance of the intertextual on how we respond to language's constitutive power, we may question which discourses have been granted the authority to condition our responses to the emotional power of style. At the same time, because styles *do* affect our sensibilities, their status is more than conceptual. While style is a locus for narratives that naturalize the embodied experience of political judgment, its analysis can also testify to the human capacity to refuse the lessons imposed by culture, particularly since our responses to rhetorical styles will also be partly spontaneous and experienced during our acts of reception. This lived part of our interpretive experience cannot be encapsulated within narrative and need not be explainable with reference to pre-established frameworks. In this regard, style functions as a site for theorizing the possibility of democratic dissent. For many contemporary theorists of rhetoric, style serves a critical role in enabling disagreements about whether a given version of an idea or event has validity. We may reject those premises that do not conform to our own "image" of what is at issue, the terms invoked failing to re-present what we think should be put forth for review. More generally, we can note that all representations are finally just that—narrative constructs and hence precisely not the same as facts. (On this point, see both Hariman and O'Gorman.)

A materialist rhetorical approach expands upon these ideas by envisioning language as a site of convergence between the agency of consent to symbolic artifacts, the influence of ideologies that have enculturated ways of seeing what is significant about any artifact put up for review, and the possibility of somatic responses that are not necessarily explainable with reference to cultural scripts. Materialist rhetorics dovetail with postmodern aesthetics in that both draw attention to the ways in which truth claims are perpetually disrupted once questions are raised about how, precisely, narratives about form influence perceptions of content. There are, indeed, consequences to language uses. But whatever reasons we devise to explain those consequences situates us right back in narrative and the aesthetic. Politics hovers within this paradoxical space of postmodern materialism. And so does style's ephemeral-yet-substantial significance. Even as styles may assist in the endeavor to enact persuasive power, our interactions with styles will be subjected to representational ambiguities. We cannot predict when a style will incite affiliations or inspire action or prompt us to dismiss an utterance as a hackneyed cliché. Meanwhile, the fall out of those judgments will affect political life.

It might be helpful, then, to consider how narratives about style are caught within an oscillating dynamic that fluctuates between the power of cultural conditioning and the power to refuse ideology's influence. Style is an especially fruitful topic to consider when exploring the parameters of that oscillating action because style's effects are simultaneously tied to narrative and individually (spontaneously, somatically) experienced. On the one hand, then, we may study style to consider how techne can promote the reproduction of cultural hegemony. On the other hand, it is equally important to note that visceral responses to acts of representation cannot be ascribed solely to ideological influences. The dynamic of flux opens a conceptual space in which to revise conceptions of linguistic labor.

Style demarcates a quality, perhaps unnamable, that emerges where artistry meets craft and the legacies of cultural conditioning. Its significance to political judgment is finally elusive. Acknowledging that part of our interpretive experience eludes understanding provides an occasion for reconsidering what we mean when we turn to rhetoric and rhetorical interventions as a way of engaging a democratic ethics. When exploring the discursive networks through which meaning is made and assigned significance, we might describe style an "ambivalent rupture" (J. Kelleher 78), a mode of representation that demarcates a space between the categorical divisions that would separate language and experience, signs and referents, poetics and rhetoric, practices and metadiscourses that seem to gauge whether language uses work. Style is not an object or type of representation but a way of talking about how we think form crosses borders to connect private predilections with public codes to constitute communal ways of seeing and believing.

The complex and contingent cultural forces that produce dominant conceptions of style can be examined to consider how chains of affect come to be embedded within interpretive frameworks that generate the emotions they would describe, and in the process, install a particular kind of political literacy that seems to adequately address the question of how to negotiate representational indeterminacy when we are called upon to judge another's credibility. This is not the same as saying that we just make things up as we judge. But it is to say that any attempt to delineate "responsible judgment" about who to embrace and who to castigate will not escape the problem of narrative and the training we've received to regard some styles as harboring more signifying power than others.

Chapter Summaries

In the chapters that follow, I identify how a rhetoric of value-neutrality and cultural impartiality was disseminated within media narratives that simultaneously broadcast stories about speech failures that presumably engendered emotional outrage. Each chapter explores how media narratives naturalized the idea that speech acts may be discredited when they stray from normative standards of legitimation expressed stylistically. Failure to abide by norms of stylistic protocol engendered public responses of ridicule, indicating how a dynamic of expulsion has itself become normalized. Not only do dominant conceptions of what rhetorical style *is* help to reproduce this norm, attitudes about style help to ratify the idea that the practice of publicly shaming those who fail to obey conventions of style is a natural byproduct of audience responses to signs of failure.

Chapter 1 analyzes the arguments used by Congressional leaders that claimed that President Clinton's "silver tongue" posed a national threat. Officially Clinton was charged with perjury and obstruction of justice, but public debate about his speech acts involved larger questions about how to signify truth. Impeachment debates offer an occasion for considering whether to continue to trust positivistic analytical models when assessing who is doing what with words. The call to linguistic clarity advanced in pro-impeachment arguments failed to persuade a majority to remove the President from office but the logic of those arguments was never challenged. Indeed, rather than generate a national debate about what kind of arguments should be available to support political outcomes, this historical event has been effectively trivialized. This response, I suggest, was made possible by cultural attitudes that underestimate rhetorical style's importance to judgment.

Chapter 2 examines two failed speeches: Clinton's notorious four minute national apology, delivered to TV viewing audiences once evidence emerged that proved he had had an affair with Monica Lewinsky; and the first public statement from Linda Tripp, who asked citizens to regard her act of taping private phone conversations as a performance of her civic duty. Both speeches were reviled and Clinton and Tripp were each accused of being inauthentic when looking for public sympathy. I examine how those failures can be understood with reference to rhetorical theories of propriety that envision style not as a conduit for truth but a means through which speakers locate words that fit the occasion of speech. But I also argue that even though propriety's transactional model of judgment usefully challenges some aspects of positivistic logic, it nonetheless carries vestiges of that logic by implying that "fittingness" is a quality that may be discerned and then confidently referenced when evaluating the legitimacy of a speech/text put forth for public review. The rhetoric of propriety sanctions a technology that would gather diverse elements together to craft a working theory of ethics and criteria for judgment, as if such criteria are inherently ethical. Drawing upon the work of feminist theorists such as Lynn Worsham and Wendy Hesford, I propose a feminist materialist rhetoric that would instead argue that any attempt to identify whether language fits the occasion will have emerged from the encounter between complex, historically marked narratives and habituated embodied responses.

Chapter 3 explores the ways in which protocols of style are embedded within rhetorical theories of ethos. I locate versions of ethos-as-style within the celebratory discourses formulated in response to the 2008 primary campaign of Barack Obama, whose ethos was esteemed by many in the mainstream press, especially after he delivered his famous speech on race in March of that year. The speech was offered in response to the negative media portraits of the Reverend Jeremiah Wright, Obama's former pastor, who was ridiculed for making controversial statements about national politics when delivering religious sermons. I explore how public responses to Wright's sermons referenced his style of delivery, and how a binary logic was crafted that created a discriminatory comparison between Obama's style and Wright's that influenced ways of reading their respective characters. This chapter also considers how theorizing ethos will benefit from both feminist materialist rhetorical theories as well as studies in rhetoric from scholars of African American communicative practices.

Chapter 4 explores the limits of rhetorical theories of genre that call for the replication of normative styles to facilitate audience recognition of categorical types of speech able to engender audience identification. I return to Obama's race speech to consider it from the perspective of genre studies, and then look at the 2008 public appearances of the Reverend Jeremiah Wright as he attempted to rehabilitate his public image. Those public appearances were condemned and Wright was officially and publicly expelled from Obama's campaign. Drawing upon studies from African American Rhetoric and Communication scholars, this chapter demonstrates how the apparent logic valorizing the replication of norms within genre studies was invoked in 2008 to affirm the chain of reasoning that seemed to justify and naturalize the act of denouncing Wright and the representational ethics that he promoted.

1 Authenticating the Liar

There is a curious exchange recorded in the October 5, 1998 transcripts of the House Judiciary Committee debate about whether to pursue the possibility of impeaching the forty-second President of the United States. Perhaps thirty minutes after the hearing opened, after six House members, mostly Democrats, spoke for or against the idea of officially investigating whether Bill Clinton perjured himself and obstructed justice, a speaker identified as "unknown" made the following point of order: "Mr. Speaker, this is a fairly important issue. It seems to me that if members are going to vote on it, the least they could do is be here in the chamber when it's debated." According to the transcripts, this statement generated a rousing round of applause.[1]

Arguably, this short statement encapsulates the strange atmosphere surrounding this "fairly important" historical event, its odd presence emblematic of the ways in which talk about impeaching Clinton strayed from idealized representations of conscientious deliberation. Ideally, any contentious issue is adjudicated through reasonable debate that facilitates evenhanded compromises. Public debate would seem to offer a clear method for generating the interpretive actions that could be called democratic, including reviewing what is at issue, finding facts, judging their value and significance, and from there, determining what should happen next.

The President of the United States was accused of committing an act of perjury. His job was on the line because many believed (or claimed to believe) that the nation's chief representative had abandoned his authority to lead the nation once he broke the law by lying under oath. Given the seriousness of the accusations against the nation's Commander in Chief, one might have expected a rousing discussion from critically informed political leaders weighing the evidence while patriotically contemplating the needs of the country. One might at least have expected a gathering of riveted participants and spectators acting as national witnesses, fighting for seats to behold an extraordinary and historically rare event. How strange, then, to read the transcripts and discover that someone found it necessary to scold his colleagues and urge them to engage in democratic inquiry's most basic practice: pay attention.

Perhaps Congressional leaders had already given this issue a lot of thought. Impeachment arguments had been circulating for months, as had evidence to inform judgments about Clinton's fate. But there was also a perception of partisanship overshadowing these deliberations. Many voters believed that House members had their minds made up before any formal debate ensued. To the skeptical, the impeachment proceedings seemed to be propelled by theatrical performances from Congressmen who engaged in an act of pretense—playing the role of concerned and inquiring national leaders while intending to cast a vote that conformed to party dogma. This is, in fact, what happened. On December 19, 1998, the vote to impeach on grounds of perjury was approved by a 228–206 vote and on the grounds of obstruction of justice by a 221–212 vote. Had the Democrats controlled the House, there would have been a different outcome.[2]

That result, along with the nameless comment recorded in the transcripts, is notable for encapsulating the problem the impeachment raised: how to distinguish appearances from reality, a problem that reverberated through every facet of this event. Was the discussion at those preliminary meetings *for real*? Organized as a true attempt to excavate a scene of high crimes and misdemeanors? Or, as opponents argued, was the impeachment a political stunt orchestrated by one political party to undermine the authority and credibility of the opposition? Indeed, the endeavor to differentiate appearances from reality implicated the very charges against the President who, many agreed, might have misrepresented facts when testifying, but did not commit a bona fide impeachable offense.

Contemporary critical theories (philosophical, feminist, rhetorical) have left us "spinning in 'textuality'" (Pollock 114), unable, it would seem, to do much but observe that appearances and realities are theoretically indistinguishable. How this premise implicates political life has raised concern for those who are invested in the idea that standards of judgment exist and should be consulted by citizens facing contentious issues. Indeed, while the impeachment inquiry investigated a specific speech act delivered by a particular person, it also posed a general question about whether and how conceptions of political discourse should incorporate the perplexing idea that, as put by Della Pollock, "words don't stick. They are 'Janus-faced,' 'fickle,' indifferent to discourses of truth and meaning" (114–15). If words don't stick, then the very charge of perjury would seem to be impossible to prove. And with no standards to reference, we may be confounded about how to judge arguments that seem to be contrived. The question the impeachment raised is whether that all or nothing perspective is the only option available to us when we evaluate political controversies.

In this chapter, I argue that impeachment discourses staged two epistemological encounters. In one, the styles associated with representations of realism collided with those rhetorical elements that signify inconstancy and mercenary strategizing. The other staged an encounter between rhetoric's "practical" aim to use language for desired ends and postmodern theorizing about language's incapacity to be pinned down to meet desires. In both contact zones, rhetorical style had a central role to play but its status was paradoxically central and ambiguous. Because style's influence on judgment is undertheorized in both conventional and theoretical conceptions of political debate, the point of public debate gets characterized as the endeavor to distinguish mere style from arguments of substance and *through that process*, identify what really matters, which will inevitably be the argument over the mode of delivery. Indeed, democratic deliberation itself could be described as the endeavor to distinguish the substantial and significant from the sham appearance, to take note of and dismiss the mechanistic production of stylized platitudes and contrived realities. The technologies of evaluation that appear to facilitate those practices would seem to be *substantial* themselves, giving us the tools we need to differentiate between reality, pretense, what has merit or may be ignored.

Such interpretive maneuvering, however, brings us back to the polemics intrinsic to any endeavor to determine what should matter. Because even as we might want to believe, in general, that public debate is a bona fide practice that truly enables democratic inquiry, we will be beset by the power struggles inscribed within any attempt to step "beyond" language when explaining how our interactions with language should organize our interpretive experiences, including that of judgment.

Given that the impeachment provoked anxieties about whether it was possible to know who was doing what with language, we can look to the discourses that circulated in 1998 to see how they exposed the limits of our ability to see beyond "mere" appearances when called upon to definitively render a verdict about whether any statement fails to exhibit commendable discursive obedience. Impeachment discourses explicitly addressed questions about how to differentiate false claims from true ones and how to determine if a given speech is genuine, as if that quality is itself identifiable and valuable. Public arguments relied upon dominant interpretive methodologies that work by preserving the binary that would distinguish the stylized political platitude from the statement of substance. But the question of authenticity proved to be an unctuous one. Rather than demonstrate that we have the capacity to see clear differences between substance and style, impeachment discourses ventured into a world of fun house mirrors and their myriad distortions.

This chapter explores the ways in which style is invoked within narratives about political judgment as a placeholder for a complex and ephemeral interpretive process whereby speculations about language's persuasive power get transformed into judgments of the significance of any given representation put up for review. At the center of this work of translation is a narrative depicting style as a provocateur that indicates whether a given representation is acting responsibly. In effect, styles act as metaphors for conceptions of how we think language functions to facilitate communication itself. But when it comes to style, we tend to confuse the metaphorical with the real. To look at rhetorical style is not only to explore conceptions of how language acts to communicate, style's study also reveals how cultural preferences for particular representational modes get sanctioned when we pretend that reigning interpretive technologies move us past the speculative to the authentic.

THE STRAIGHT PATH AND THE SPIN

In 1998, Clinton faced several charges. He was accused of lying under oath when testifying in a prior case led by Paula Jones, who alleged that Clinton, when Governor of Arkansas, had sexually harassed her. The impeachment, however, did not address sexual misconduct but speech misconduct. At least that was the official distinction, but it soon became apparent that when arguing for Clinton's removal, the two categories often blurred. Had the president perjured himself when he testified that he never had a sexual affair with another young woman, Monica Lewinsky? Clinton was also accused of obstructing justice by attempting to cover up their affair. A summary of Clinton's linguistic infractions included, among other charges, that the President coached false testimony from witnesses speaking on his behalf; that he obtained gifts, then hid them once they were deemed to be evidentiary and subject to subpoena (hence a lie of omission); that he continued to lie about his liaison with Lewinsky in both public statements and to his staff, leading them to then give false testimony in subsequent legal proceedings; and that he bought Lewinsky's silence by obtaining a job for her after convincing her to sign an affidavit in the Arkansas Federal Court that falsely testified to the status of their relationship.

Each of the charges linked criminal behavior to an act of representation, suggesting that methods are available to identify the kind of linguistic comportment that should be penalized. From the GOP perspective, there should have been no dispute at all. Perjury would seem to be a discernible crime, requiring a straightforward act of adjudication. Either a person lied under oath or did not. The evidence will be clear. This stance relies upon a conventional view of representation: that it involves an act of substitution in which words *stand in for* and hence represent a prior, already established referent, imagined, for example, as a concept, a concrete phenomenon, a historical past. The work of representation means bringing the prior referent "to presence" within whatever symbolic medium one is using (speech, writing, film, etc.).

Hence, when testifying, the President took an oath to re-present the truth but instead made statements that misrepresented *what really happened* when he claimed that there was no sexual relationship with Monica Lewinsky. And he repeated that same stance to the public once news of an investigation into his testimony became public. Of all of the memorable televised moments brought to us in 1998, many will likely recall that January 26 news conference during which Clinton stood, finger pointed, hand hitting the podium as he ardently denied the rumors that were circulating. "I want to say one thing to the American people. I want you to listen to me. I did *not* have sexual relations with that woman—Miss Lewinsky." No ambiguity there, it would seem. His subsequent recanting of precisely that statement seemed to prove the GOP argument: The President's initial representation of a historical past failed to match a prior reality and we had evidence of the disconnection.

But the attempt to pin down the fact of criminality and then the accompanying consequences remained as slippery as a wet bar of soap. The very arguments supporting impeachment equivocated when naming what was at issue, and incorporated reasons that addressed concerns other than the execution of a crime. Clinton's punishment was necessary not only because he needed to pay for his actions but also because citizens needed to know that there are enforceable laws governing language practices. Impeachment proponents referenced a positivistic view of representation when they portrayed those laws as immutable and transcendent rather than as social constructions, and their concern about presidential misconduct was pitched as a moral concern about social order achieved through compliance with a representational code. All of which suggested that the real crime pertained to a realm well beyond the legal proceedings initiated by Paula Jones. At the February 1999 closed-door Senate Hearings on the Articles of Impeachment (subsequently published in the Congressional Record), Sen. Mitch McConnell (R-Kentucky) explained that he was compelled to vote to convict Clinton because "the President would seek to win at any cost. If it meant lying to the American people. If it meant lying to his Cabinet. If it meant lying to a federal grand jury." Conviction was necessary, he added, because "the road" the president "has traveled" was not straight but "twisted, tortured"—one that "forced the American people and their government to plod along—for what seems to many of us like an eternity."[3]

Sen. Richard Lugar (R-Indiana) voted guilty because "our President must be trustworthy—a truth teller whose life of principled leadership and integrity we can count upon." Clinton "betrayed that trust" that must be believed "if we are to follow him. . . . His leadership has been betrayed because most Americans have come to the cynical conclusion that they must read between the lines of his statements and try to catch a glimmer of truth amidst the spin."[4]

"The spin," of course, is a code word for the rhetorical or that which stands in opposition to the disinterested, timeless, and transcendent. "The spin" is precisely the realm of the spurious and the fraudulent, inhabited by charlatans who claim to speak truly but instead use language to seduce and manipulate audiences to take up perspectives that go against their better judgment. The spin implicates representational styles that abuse power when they act to turn heads away from "hard" facts or "reason's harsh light." Accordingly, we should attempt to escape the spin of seduction and seek access to reason and truth by invoking discourses of realism. We should engage in the practice of representation that endeavors to separate the spin from the truth by deploying a style that connotes a purposeful ordering and presentation of signifiers meant to reflect a prior reality. We might call this kind of engagement Mimesis 101.

From this perspective, the abstract goal of "bringing truth to presence" will be achieved when rhetors insure that the signifier acts as a substitute for the reality that is not visible or no longer literally present, such as an abstract ideal (justice) or a historical event (a prior occasion of speech). The act of re-presentation appears to be accomplished when language users reference an invisible and yet discernible structural order that presumably exists to insure that the representational form journeys to where it should—out of the spin zone and back to truth's domain. To follow a (straight) path to the real and authentic, language users should endeavor to correlate the originary referent with the signifier that would re-present it by crafting a proper correspondence. The straightforward and honest speaker is the one who clearly charts clear correspondences and chooses words that do not impede the audience's perception of what a signifier represents.

This version of discursive responsibility implicates not only how to use language but also how to receive it. Audiences are expected to "take a hard look" at the represented object to determine if the words being used are in alignment with the source material. Such discernment involves acts of recognition characterized as re-cognition—a cognitive act that involves taking a careful look at an object of representation to see if the essence of truth has appeared along with the signifiers that represent a given premise. Once speakers create a proper correspondence between words and referents, then the aesthetic and rhetorical dimensions of language use fall away, dislodged by the weight of what is indispensably valid.

Visual metaphors underwrite this conceptual model. By directing audiences to search for truth's nugget and to decry its absence, this interpretive methodology also promotes a hierarchy of values wherein a representation's form is regarded as subservient to content and therefore not as significant as the referent that precedes it. (See Panagia 7). Audiences are on call to look past the surface style, especially when it is deceptively seductive, so as to assess whether the rhetor has engaged the right procedures and endeavored to establish discernible resemblances between signs and referents. Credibility is ascribed to speakers who seem to follow governing procedures while those who do not may be deemed reckless and negligent. The value system encoded within this apparatus seems to neutrally authorize the dismissal of those who do not engage representational properties as they should.

Such was the logic organizing the campaign to unseat the President, whose speech acts were maligned because they gave no evidence of even attempting to conjoin words with referents. The GOP stance conveyed all of the suspicions of representation expressed by Plato as House and Senate members sounded an alarm about the dangers of figural excess that presumably will be eliminated when all emulate correct representational practices. Clinton's apparent indifference to a governing representational order needed to be curtailed because its threat implicated more than his ways with words. The public's apparent indifference to his crimes was read as emblematic of a national crisis involving a general disregard both for procedural fealty and for having simple faith in truth's omnipresence.

"What has been happening, not just here in Washington, but all around the country is something far more disturbing than the trial of a President," stated Sen. Frank Murkowski's (R-Alaska) at that Senate closed-door session that would determine if the nation's choice for president would be upended. "What we have been witnessing is a contest for the very moral soul of the United States of America—and that the great casualty so far of the national scandal is the notion of Truth. Truth has been shown to us as an elastic commodity." In another context, Rep. Bob Inglis (R-SC) expressed the same concern. "There are some who seem to be saying that truth doesn't matter." When voting to impeach Clinton, Rep. Robert Aderholt (R-AL) described the issue as being not about "the relation that Bill Clinton had with Monica Lewinsky, but rather the credibility and the honor under oath that must exist within the institution of the presidency, and which has been squandered by the current occupant of this high office. There are absolute applicable standards by which we all must live. If we do not live up to those standards, we will no longer be that nation which stands as a beacon of hope for all the world."[5]

It should be noted that a realist conception of representation is not party affiliated. The idea that modes of expression should deliver truth and reality in *a straight way* is one of those commonplaces that structure basic conceptions of language use in U.S. culture. Contemporary representations of political issues within media representations, for example, regularly draw upon the idea that there is a mode of speech that can be characterized as "straight" and because straight, effective and honorable. "Straight Talk Wins Votes in Wisconsin" ran a headline in *U.S. News and World Reports* three weeks before the 2012 presidential election between Barack Obama and Mitt Romney.[6] On the other hand, it is also true that the GOP has crafted a party identity that is wedded to a preferred style of speech called "straight talk"—the kind that seems to be most invested in delivering "the hard facts" to audiences. "Sign up for Ron Paul's Texas Straight Talk" declares the Congressman's official website, which, in issuing this invitation, links Paul's identity to his mode of delivery. Similar qualities are attributed to New Jersey Governor Chris Christie, who, according to CNN, was expected to deliver at the 2012 Republican Convention a "straight-talk speech that Republicans have come to expect from the straight-talking Christie." "Laura Bush Delivers Feisty GOP Straight Talk" ran a 2008 *People Magazine* story favorable to the first lady at a time when her husband's White House tenure was largely ridiculed.[7]

Presumably, unlike Clinton, the straight talker has nothing to hide. Emboldened by the courage of his convictions, he expresses ideas without pandering and without fearing the backlash that his perspective might generate. Clinton's unwillingness to get his words straight not only refused to engage virtuous mimicry, many believed that he purposely twisted words in a resolute attempt to mislead citizens with statements that gave the appearance of being forthright while only pretending to do so. As put by William Kristol, editor of *The Weekly Standard* and panelist on ABC's "This Week":

> Bill Clinton has acted for the past year on his deepest beliefs: that law is merely politics, that the truth is merely spin, that an oath is merely rhetoric, that justice is merely power. These doctrines are deeply corrosive of free government. They corrupt us and degrade our constitutional order in a profound way. This fundamental disdain for his presidential oath is Bill Clinton's highest crime and misdemeanor. And the remedy for high crimes and misdemeanors is impeachment.[8]

According to *Dallas Morning News* commentator Richard Estrada, "Like Nixon, Clinton is his own worst enemy. He is an equal opportunity bully, smirking at political enemies and the victims of his personal whims. He may survive the latest threat to his political life, but his reputation will not survive his diminishment of his presidency, nor his hubris."[9]

The idea that speakers should be punished for misrepresenting reality is not unique to the events of 1998. Here we can take a cue from Scott

Durham who notes that historically, many cultures have devised narratives about ideal speakers and a corresponding injunction against those who claim to enact a cultural ideal but only pretend to do so. Indeed, the idea that democratic life demands a kind of vigilance that will unmask charlatans has been deemed so vital to maintaining social order that punishments have been devised within Western philosophical traditions for those who fail to demonstrate a commitment to establishing resemblances between speech and Truth. Durham's observations about this dynamic are worth quoting at length:

> In the metaphysical and theological traditions, the appeal to narrative is made by the philosopher or 'truthful man,' whose attempt to grasp the 'beyond' of the image is formulated as a problem of passing judgment on the image as a truthful or deceptive representation, which either reaffirms or subverts the founding truths of the prevailing order of things. Does the lineage of the image participate in the essence of the original or is it merely a sophistic counterfeit or a demonic usurper? Does it lead us back to our foundation in the Good and the True or does it cause us to lose ourselves in error and perversity? (19).

Media reports circulating in 1998 often expressed exactly the concerns outlined by Durham, including the following op-ed that ran in the *Philadelphia Enquirer*:

> Doublespeak, particularly of the political and legal kind, of the Clinton kind, is language that pretends to communicate but really doesn't. It is the product of clear, calculated thought, intended from the outset to control and pervert reality. It is language that avoids or shifts responsibility and undermines honest public debate. It is an oppressive form of communication that ultimately confines our thought and suffocates our ability to express ourselves freely. It breeds suspicion, distrust, cynicism and ultimately hostility.[10]

The remedy to the threat of perversion: expulsion. Expel the pretender—the one who promises to speak truly but instead steers listeners away from truth's domain (Durham 19). Expel those who fail to adopt proper purposes and banish the desire to engage in language practices that forsake the honorable and principled. "Most officers of my acquaintance would have resigned their commission had they been discovered violating their oath," declared Senator John McCain (R-Arizona) during the Senate debate that followed the House impeachment. "The President did not choose this course of action. . . . As much as I would like to, I cannot join in his acquittal."[11]

The act of expulsion attempts to make the problem of representational indeterminacy disappear by doling out punishments to those who fail to demonstrate that they have endeavored to secure the "lineage of the copy" (Durham 19) and through that process, take part in a ruling interpretive order that guarantees that distinctions between meritorious and abusive speech will be unambiguously maintained. But while GOP arguments rested upon the idea that an *a priori* representational order (or self-evident logic) prefigures any cultural production and should govern how language is used, in the wake of poststructuralist challenges to the metaphysics of presence, questions arise about how to distinguish the existent *a priori* from the cultural signifiers people invent to describe representational action. Interpretive technologies are also representations and the processes they delineate are linguistic descriptions that function like any other discourse that is historically situated and socially sanctioned. And because discourse cannot escape the social, meanings are not conveyed via a straightforward lineage but when words are positioned within rhetorical contexts and in relationship to other socially sanctioned terms. The technologies we use to enact interpretive processes are fully mired in these complex acts of positioning, unable to stage an act of independence that would separate representational forms from their meanings. This principle applies to all of those words that seem to have self-evident content—logic, reason, straight talk. The content of such terms cannot be categorically distinguished from the signifiers that would give that content expression.

With no ability to escape narrative, all methods of interpretation engage acts of translation. Indeed, as Jean Baudrillard has observed, a problem of translation will be raised whenever we communicate because the attempt to delineate what a given representation has conveyed will not encounter a question about truth's appearance but a question about how to perceive where we think a given representation aims. Is the representation attempting to re-present truth or only pretending to or perhaps aiming somewhere else entirely? Baudrillard's attention to perpetual translation underscores a critical caveat within the narratives that engage metaphors of vision to describe interpretive labor. Even Plato maintained that language is incapable of displaying truth's raw essence. True visions of truth are only available to the gods. Since humans cannot discern whether truth's essence is present, when they judge, they assess whether it seems that an interlocutor's language use has *attempted* to mimic *a priori* forms. (On this point, see Panagia and Durham.) In other words, when we assess a representational aim, we "look at" that which remains stubbornly invisible—an attempt at a kind of participation that would align with the divine realm that is unavailable for human review. We're at least three steps removed from any straightforward vision of truth's presentation. Hence, when gauging ethical comportment, we can only evaluate what cannot be seen: whether a rhetor harbors a goal of being true to the *idea* that one should attempt to convey what is genuine and authentic.

Baudrillard's use of simulacra calls attention to this knotted but crucial caveat. Because interpretive methodologies cannot definitively locate truth's presence, procedures overseeing judgments about whose speech aims in the right direction are based upon speculations, not facts. "Simulacra" confound orders of representation by introducing the possibility that pretense—the fake show of obedience to an order of representation—will be mistaken for a genuine act. And they introduce the further possibility that the lineage of the copy should not be automatically esteemed. The term simulacrum identifies symbolic constructs/representational modes that forego the demands of Platonic mimesis by making no claims to a domain beyond interpretive mediation. The simulating action that produces linguistic signs and visual artifacts need not ascribe value or ethics to the endeavor to mirror truth. Simulacra implicate style because the putative abandonment of any attempt to retrieve the "true referent" would seem to empty the signifier of content, leaving only a formal appearance that does not engage with the ideal but offers only an imitation of bona fide act of engagement. Simulacra could potentially mean anything.

When cultures embrace simulacra as valid linguistic signs, they re-order the value system that would determine which language practices matter. In contexts in which simulacra circulate, no premium is placed on the attempted act to re-present reality and the referent is not given priority over the signifier that would represent it. The speech that heads back to truth is not preferred to the one that spins. Rather, all representational endeavors are equally regarded no matter what direction they take. Baudrillard maintains that a problem of translation arises when people fail to see the difference between the evaluative equity implicated by the production of simulacra and the order of evaluation imposed by the conventional work of distinguishing categorical differences between the true, the false, the real, the imaginary. Further, because simulacra look like genuine signs of truth, they can fool us. They will feign the requisite work of mimicking a higher order but offer a mere appearance, a thin surface rather than a core essence.

Baudrillard advises caution: Through the power of simulacra, we risk privileging artificiality over reality. We live at a cultural moment that has been influenced by the lessons of postmodernism and that embraces hyperreality as a component part of any communicative context. He argues that we are in danger of preferring representations that are pure contrivances, relying upon them as points of reference informing conceptions of what has value and significance. Letting go of the ability to make truth claims threatens to render systems of interpretation "weightless" (Simulations 10).

The GOP's fear about the nation's "soul" veering away from truth could be characterized as expressing a similar concern. On the other hand, to many of us watching the impeachment spectacle, the endeavor to punish the President for an illicit speech act enacted the very problem of pretense that GOP leaders claimed to fear, leaving us once again spinning in textuality.

THE REALITY AND THE CHARADE

I have been arguing that GOP arguments about the need to trust in the absolute authority of the law conflated a culturally produced social practice with a transcendent order that presumably oversees and guides how human beings respond to representations of ideas and events. On one level, such arguments remain persuasive because the idea that all should abide by the law *is*, after all, critically significant to the functioning of democratic life. Perjury *is* a serious offense and should be punished. We need to be able to count upon the idea that testimony given in a legal setting should be as faithful to the truth as possible. Further, the rule of law, in general, should be sacrosanct if we care about preventing despotism.

But when the concepts of governance and obedience were incorporated into public arguments in 1998, the idea that the law's authority should absolutely and resolutely govern both the production of speech and audience reception not only failed to persuade a majority, the dedicated support for this way of perceiving issues cost the Republican party five seats in the House during the 1998 mid-term elections. As noted by political scientist Gary Jacobson, it was "only the second [time] since the Civil War that a president's party has increased its share of seats in a mid-term election" (21).[12] Many perceived pro-impeachment arguments to be empty, overwrought, "just" rhetoric, mere pretense, and hence dismissible.

As debates circulated in 1998 about the significance of Clinton's affair with Lewinsky, GOP leaders had to convince audiences that they were sincerely raising a *question* about whether Clinton should be impeached. To appear to conduct a genuine inquiry, lawmakers gathered to talk things over, but because views about what was at issue were sharply divided along party lines, precisely how to organize discussion in the proceedings became bogged down in controversy itself. Congressional leaders endeavored to devise terms to name interpretive procedures that presumably would keep the question of impeachment open rather than rationalize a predetermined verdict. A language was needed that could clearly describe interpretive practices that truly enacted *inquiry*. Presumably, during the October meetings that took up the question of how to stage an impeachment inquiry, House members would be able to skirt the problem of simulacra by proposing deliberative procedures that would establish something akin to "best practices." (Or, to put this in the language of mimesis, any speaker's description of how to evaluate the meaning and significance of the evidence to impeach would correspond to that speaker's actual conception of how representational processes work to facilitate a genuine inquiry within a legal proceeding.)

Debates in 1998, however, demonstrated precisely the inverse—that languages about procedures did not neutrally transmit uncontroversial depictions of evaluative practices. Once the House Judiciary Committee voted (21–16) to pursue an *inquiry* into the question of impeachment (Oct. 5, 1998), the House as a whole met to address the question of whether to approve the Judiciary Committee findings. Disagreements followed as Congressional leaders found themselves not only arguing about how to regard Clinton's speech acts, but also about how to determine a method for exploring the question of whether criminality had made an appearance.

Rep. Henry Hyde (R-IL) opened that judiciary committee meeting with a statement that attempted to set parameters:

> We have another ideal here: to attain justice through the rule of law. . . . And so here today, having received the referral and 17

cartons of supportive material from the Independent Counsel, the question asks itself: Shall we look further or shall we look away? I respectfully suggest we must look further by voting for this resolution and thus commencing an inquiry into whether or not the president has committed impeachable acts. We don't make any judgments. We don't make any charges. We simply begin a search for the truth.[13]

On the face of it, this statement might sound reasonable, if not rudimentary. If objectivity is obtainable, then we all might agree that the October meetings were, indeed, quite directly about establishing procedures and not about determining who was engaged in this historic event *just for show*. Hyde's opening statement attempted to avoid that thicket of ambiguity by clearly describing the situation at hand. Ostensibly, facts about the alleged crime had been collected and were available for review. At least sixty thousand pages of evidence had been produced by Independent Counsel Kenneth Starr to demonstrate that a crime had been committed. The evidence, meanwhile, was treated as a re-presentation of a "fact-finding" mission, delivered in narrative form, presumably neutral, presumably reasonable and hence devoid of any language uses that would persuade audiences to adopt a particular view of what the facts meant. When considering whether they were compelled to look at that evidence in the first place, Congressmen advocating an inquiry responded: Of course. How could a responsible inquiry move ahead but by taking a look at the evidence collected?

We might, then, expect few to disagree with the seemingly reasonable response from U.S. Rep Tom Delay (R-TX) about why legislators should always take a look at the possibility that a political leader has engaged in criminal activity: "Closing our eyes to allegations of wrongdoing by voting no or by limiting the scope or time constitutes a breach of our responsibilities as members of this house."[14]

When proposing to take an objective look at the facts, both Hyde and Delay invoked what might be described as a scientific model of deliberation that envisions inquiry as objective and guided by an empiricist process in which a search for facts is made possible because "facts speak for themselves." This version of realist discourse implicates style in that it maintains that forms of representation should facilitate the endeavor to both engage responsible deliberatory practices and signal one's true intentions to others. The words we use to name this kind of engagement describe actions such as categorization, differentiation, logical clarification. These words tend to be read not as words but as clear descriptors of bona fide actions that correspond exactly to what is named—scrutinizing, clarifying, ordering, establishing causal links between various points of a perspective. Typically, the realist strategy is not read as a strategy but as the means for conveying and activating a rational process that makes it possible to obtain the objective overview the critical thinker is expected to take.

The practices that appear to actualize rational procedures of deliberation draw upon the same scopic paradigm (see Martin Jay) that invokes a metaphor of vision to depict political judgment as an act of critical scrutiny. Impeachment advocates were able to summon this paradigm because it is a familiar one with a long and venerable history that, according to Davide Panagia, extends from the writings of Thomas Hobbes to Jeremy Bentham to the contemporary theories of Jürgen Habermas, whose ethic of communication calls for open debate that enables interlocutors to mutually recognize and validate the most reasonable premise. The organizing logic conflates democratic practices with public scrutiny and affirms the validity of the mimetic act of "presencing" while rendering its reception as tantamount to deliberation's very character. Once this narrative depiction is referenced as a real descriptor of deliberatory practices, then it will seem both logical and ethical to expect that language users should put forth acts of representation that facilitate a straight forward review.

But rather than prove that the language of empiricism is available to buttress deliberatory processes, the October meetings demonstrated that proclaiming a desire for representational order will not necessarily instigate it. Disagreements arose about every aspect of the inquiry in ways that implicated the role of narrative in establishing visions of what actually constitutes critical scrutiny. When Republican members effectively said, "yes, let's look at this," Democrats responded, "at what?" and "for how long?" As summed up by U.S. Rep. Barney Frank (D-MA): "The chairman said we shouldn't look away, we should look further. I agree. What we shouldn't do, however, is adopt a resolution that says, 'let's look around. Let's see what we can find.'"[15]

Democrats who did not want to pursue an inquiry at all—those who felt that the calls for impeachment were *a charade*—raised objections to Republican methods of obtaining and processing evidence. They posed questions that, initially, seemed to be straightforwardly procedural: How much time to devote to deliberation? *What* evidence should be examined to insure that a look at facts took precedence over innuendo? But even these seemingly simple questions encountered the problem of translation that accompanies the endeavor to distinguish style from substance. Rather than generate an unassailable linkage between a narrative describing an ideal inquiry and an actualization of that ideal, the October debates about whether to even consider the option of impeachment revealed a fundamental inability to demonstrate that words connect to practices in ways that would enable the spectator to ascertain differences between the fake and the true. How, for example, to represent and bring to full presence the intangible and fluid experience of *deliberating*? What to do to insure that legislators were truly engaged in the labor of thinking and not delivering preformed stylized performances?

When, for example, Hyde opened the meeting of the House and mentioned that thousands of pages from investigating attorneys had been made available for review, he suggested that the pages themselves should be regarded as an unprejudiced object of scrutiny. But many had doubts about the impartiality of that evidence and what it represented. The objectivity of the Special Prosecutor who collected "the facts" was also rendered suspicious, and that sense implicated feelings about whether a straightforward look at the evidence would instigate an unbiased review. Further, the question about how much time to give to debate posed a secondary question of whether we can know, for sure, whose look has been critically engaged rather than cursory—the mere show that aimed to validate a foregone conclusion. How to tell the difference between the look that would truly deliberate from that which only appeared to do so?

The suspicions of Democratic congressional leaders about the legitimacy of the inquiry were articulated by U.S. Rep William Delahunt (D-MA), who, at the House debate about the impeachment inquiry, objected to the restrictions being placed upon the kind of deliberation that was to take place:

> I'm aware of the fact that there is a limited time for this debate. I think that is indeed unfortunate, because I was going on to talk about how we have abdicated our constitutional duties to an unelected prosecutor; how we have released thousands of pages that none of us in good conscience can say that we've read; how we've violated the sanctity of the grand jury so that we can arrive here today to launch an inquiry without an independent adequate review of the allegations by this body, which is our constitutional mandate. . . . That's not a process, Mr. Speaker; it's a blank check. That's what I was going to talk about. But out

of deference to others that want to speak, I will conclude by saying that one hour to begin only the third impeachment inquiry in U.S. history is a travesty, and a disgrace for this institution.

This was followed by applause.

Hyde's reply:

I just want the record to be clear. My good friend Mr. Delahunt talked about 60,000 pages that were released that weren't reviewed or looked at. I want him to know and I want everyone listening to know every single page of anything that was released was reviewed and things that weren't released were reviewed by our staff. . . . Six (Democrats) never came over to see the material. On the Republican side . . . every member came over to look at the material.[16]

The actions undertaken in this House inquiry had all of the hallmarks of fairness and yet, from Delahunt's perspective, what they produced was precisely the opposite—a rush to judgment. The implication here is significant because of what we may extrapolate from it: that the very procedures that seem to demarcate and generate a responsible and ethical democratic process can instead instigate an abuse of power. Indeed, rather than prove that due deliberation should be configured with reference to a mimetic theory of correspondences, the October meetings raised ethical questions about whether to connect Congressional deliberatory practices to the languages that would describe them. Doubts about such connections implicate how to apprehend the relationship between narrative, experience and discourses of authenticity. Do the languages that would represent acts of deliberation adequately and accurately portray a just (and repeatable) political process? If connections between discursivity and event remain tangled and elusive, then an action does not necessarily indicate a "doing" that correlates with a narrative depiction. Not all acts of looking will realize the ideal of fairness or constitute proper attentiveness. And if concrete practices cannot be fully or precisely *described*, there are narrative gaps within any judgment of whether a practice such as deliberation has made an appearance. How to fill in those gaps is precisely the ethical question.

Hyde's response effectively avoided any consideration of ethics and representational ambiguity and instead asserted an automatic linkage between looking and testimonials to practicing diligence. The review of the sixty thousand collected pages was presented as concrete evidence of an intangible quality that might be called "thoroughness." In proclaiming that members of his party had taken a look at the evidence, Hyde delineated a specific technology that promised to transform what some had called a "partisan witch hunt" into a model of judicious review. In effect, he suggested that the act of looking itself inaugurates an ethical stance, and that the presence of an amorphous concept such as *deliberation* will be demonstrated via a testimonial about its importance. Hence the very phrase "due deliberation" would seem to designate in a straightforward way the ethical actions practiced under its name. Presumably, not only will the facts be discernible and recognizable to spectators, so will the methods deployed to engineer their unbiased review. The style used to designate fidelity to the representational processes depicting facts would seem to be of little significance.

It is important to consider how this model is referenced regularly within political debates as if it does indeed offer a neutral means for adjudicating differences in perspective and as if audiences *do* follow a neutral order when judging about which positions have substance. The discursive conventions associated with rational argumentation seem to make it possible to cut through stylistic excess and retrieve what is essential about core issues and to deploy truth's harsh light to excavate what exists, no matter how disturbing or ugly. And, presumably, when language is stripped of its excesses, we should be able to notice when substance is missing. But it is also possible to read those conventions as conventional, a portal to instrumental thinking that gives the appearance of bona fide engagement while instantiating the mechanistic repetition of practices devoid of scrutiny that might be called *critical*.

Delahunt's statement registers the difficulty of knowing whose use of language is, indeed, practicing due diligence. If it is possible to regard the very claims of fairness as an abuse of power, then we may question whether to automatically place a higher premium on the discursive practices that claim to aim towards truth's revelation. In effect, discourses about the impeachment asked citizens to determine *whether* having faith in language's ability to convey truth neutrally should underwrite the nation's representational agenda.

Idiosyncratic Action

Once the President's use of language was targeted for critique, it became paramount for the GOP to exhibit a mode of representation that did not dissemble and that instead fulfilled moral obligations to *be* true. One notable attempt to illustrate what "straight talk" looked like could be found in the Articles of Impeachment, the legal document that officially represented what was at issue and in so doing, promised to provide a clear demonstration of how argumentation is structured by correspondences between signs and referents. There were four articles, but I will cite only Article One:

> In his conduct while President of the United States, William Jefferson Clinton, in violation of his constitutional oath faithfully to execute the office of President of the United States and, to the best of his ability, preserve, protect, and defend the Constitution of the United States, and in violation of his constitutional duty to take care that the laws be faithfully executed, has willfully corrupted and manipulated the judicial process of the United States for his personal gain and exoneration, impeding the administration of justice, in that: On August 17, 1998, William Jefferson Clinton swore to tell the truth, the whole truth, and nothing but the truth before a Federal grand jury of the United States. Contrary to that oath, William Jefferson Clinton willfully provided perjurious, false and misleading testimony to the grand jury concerning: (1) the nature and details of his relationship with a subordinate government employee; (2) prior perjurious, false and misleading testimony he gave in a Federal civil rights action brought against him; (3) prior false and misleading statements he allowed his attorney to make to a Federal judge in that civil rights action; and (4) his corrupt efforts to influence the testimony of witnesses and to impede the discovery of evidence in that civil rights action. In doing this, William Jefferson Clinton has undermined the integrity of his office, has brought disrepute on the Presidency, has betrayed his trust as President, and has acted in a manner subversive of the rule of law and justice, to the manifest injury of the people of the United States. Wherefore, William Jefferson Clinton, by such conduct, warrants impeachment and trial, and removal from office and disqualification to hold and enjoy any office of honor, trust or profit under the United States.[17]

Ostensibly, the Articles of Impeachment offered a legal representation that straightforwardly delineated the charges and their reasoned justifications. But like much of the discourse involved in this event, the very language in these documents seemed noticeable. Rather than solidify a sense that a crime had been committed, the Articles renewed doubts, at least for some citizens, about whether this issue deserved attention at all. Indeed, rather than provoke recognition of a severe crime, the legal language highlighted the difference between narrated descriptions and lived perceptions of Clinton's behavior. Humiliating? Yes. Disgraceful? To adherents of a particular version of propriety, yes. But was a lie about a sexual liaison equal to a violation to protect The Constitution? Should a refusal to fully cooperate in an inquiry about one's sexual dalliances be represented as an "obstruction of justice"? To some, Clinton's responses to the grand jury in the Paula Jones case had to be measured against the dubious merit of *that* proceeding. If Clinton did lie (fudge?) about his relationship with Monica Lewinsky, then was that a crime at all? A high crime?

Arguably, the Articles of Impeachment failed to enact a *logic* of substitutions. For many readers of House Resolution 611, the words did not seem to correspond with the deeds being described. Nor did they seem to retrieve and bring forth any esteemed abstract qualities such as a higher order of reason. Indeed, one could make the case that the verbs in the Articles seemed to be stylistically excessive, even hyperbolic, and hence dismissible for failing to execute a systematic and neutral method that allowed for the identification of the issues and their importance. And if *legal* language—that which promises objectivity and equity—can seem excessive, then what does that suggest about the prospect of formalizing abstract conceptions of how to think in other, less narrowly defined contexts?

The Articles exposed a rift between the generalized narrative that depicts democratic inquiry as an act of scrutiny and the specific material practice of scrutiny exercised in this particular case. Many citizens may have wondered about whether *this* was the kind of look that vigilant citizens should be expected to take when inspecting the comportment of their national leaders. When puzzling that out, they encountered the textual limits to acts of translation, where the implicit rational order arranged through narrative encounters the potentially unwieldy experience of human interpretation. In rejecting the claims of neutrality by those who wrote up the formal charges, there was a simultaneous refusal to see a straightforward connection between the legal language used to name this issue and give it visibility and the enactment of justice.

A number of polls suggested that voters instead read the drive to impeach as political theatre. Immediately following the December, 1998 vote to impeach, pollsters endeavored to register the mood of the citizenry and found expressions of discontent. As put by a headline in *USA Today*: "Public Likes Clinton More, GOP less in Wake of the Vote." The article cited a *USA Today*/CNN/Gallup poll that showed "public support for Clinton jumped to a personal high of 73 percent" and that "fewer than one in three has a favorable view of the GOP, its lowest since 1992." Other polls concurred. A CBS-*New York Times* poll taken after the vote to impeach found that sixty-six percent of those polled said that Clinton should not resign; thirty-one percent said that he should. In an NBC poll, seventy-two percent of respondents approved of the job Clinton was doing, while twenty-five percent disapproved. Sixty-two percent maintained that Clinton should complete his term, a number that had risen eleven points from the previous Tuesday.[18]

Because the charges were not demonstrably valid, they appeared to be baseless and hence the case itself was "logically" dismissed. This, of course, was a relief to those of us who viewed this event as a journey into the land of the surreal. But that response did not contend with the problems of representation that impeachment discourses otherwise raised. Embedded within purported explorations of "the facts" of criminality was a speculative question about how discursive practices manifest intangible qualities such as guilt. Arguably, the possibility that ambiguities are embedded within speculations about how language communicates meaning was exactly the point of contention within impeachment debates. Any exploration into the guilt or innocence of a person charged with lying under oath raises a philosophically opaque conundrum about whether it is ever possible to tell the difference between "the spin" and its presumed opposite.

Given that the vote to impeach Clinton was rejected because, to those polled, the charges seemed to be *excessive*, then it is possible to conclude that style plays a formidable role in determining representational legitimacy. Rather than clarify why Clinton deserved to be impeached for an aberrant act of speech, arguments that called for straight talk instead illustrated that a strange doubling accompanied public discussions about crime and representation. The strange part included the sense that a principle of negativity permeated the presentation of the issues, wherein the style of pro-impeachment arguments promising to deliver straight talk seemed instead to call out its absence. Every attempt to establish an indisputable "reality" about Clinton's criminal activity or the authenticity of the impeachment inquiry itself veered into what might be called the gestural, theatrical, and aesthetic aspects of political discourse. Warnings about the dangers of Clinton's linguistic impropriety simultaneously registered a query about how to read the language use of those making the accusations. Indeed the very style of those claims contributed to their rejection.

After the impeachment effort failed, for example, Hyde repeated the idea that impeachment proponents were motivated by a noble desire to uphold standards, and this time referenced history when defending his actions in a *Chicago Tribune* editorial:

> The impeachment ... was not a political struggle ... but a historic constitutional test. A bedrock principle of democracy, first formulated by our Anglo-Saxon legal tradition in the Magna Carta, was a stake: the principle that no person is above the law. Birth, wealth and social position do not put someone above the law. Neither does public office. ... This was a constitutional test of whether the United States government remains a government of laws, not of men.[19]

This kind of pronouncement, one that aimed to seamlessly organize political life by connecting past to future, instead called attention to itself via the attempt to craft an equitable correspondence between this sorry event and that awe-inspiring document from a historical past that stands as an emblem of human progress toward shared governance and individual freedom. Indeed, this was exactly the kind of comparison that was regarded (by that apparent majority) as violating the correspondence theory that seeks resemblances between terminologies and the ideas words would represent. By formulating dissonant linkages, Hyde's commentary became stylistically noticeable for its overreach rather than for his argument's ability to nail a point of view and demonstrate how straight talk ought to appear. Once a representational mode becomes noticeable, then how to situate it within the organizing logic of substitutions is not immediately apparent.

But rather than mull over this conundrum, we tend to consign such stylistic dissonances to the realm of the unpersuasive and dismissible. This outcome is a byproduct of the value system that prioritizes the delivery of substantial content by characterizing style as a surface feature of language, its concerns relatively meager and insubstantial, both qualitatively different from information and knowledge and potentially an impediment to their apprehension. We are expected to uphold the idea that rhetorical styles should be invoked to guard citizens against "two kinds of corruptions—vagueness and artificiality" (McCrimmon 6) that indicate that the rhetor has "settled for a superficial view" (6). Typically, after deciding that a given style, like that of Hyde's, is "artificial," we draw upon such perceptions to determine what happens next, which usually means losing interest rather than deliberating about how styles affect evaluations of an utterance's content and significance.

How to theorize style's role within acts of persuasion is a question that rhetoricians have puzzled over since antiquity and found difficult to answer. As Edward P.J. Corbett observed, style is a "vague concept" that we think we grasp but then find impossible to encapsulate within neatly sorted descriptions. To characterize style, we often borrow familiar descriptors such as "'lucid,' 'elegant,' 'labored,' 'Latinate,' 'turgid' or flowing" (209). Or, as phrased within impeachment discourses, "plain" and "honest." Our conceptions of style, Corbett concludes, include "a curious blend of the idiosyncratic and the conventional" (210). When idiosyncrasy and convention blend, then a question is raised about the purpose of stylistic standards and whether their application helps to identify what a style is and does. Styles may be identifiable when discursive protocols are followed, but the effects (or consequences) of re-presenting forms of representation are not. Styles are *present*. They are material embodiments of ways of seeing that can carry forceful persuasive effects by provoking our senses. But what a given style *conveys* is conspicuously (and perhaps tortuously) ambiguous. Meanwhile, because that curious blend between the idiosyncratic and the conventional cannot be standardized to guarantee interpretive results, it contributes to the contemporary tendency to downplay style's role in political judgment.

But as we move from apprehension to dismissal, we are apt to lose sight of a critical moment of interpretive conversion. Style's role in judgment is minimized when meaning and significance get ascribed to entities that appear to *have substance*. This apparent order of cause and effect offers another occasion for considering how interpretation engages acts of translation. Our encounters with the domain of "the substantial" would seem to require no translation at all, as substance would seem to be self-evidently present, unambiguously noticeable, forging a clear and direct relationship between the signifier of substance and its substantial quality. The judgments we make about what has substance seem to be organized by the terminology we've devised to designate that quality, while the possibilities for identifying what has substance seem to rely upon the procedural—a neutrally deployed process that constitutes the experience of feeling (knowing) what has weight.

Arguably, this tidy model is packaged for easy consumption, but it overlooks component parts of interpretive technologies that are significant yet impossible to substantiate. Elizabeth Grosz explores one example of the ways in which an insubstantial significance inheres within conceptions of narrative's relationship to interpretation in an article that considers whether the discourses of philosophy and those of architecture can speak to each other in discussions that consider how to conceive of space. There are radical differences between these discourses. One aims to design material objects that will inhabit a physical landscape while the other imagines the mind as an object, a landscape that may be mapped, traveled upon, situated, and occupied. We draw connections between these two discourses as if their associations are automatic, but any correlation will be conceptual only. Any (virtual) comparison will contain unanswerable questions about whether concepts have inherent relationships to reality and whether the virtual ever gets converted into the actual. *If* a shared conceptual space can be forged between these disparate discourses, its status will be tentative, perpetually unsettled and not hospitable to clearly enunciated indications of *what* is shared.

The tentativeness of any formulation about what these divergent discourses share calls attention to a dynamic of conversion within the interpretive processes that enable a proposed possibility to be treated as an actuality. In tracing what that conversion entails, Grosz contemplates the significance of the time of translation that seems to establish its own substantial dimension occupied by mental processes that get activated as an aspect of contemplation. This time/space is ephemeral as well as multifaceted. It involves (at least) the time of "before" that encapsulates preconceived notions, the time in which thought emerges, takes note of, assesses, etc., and the time of deliberation wherein we consider whether an object of representation has merit, significance, gravitas.

I bring up Grosz's argument because it foregrounds an aspect of interpretive action that tends to go unnoticed. In the context of political disputes, the dynamic of time also includes the time it takes for an apprehension of a particular material/stylized marker to emerge into a judgment of its quality and significance. Within that time of transition, the ephemeral potentiality of a style to mean any number of things will be converted into a narrative declaring its actual significance (whether it is classified as idiosyncratic, conventional, helpful, an obstruction, etc.). These judgments occur in the time of "retrospect"—when we appear to look back at a prior (preconceived) order of meaning to determine the significance of any signifier made anew. The endless possibilities of meanings that might be derived from style's idiosyncratic features get domesticated within interpretive orders that look for stylistic conformity *in order to* put forth a narrative about standards. In that particular time of conversion, we will likely forget those other potential meanings, especially when we are encouraged to connect the act of *finding* meaning with that of being ethical. We will also likely forget what occurred *during* the interval of time between the possible and the actual, "an interval that refuses self-identity and self-presence to any thing, any existent. This interval, neither clearly space nor time but a kind of leakage between the two, the passage of one into the other" (Grosz, "Future of Space") will be forgotten once the final judgment takes hold and becomes the point of reference in subsequent narratives about the judging event. Within that realm of leakage between space, time, and judgment, we undertake acts of translation that then inform the decisions we make about whether a given style fits the occasion of its use, decisions that are perhaps flitting and transitory, but remain radically consequential to estimations of what seems to exist.

Judgments of what exists (such as whether legal language identifies just causes for impeachment) engage an aesthetic dynamic wherein narratives appear to correspond to experiences of deliberatory processes only when we overlook what cannot be represented—the very act of converting an apprehension into a resolution. Such conversions entail drawing connections between diversified discursive elements and then neglecting to consider the stylistic strategies that get deployed to enable them to appear to connect to judgments of meaning. Arguably, we do not consider how that time of conversion influences judgments of what exists because of the tendency to conflate the act of naming an interpretive result with the act of apprehending its significance. Rather than remember that narratives have contributed to how we convert the possible to the actual, we instead align an idea of actualization with an idea of "being substantial," and then attach that conceptual connection to specific representational forms that we have learned to regard as *having substance*. In the process, style's specific contribution to how potential meanings get channeled into resolute judgments of what has merit or fails to carry weight disappears. Indeed, we mostly ignore the particular ways in which our sense of what has substance emerges partly because we are prone to look for "the substantial" and overlook all that will not settle into any recognizable form —time, the action of conversion, style's potential and ineffable ability to affect our senses.

The thicket of debate that arose in the 1998 impeachment proceedings demonstrates that taken-for-granted conceptions of deliberative time did not work in conclusive ways to clarify what was at issue and how it should be addressed. The question of who was doing what with language created numerous messy entanglements, all of them poised for judgments about which, if any, had significance. The act of categorizing what was at issue did not automatically propel citizens toward a neutral time of deliberation in which all considered the legitimacy of terms being thrown around to name what was at issue. Instead, the potential categories conveyed attitudes about how to ascribe substance. Was perjury at issue? A linguistic evasion? A deft response to political theater? The terms established how to "look" at potential meaning, and *the look* (the "surface" appearance) influenced what happened in the deliberatory time that then generated judgments about the impeachment's (lack of) significance.

STYLE AND SIGNIFICANCE

This is, of course, Kenneth Burke's point. Burke attends to the constitutive role of language that delivers meaning neither transparently nor neutrally but by provoking audiences to experience an embodied sense of identification to signs that they will potentially accept (and with which they will become "consubstantial"). Any form of discourse engages a representational dynamic that facilitates not only an act of recognition but also the potential for shared participatory responses. Words constitute communities not because they reflect connections that already exist but because they offer sites for inducing shared perceptions about what matters. Unlike Plato, Burke does not banish the aesthetic from the serious work of political judgment but emphasizes its centrality to facilitating the appearance of having shared perceptions of whether something as amorphous as *significance* is on hand. Hence Burke positions rhetorical style at the center of the discursive give and take that comprises democratic deliberation, and he effectively revises conceptions of how styles influence judgments about which representations should earn our intellectual and emotional commitments. Not only do styles establish the textual protocols and grammatical conventions that craft cultural productions, more importantly, rhetorical style is key to the social practice of communication.

Hence, a crucial difference between positivistic views of representation and rhetorical ones can be located within attitudes about style's significance to judgment. While impeachment advocates condemned the bad attitude Clinton conveyed when refusing to forego rhetorical flourishes and straighten out his speech acts, rhetoricians rehabilitate conceptions of style by configuring stylized speech as ethically motivated speech. The seemingly surface features of rhetorical styles provide a gateway to a most important element within judgments of who is doing what with words—our perceptions of how people participate with language. We read styles as exhibitions of that which remains invisible: one's intentions, aims, attitude about how language should be used. Indeed, as rhetoricians have long argued, it is through style that we determine whether a rhetor seems to be communicating genuinely, is concerned about us, the nation, or even approved modes of expression. Our entrée into acts of judging begin with our readings of a speaker's motives. If we do not trust or believe the speaker's motives, we probably will not be convinced by what he or she says, even if the ideas might otherwise seem perfectly reasonable. Style is neither superficial nor an obstacle to truth's delivery but endemic to communicative action. Styles convey ways of seeing what matters within a scene of representation and enable audiences to get a sense of what a speaker (writer) cares about when putting forth a premise that others might share. For Burke, style is a means for getting others to collaborate with you when determining what to esteem and/or overlook. "You persuade a man only insofar as you can talk his language by speech, gesture, tonality, order, image, attitude, ideas, identify your ways with his" (Rhetoric of Motives 55). One learns to speak in ways that audiences will recognize to encourage their acceptance of one's point of view.

Burke's rhetorical theorizing about style's role in judgment is wonderfully complex and difficult to pin down, unlike the convention that treats style as a coherent and uniformly conceived resource for decisions about who speaks authoritatively and truthfully. Arguably, a more complex conception of style's role in judgment is better suited for contending with what the impeachment arguments show—judgments that appear to be substantiated by solid interpretive methods can quickly dissolve into the illusory and ephemeral. We project motives onto speakers and those projections are only speculations. But they are of the kind that can have significant political consequences. Because political speech cannot escape the aesthetic and socially constructed dimensions of evaluative methods, an ethics of representation cannot eliminate the contributions of rhetorical strategizing.

When we invest in interpretive frameworks to substantiate judgments, we should not lose sight of the ways in which acts of judging begin with artifice. Judgments begin with narratives that imply acts of conversion (and translation) that cannot themselves be represented and that remain paradoxically imaginary and substantial. As we engage with styles that aim to signify motives and attitudes, we enter into a dynamic of symbolic action that, in Ned O'Gorman's reading of Burke, does not work in a definitive and singular way but might instead be envisioned as traveling along a spectrum that moves between the sublime and the ridiculous. According to Burke,

> Some vastness of magnitude, power, or distance, disproportionate to ourselves, is "sublime." We recognize it with awe. We find it dangerous in its fascination. And we equip ourselves to confront it by piety, by stylistic medicine, and by structural assertion . . . The ridiculous, on the contrary, equips us by impiety, as we refuse to allow the threat [of] its authority: we rebel, and courageously play pranks when "acts of God" themselves are oppressing us (qtd. in O'Gorman 452).

O'Gorman builds upon this quote to describe a democratic style that embraces the "sublime-ridiculous" spectrum as a component part of political judgment, "a continuum" that, when embraced, "equips people, whether political leaders or everyday citizens, to move with agility across it. . . . Democracy encourages movement across this continuum by cultivating a strong, albeit somewhat paradoxical, sense among citizens that appearances and surfaces matter even as they are dispensable" (453). When attending to conceptions of democratic inquiry and judgment, keeping an eye on precisely the continuum of a paradoxical spectrum of potentialities offers one way of countermanding dominant scripts that too often "confuse difference with negation" (Panagia 60) in an effort to resolve what is paradoxical and replace it with a representative and narrativized postulate. When difference is conflated with negation, then it would seem that we must decide between two opposing options. Does the issue have substance or is it insignificant? Does a speaker's use of words bring about the sublime or the ridiculous? Presumably, only one quality may be chosen at a time. But keeping an eye on the paradoxical spectrum of possibilities that inhabits acts of translation would forestall the drive to differentiate the potentially sublime utterance from that which is potentially ridiculous within a narrative that would appear to enact a resolution but would be only able to manage this stylistically rather than authentically.

Of course positing an interpretive framework that recognizes paradoxes and interpretive ambiguities offers precisely the kind of "opaque" approach to language that agitated impeachment proponents, who doubled down on issuing big pronouncements that would explain, justify, and clear a path for language's sublime power to travel and propel meaning and significance to the forefront of deliberations. Congressional leaders explicitly and directly declared a commitment to exalted and immaculate standards of evaluation, as if making that point over and over would definitively prove that the cause of their actions was not, as put by Hyde, "the ravings of some vindictive political crusade but a reaffirmation of a set of values that are tarnished and dim these days."[20] Republican leaders delivered solemn testimonials that aimed to convince audiences of their somber devotion to a sacrosanct "rule of law," as if such declarations would inspire citizens to take seriously the GOP's stated concern about the nation's welfare.

"We must remain blind to bias and other distractions when applying the law—no matter whether we are applying it to an average citizen or to the President of our country" stated U.S. Rep. Howard Coble (R-NC) at the October 5 judiciary committee meeting. Three days later, at the meeting of the House, U.S. Rep Asa Hutchinson (R-AZ) concurred: "People say this is not Watergate. That's true. Every case is different. But the rule of law and our obligation to it does not change." So did U.S. Rep. Charles Canady (R-FL): "It is our solemn responsibility under the Constitution to . . . set an example that strengthens the authority of the laws and preserves the liberty with which we have been blessed as Americans." And so did U.S. Rep (R-TX) Tom Delay: "Let history judge us as having done our duty to uphold the sacred rule of law."[21]

The articulation of a desire to be in accordance with the law would appear to make that desire present and in the process prove that one's motives are not only politically innocent but also concerned with issues that are substantial, indeed, vital to the nation's future. A testimonial to the rule of law, if genuine, would presumably act as a rallying point for anyone who agrees to uphold law's sacred rule. And yet, like the Impeachment articles, it was precisely the endeavor to explicitly demonstrate the authenticity of "virtuous" aims that undermined the credibility of the proclamations and rendered them, at least for some citizens, as signifiers of the ridiculous. The form rendered formulaic through citational repetition, converted into a command to *be* literal, became ideologically suspect. The paradoxical element of "positive" negativity within those testimonials inspired not affiliations but suspicions about the motives of those pushing for this drastic political outcome, and the stylistic repetition contributed to solidifying that sense. In this case, the very phrase "rule of law" took on an incantatory quality that communicated neither true devotion to an ethics of representation nor transparency but an act of impersonation, a kind of engagement that might be called "aesthetic" in a pejorative sense—a formalized, indeed mechanized, mode of participation that veered into the ritualistic. In this context, the phrase "aesthetic engagement" recalls Terry Eagleton's definition—a kind of participation processed in accordance with its own internal logic, rendering only an appearance of having truly engaged with the issue put before the public about how to judge errant speech acts.[22] Mere style, we might say. Pure bombast.

Here is where conceptions of style become especially complex because those conceptions will be derived from cultural narratives that teach what to look for when assessing the legitimacy of representational forms. To push O'Gorman's point a bit further, besides envisioning judgments as traveling between a spectrum charting the sublime and the ridiculous, we need also to attend to the question of how to determine where to land. When we decide whether styles let us soar beyond the worldly or trap us in the matter of the mundane, our judgments of style's effects will be influenced by the cultural narratives that prioritize the substantial and actual over the speculative and the unrealized potential. Style straddles a spectrum as well. Styles are both textually material and merely textual—merely the representative of a prior conception about how symbolic forms inform ways of seeing what has merit. But because styles do affect our senses, they are also imbued with awesome potentiality. Styles can help instigate "new" perspectives, "shocking" us out of complacent worldviews, as Kant would suggest. Or, as Burke suggests, styles can act to console us when familiar. Or, in the case of the impeachment, styles can act to alert us that something feels "off" about the purported connections between the propositional content of a speech and the motives underwriting its expression. By overlooking how we apply a sense of substance or its lack to our evaluation of style, we overlook a subtle but critical element of an interpretive encounter that can influence how we come to believe or lose faith in the languages that would speak on our behalf.

Pragmatism and Positivism

Rhetorical study engages in speculations about how to use language strategically to achieve desired ends. It's not that truth does not matter. But facts are not necessarily available and even when they appear to be, their presentation does not necessarily persuade. In rhetorical formulations of how to use language, the act of speculating about what makes an argument effective is treated as an act of substance, as part of one's civic duty. Rather than denounce speculation and then consign style to the realm of the superficial, style's importance is reframed through the lens of the pragmatic. Accordingly, style acts to serve an identifiable social purpose. Its value is located not in its aesthetic qualities but in its ability to be socially productive by acting on behalf of the formation of a majority view.

As a starting point for an interpretive framework, this insight offers both a promising and a problematic way of contending with the paradoxical positive negativity that animates style's place in judgment. Rhetoricians often endeavor to demonstrate that rhetoric's contribution to acts of communication matter and are about more than "mere" style. How this outlook is validated allows for a consideration of significant differences between postmodern and rhetorical delineations of ethics in relation to acts of representation. For example, James P. McDaniel and Bruce E. Gronbeck maintain that it should be possible to both allow for civic disputes and find a path toward reconciliation by advocating "the imperative of the doxastic"—those "species of communal thought and values that must fill up the abstracted self of the citizen if he or she is going to have rhetorical efficacy in localist political environments" (36). Gerard Hauser, meanwhile, clarifies what "species" might mean when he promotes a specific style—vernacular rhetoric—as a central agent within political judgment that generates "a common understanding about the reality of experience, including its intended and unintended consequences" (297). To make rhetorical inquiry relevant, Hauser proposes that rhetorical models be based on actual discursive practices. "To overcome the reification of publics found in the Rational Deliberation model, a discourse-based theory of public opinion must *widen its scope* to include vernacular exchanges in addition to those of institutional actors. . . . A rhetorical model locates public opinion—a civil judgment—in the manifestations of common understanding within a public sphere," which he adds, is "fashioned through the dialogue of vernacular talk" (297—original emphasis. See also, Ivie 455).

In practice, rhetorical attention to style has promoted the idea that styles should bear recognizable forms, especially those that have come to be regarded as signifying reason or rational norms. Vanessa Beasley makes an explicit case of "a democratic style" that "must foreground reasons, recognition and imagined relationship(s) to promote the discursive environment necessary for the most fundamental democratic processes to flourish" (466). She argues that "the public articulation of reasons promotes education, legitimation, and accountability . . . Democratic style should offer recognition to audience members" and should "activate certain relational commitments to other people whom one does not know" (466). (Beasley eventually wonders if she should reject this schematized approach but does not fully do so.)

We will find echoes of this kind of thinking within countless textbooks that advise college writers about how to represent their ideas on the page by adhering to discursive protocols that have been culturally sanctioned. In his opening chapter, "Understanding Style," Joseph M. Williams begins by noting that his book on style, clarity, and grace is "based on two principles. It's good to write clearly, and anyone can" (1). That democratic pitch to "anyone" delineates an ethics of equity that in turn bears upon the kind of style that presumably should be valued—that which assists the act of persuasion and the enactment of community. And that assist is typically given stylistic expression when one attempts to represent with clarity forms that follow a logical order, elucidate definitions, and invoke "if, then" clauses that are sensible. The cause and effect logic that structures an argument should enable a majority to tell where one's thinking leads. Audiences should be relieved of the burden of having to struggle to understand what one is saying and why. Once freed from an interpretive struggle, audiences will be able to decide on the merits of a position put up for review. Paul Butler offers similar advice when he encourages compositionists to use the study of style as a way of claiming expertise about language issues and through that claim, to fashion the identity of the public intellectual contributing to public conversations about language controversies that take place outside of the academy. Butler traces how composition scholars lost an interest in style because of an association between style and a much-critiqued rhetorical tradition called "current-traditional rhetoric" that, scholars have argued, was too rigidly invested in Enlightenment mythologies. Because of this historical association, rhetoric and composition scholars "have failed to see the study of style for what it actually represented . . . a set of innovative practices used to generate and express language through the deployment of rhetorical features" (143). He adds that returning to a study of canons of style as a mode of invention "could be used profitably together in current discourse" (143).

To render style's role as pragmatic means discarding the expectation that one should chart a path back to universal truth. Rather, language use aims to activate audience consent. Accordingly, meanings evolve as audiences decide whether to adopt a particular version of truth in spite of a perpetual representational inconstancy. (See Hariman on this point as well.) Without the capacity to choose whether to believe in the validity of any given representation, the democratic part of public argument is effectively annihilated. Hence, rather than function as a reflection of meanings that are already intact, styles act as agents that generate the reasonable, democratic give and take of ideas, the kind that allows ideas to be represented, weighed, judged, and also abandoned. Styles help audiences evaluate whether representational forms facilitate actions that engage democratic practices, like aiding communication or showing concern for the nation and the citizenry.

While this reflexive approach to language studies is supple enough to allow for the possibility of dissent, it does not necessarily address the question of which specific styles will be anticipated, accepted, or dismissed, for what reasons, and to what effects. And while the acknowledgment of representational inconstancy also addresses style's significance to democratic processes in ways that expand conceptions of political judgment beyond the simple logic of substitutions, it nonetheless retains allegiances to the scopic paradigm that it presumably challenges. It affirms a hierarchy of values that delineates what kind of styles should receive cultural preference—i.e., those that identifiably serve specific purposes, that may be "used profitably" to signify qualities that have been culturally sanctioned, such as *being reasonable*. If it is "profitable" to convey styles that get read as reasonable, that is because there is a preset conception of what reason will look like linguistically and how its look will facilitate judgments about whether "reasonableness" has, indeed, appeared.

The "use language profitably" premise also implies an inherent connection between the idea of accountability and the priority of representability. Any judgment about "the look" of reason will then influence a secondary judgment about what cannot be seen: whether the rhetor is motivated to use language responsibly and with a reasonable attitude. The metaphor of vision reappears to support the idea that accommodating audiences means presenting those reasonable forms that, presumably, are recognizable and that, because communally accepted, get around the problem of ambiguity by generating thought processes that all have agreed to call "reasonable." In effect, political participation is positively measured through the evaluation of forms that signify invisible aims and motivations. Style continues to be situated as evidence of whether a speaker desires to be held accountable for his or her language practices. One's willingness to participate with socially sanctioned modes of representation is read as evidence of having good motives, while the motives that are good presumably coincide with socially redeemable aims. So that, even though attitudes are invisible, we tend to believe that making something representable means *being* accountable and that accountability is communicated stylistically.

It is style, then, that we rely upon to represent a moral image of thought. Having a commitment to styles that appear to be moral seems to tell us about what the speaker/writer intends to do with his words and whether those intentions are nefarious or honorable, and we make such determinations by deciding whether formalized expressions are cogent, orderly, pointed, etc. Such stylistic features seem to tell us whether a speaker, for example, aims to communicate rather than seduce, be earnest rather than playful or ironic, inform rather than please.

But is there a difference between the aim to use language to constitute a community of agreeable listeners and the expressed aims of GOP legislators to find a shared language that would communicate noble representational purposes?

Consider, for example, the following statement from U.S. Rep. Bob Barr (R-GA), delivered at Clinton's impeachment trial in December 1998, to justify Barr's vote to impeach:

> You know as children, all of us believed certain things with all of our hearts. We knew there was a difference between good and evil. We knew it was wrong to lie, and equally important, that if we got caught, we would be punished. . . . What happened to these simple truths that we all knew in our hearts just a few

short years ago? Why do so many adults now find it so hard to call a lie a lie, when as parents, teachers, and employers, we have no hesitancy?[23]

What to make of this expression of yearning? Arguably, it articulates a longing to find a way back "home" to truth, the same longing that has preoccupied philosophers, poets, and priests, many of whom have also longed for signs of origins, evidence of a continuance between this life and another, past and present, a connection between what we can imagine and what we can know. And yet, while it is possible that Barr's statement conjured such reflection, it is equally possible to imagine many of us sitting there on our couches watching the impeachment hearings unfold, the second one in the nation's history, having a less than sublime response, muttering, perhaps, something along the lines of, "You've got to be kidding."

Dismissing the value and significance of Barr's locution does not necessarily translate into a rejection of the value system informing his perspective. Presumably Barr, described by one reporter as "leading the charge to impeach a popular president," [24] offered his rendition of a common enough motif in this proceeding to repudiate interpretive ambiguity that could interfere with the goal of being a straightforward, objective, and fair adjudicator of the issue. But for anyone who was hoping to witness justice at work, what may have seemed notable was a sense of dissonance between an expectation and an experience—expecting to bear witness to the exhibition of reason's signs; encountering instead a nostalgia-inflected homily about simplicity and innocent children as a way of justifying a draconian outcome. In a legal proceeding that purported to address presidential misconduct, this blend of convention and idiosyncrasy may have been curious if not bizarre, offering (to some of us) absurd imagery when juxtaposed against preconceived notions of what form reason should take. Nonetheless, there are plenty of cultural practices—including those from rhetoric's traditions—that lend support to Barr's larger claims about the need for speakers to speak clearly and get to the point. Indeed, borrowing from Hayden White, it is possible to consider how the propositional content of Barr's statement compares to discourses of history that claim to engage models of discourse "purged of all figurative and tropological elements, and subjected to tests of logical consistency as an argument and of predicative adequacy as a body of fact" (5).

Barr advocated for the use of recognizable modes of speech to allow for determinations of who may be held accountable for language choices. As such, he made a case *for* representability in general, and more specifically, for representations that present a systematic order of cause and effect in which "good" reasons lead to "good conclusions." Far from seeming like pure nonsense, Barr's statement and the principles that he defended were both intelligible and representative of dominant discursive conventions, including those touted within rhetorical studies of style's role in generating audience adherence. Within Barr's call for simplicity was a presumed inclusionary motive made evident via the "plain" style that extends a democratic "welcome" to everyone and conveys a bona fide desire to reach as many in the audience as possible. The question, then, is whether and how Barr's particular call for clarity differs from, for example, the Rawlsian or Habermasian idea that communication should be *oriented* towards producing understanding, or how it differs from the rhetorical concern with devising styles that signify one's desire *to* communicate and to use language for the purpose of community formation comprised of mutually shared perspectives.

There are dissonances. When comparing Barr's statement to rhetorical theorizing that positions rational and vernacular norms as signifiers of socially responsible communicative practices, we might observe that Barr's demand for innocence expressed through the elimination of verbal excess is precisely at odds with a rhetorical framework that valorizes flexibility and representational inconstancy. Rather than advocate for particular representational forms, rhetorical approaches to language study address how context is an element within any decision about which forms are suitable to speech occasions. Hence, a rhetorical take on Barr's justification for an impeachment would deem it unpersuasive because a majority would probably reject the allusion to a child's perspective as being suitable in this case.

Further, while Barr conflated linguistic transparency with a kind of literacy that is elemental and denuded of strategic calculating, rhetors would note that this paean to rhetorical innocence represents its own specialized discursive practice, or what Stuart Hall would call "a cluster (or formation) of ideas, images and practices, which provide ways of talking about forms of knowledge and conduct associated with" knowledge production (see Webb 56). Hall's account is congenial with Burkean studies in that both ask us to question how we draw relationships between "knowledge" (culturally defined) and the representational technologies that would presume to bring that knowledge to presence. None of this is artless. To understand Barr's comment, audiences would have to know something about the value attached to the idea of innocence, and that it is common to configure the idea of innocence in the form of children at play. Barr's presumably inclusionary "we're all children at heart" premise also delivers a reprimand to those who practice verbal complexity, implying that they may be rightly judged as elitist, pretentious, out of touch, and worst of all, inauthentic. Audiences further will be expected to be able to sort through the interrelated premises that suggest that identifying how speakers should conduct themselves linguistically will also identify the audience's coordinating obligations: to be on the look out to see if the "authentic" "simple" and "clear" (or vernacular) statement has made an appearance. Audiences would be expected to comprehend, if not commend, the idea that when we follow our hearts when judging, we endorse the most noble descriptor of "the American" democratic spirit—a spirit that fosters community by championing the plain style that speaks to all, does not exclude, patronize, confuse, or deviate from the goal of calling everyone an equal. The ability to understand all that Barr's homily communicated is not achieved in any simple or direct way but by connecting in complex ways to experiential contexts that influence how we judge whose act of representation seems to be honest, presented for political purposes, or some mixture of both.

But even when rejecting the reductive trajectory informing Barr's veneration of simplicity, its kinship with rhetorical claims about how to engineer language uses that will enact identification might give us pause. Barr's investment in a specific version of representational normativity is oddly congenial with the rhetorical valorization of discursive normativity as being benevolent, well-intentioned, and democratic. Rhetorical positivism is not the same as the empirical positivism within Republican arguments that contended that propositional content trumps style. In rhetorical theories, both style and content matter to the endeavor to persuade. The positivism within rhetorical theorizing situates style as morality's identifiable agent, albeit in ways that are not straightforward. Rhetoricians envision style's role as helping to negotiate intricate interconnections between private individual interest and public concerns. Signs of eloquence, in particular, are expected to smooth over differences in perspective and craft affiliations that facilitate interpretive resolutions. The question, then, is whether a rhetorical appreciation of the eloquent representation has a different political *effect* than that of a Platonically-inflected positivism that valorizes stylistic transparency.

A look at the trajectory of Barr's call to community helps to illuminate the ways in which rhetorical theorizing about how to use styles to promote social cooperation are informed by a subtle yet persistent faith in the priority of that which is representable; rhetoricians tend to trust in a narrative that maintains that enacting (orderly, eloquent) representations is tantamount to being socially responsible because it indicates one's willingness to be held accountable for one's ideas. Barr's depiction of this premise may have been stylistically simplistic, but his argument propositionally concurred with the call to rationalist norms within rhetorical theories of style that would explain how audiences might know if "the reasonable case" has made an appearance. Rationalist norms are also "clusters (formations) of ideas, images and practices" that encourage particular types of rhetorical action that will (presumably) produce recognizably legitimate interpretive results. Comparing Barr's nostalgia to rhetoric's enthusiasm for rationalist norms helps to illustrate how the narratives we devise to organize conceptions of how to participate with language will engage acts of fantasy when they suggest that the use of the familiar form will facilitate the conversion of representational ambiguity into credible judgments about discursive aims. We are expected to believe those explanatory narratives as if they truly do tell us about how to enact inquiry that can be called democratic. But if responses to Barr's justification for impeaching Clinton demonstrate anything it might be that signifying obedience to stylistic protocol will not definitively indicate if a speaker's aim is either conscientious or socially beneficial.

Hence, the pertinence of Richard Lanham's observation: styles do not just operate as vehicles that put verve into how we express ideas. They are also representative of value systems that will have emerged from disciplinary and social contexts. Lanham maintains that social contexts will dictate how styles will be evaluated while rhetorical styles will convey attitudes about a given culture's sense of what is linguistically (stylistically) permissible. "By a sense of style we socialize ourselves. Style finally becomes . . . social custom. . . . Style defines situations, tells us how to act in them" (178).

Styles, then, reveal more than style when they disclose how hierarchies of value get attached to linguistic comportment. When styles are expected to be readable, familiar, a site for generating a sense of equity, and hence commonality, their appearance seems to signify a rhetor's aim to get along with others and facilitate democratic communication. But judgments of aims require speculation about how to transform the apprehension of a given text into an evaluation of its meaning and significance. Any response to Barr's homily—either acceptance or rejection—will have been influenced by narratives that situate stylistic protocols within social hierarchies and then underestimate the significance of style's contribution to the interpretive conversions that will get made when speculation gets transformed into a conclusion about whose words are behaving reasonably and/or preposterously. Meanwhile, like Barr, rhetoricians who champion narratives that specify representational goals like "democratic participation" also express anxiety about whether representational inconstancy can be partnered with linguistic virtue.

Pragmatics Meets Inconstancy

If interpretive acts are social customs, they may be analyzed to consider how style's deployment helps to naturalize ways of seeing what should have value and credibility. A circular logic animates the idea that styles help to express representational goals and instigate the interpretive methodologies that allow us to substantiate when those goals are met. The potential of a given style to provoke any number of responses appears to be subdued once the explanatory narrative directs conceptions of how to negotiate what can be known with what is impossible to know about any motives propelling where an act of representation is headed. When we believe that style helps us assess whether a speaker has fulfilled an intangible aim such as "taking responsibility," we are effectively tasked with deciding if a contemporary representational act is in accord with past models and preestablished standards that exhibit stylistic forms that have earned cultural regard because we've already seen them circulating in public discourse. But this method of comparison can also prompt us to glide past the speculative question of how precisely representative styles communicate purposes in ways that will be recognized.

The shortcomings of this interpretive framework were evident in one of the more notorious public moments in 1998—when Clinton testified (via satellite) before a Grand Jury, the first sitting President who was called upon to do so. Grand Jury testimony is one discursive practice that seems capable of achieving the goal of converting an idea of accountability into a reality. When Clinton met on August 17 with Deputy Independent Counsel Solomon L. Wisenberg, many believed that the legal proceeding would create the conditions that would force the president to be held accountable—finally—for his words. Clinton's detractors most likely hoped that putting him under oath in this context would compel him to come clean about having perjured himself when he denied his relationship with Lewinsky during the Paula Jones proceedings. That goal appeared to guide the direction of the questions posed by Wisenberg, which included the following memorable exchange:

> PROSECUTOR: Mr. President, I want to . . . briefly go over something you were talking about with Mr. Bittman. The statement of your attorney, Mr. Bennett, at the Paula Jones deposition . . . "Counsel is fully aware that Ms. Lewinsky has filed—has an affidavit which they are in possession of saying that there is absolutely no sex of any kind in any manner shape or form, with President Clinton." That statement was made by your attorney in front of Judge Susan Webber Wright, correct?
> CLINTON: That's correct.
> PROSECUTOR: That statement is a completely false statement. Whether or not Mr. Bennett knew of your relationship with Ms. Lewinsky, the statement that there was "no sex of any kind in any manner, shape or form, with President Clinton," was an utterly false statement. Is that correct?
> CLINTON: It depends on what the meaning of the word "is" is. If the–if he—if "is" means is and never has been that is not—that is one thing. If it means there is none, that was a completely true statement.[25]

Derision, seemingly universal, followed. *This* was testimony? Under oath? By elaborating on multiple ways of reading the "if-then" clause, Clinton seemed to violate the basic obligation to speak directly and purposefully and then be held accountable for a prior misdirected act of representation. In posing a question of definition, Clinton seemed to rebuff the expectation that he take responsibility for the confusion caused by a prior act of speech (which also failed to responsibly convey what really happened) and hence he indicated an unwillingness to abide by the communal rules overseeing linguistic comportment in a legal proceeding. So loathed was the "is is" phrase, it has been immortalized in Bartlett's *Famous Quotations* to connote insufferable equivocation. Those two simple words became a lightening rod for everything that seemed wrong about Clinton and what his presidency represented. It was referenced by U.S.

Rep Howard Coble (R-NC) in his opening statement at the impeachment hearing to justify Coble's vote to impeach: "When I return to my district, I sometimes motor south on Highway 29 through the fox and the wine country of Virginia. And as I approach the North Carolina boundary line, my mind begins to clear, as I am at that point removed from the Beltway spin. All of a sudden I am aware of the definition of 'sex.' All of a sudden I know the meaning of 'alone.' I know what 'is' is, as do the majority of my constituents" "(soft laughter)." Journalists joined in the mockery. As Timothy Noah of Slate.com observed, "Years from now, when we look back on Bill Clinton's presidency, its defining moment may well be Clinton's rationalization to the grand jury about why he wasn't lying . . . Bill Clinton really is a guy who's willing to think carefully about 'what the meaning of the word "is" is.' This is way beyond slick. Perhaps we should start calling him, 'Existential Willie.'"[26]

By failing to deliver a response that clarified a meaning that could be grasped for immediate review, Clinton also failed to meet other expectations about what form linguistic participation should take. Arguably, his apparent refusal to abide by the anticipated obligation to explicate rather than muddle provoked the Prosecutor's follow up question, conveyed with what might be called a sarcastic tone:

> PROSECUTOR: I just want to make sure I understand, Mr. President. Do you mean today that because you were not engaging in sexual activity with Ms. Lewinsky during the deposition that the statement of Mr. Bennett might be literally true?
> CLINTON: No, sir. I mean that at the time of the deposition, it had been . . . well beyond any point of improper contact between me and Ms. Lewinsky. So that anyone generally speaking in the present tense, saying there is not an improper relationship, would be telling the truth if that person said there was not, in the present tense; the present tense encompassing many months. That's what I meant by that. Not that I was—I wasn't trying to give you a cute answer, that I was obviously not involved in anything improper during a deposition.

Ridicule might seem like a natural response to perceptions of language users who fake it—who, for example, parse terms as if doing so actually answers a question. Conventionally, we would likely agree that when a person testifies, he should not be cute. But that "given" is indicative of a chain of associations that precede expectations about how one should stylize one's speeches in order to conform to whatever contextual demands are made in a given speech situation. In Clinton's case, that meant comparing what he said to a preestablished idea of what constitutes "responsible testimony" and then jeering at his invocation of grammar rules when addressing a question about his possible culpability. But standards are also narratives, not neutral signifiers of equitable interpretive processes. They can impose potentially unfair interpretive constraints, especially when standards seem to authoritatively steer how speech acts get situated within that spectrum of idiosyncratic and conventional language uses.

Too often, the chains of associations that inform assessments of a speaker's aims lose their speculative status and come to be regarded as actual evaluative methods. Testimony tends to be regarded as a "concrete" and *actual* practice that involves a bona fide act of retrieval—as if those who testify actually take a step back to the past and find a way to deliver the content of the prior experience in terms that accurately carry the past into the present. When testifying, one is expected to deliver one's statement by subtracting any complicating desires such as taking pleasure in the act of speaking, attempting to seduce the jury, or expressing a will to triumph over an a perceived opponent. A (clever) linguistic "dodge" that asks, well, what *does* "is" reference? does not appear to communicate that one aims to helpfully render an accurate version of "the truth and nothing but." It would seem only natural to disparage a witness who not only failed to engage dominant codes but also indicated an apparent refusal to do so by manifesting a *lack of enthusiasm* to follow protocol.

But the putatively natural derision that followed Clinton's act of speech exposes not its inherent problems but the ways in which audiences are encouraged to internalize the idea that when speakers do not adhere to discursive expectations, the rest of us are given permission to disengage and be dismissive. Such assessments are authorized when mimetic models are marshaled to endorse judgments about whose language choices fail to match idealized standards. And this applies to both the Platonic versions of how to participate with language as well as rhetorical ones that reference standards to authorize speculations about whether a given speech aspires to act responsibly. In effect, we are given permission to overlook and devalue those speech acts that fail to engage our judgments in ways that we expect them to, whether they act to uphold community standards or, as in Clinton's case, use language to challenge a coercive prosecutorial strategy. The dissonance of the "is is" phrase is remarkable not because the phrase deserves either derision or praise but because it offers an illustration of the meeting point between a speech act and the expectations that inform a collective sense of what language is supposed to do to constitute legitimate purposefulness. When we don't question the legitimacy of the idea that we should speak with purpose and make use of recognizable styles to clearly represent purposes, then the demand that we *be* purposeful and show that aim by adopting normative styles will stand as legitimate, inevitable, and not itself abusive. Clinton's "is is" phrase did not easily fit into any preestablished identity category that would legitimate its articulation. It was not especially witty. Few would likely regard it as a courageous example of "speaking back to power." As President, Clinton was not being oppressed in any conventional sense of the word; his words continue to be influential. Evaluating his "is is" phrase according to a preestablished hierarchy of values that has staked out what counts as a salient purpose gives "the community" permission to disregard and effectively render insubstantial any locution that refuses to go along with enforced institutional conventions.

When we are speculating about a speaker's purposes, we not only make judgments as if we have, indeed, identified those purposes, we also make judgments about whether identified purposes seem to be significant (or have "substance"). But given that ways of reading and evaluating significance have been shaped by cultural imperatives—including the one that effectively counsels rhetors to *show* significance by obeying discursive protocols—the answer to the question of whether and what kind of significance actually appeared will carry the imposition of cultural ideologies. And while that observation may be itself familiar to readers of critical theory, what may not be as common is a more specific meditation about how rhetorical technologies of evaluation that promise access to all instantiate biases by conflating particular acts of representability with accountability and then drawing upon that conflation when converting speculation about motives into judgments of who is credible.

When engaging in rhetorical analyses of who is doing what with language, we should not lose sight of the ways in which rhetorical responses to Platonic logocentrism also counsel punishments for speakers who fail to represent viable purposes and that these punishments also include acts of expulsion, albeit in more subtle ways—expel by rendering insignificant. Much of the exchange between Clinton and the Independent Counsel involved skirmishes about the way that Clinton responded to questions and included the complaint that Clinton's responses were too long, as if to suggest that his responses were designed to distract listeners and turn their attention away from the heart of the matter. In the following exchange, the President and the Independent Counsel interrupted each other but eventually, Clinton began to offer the short responses requested from counsel, and those responses followed legal protocol that allowed him to exercise his right to refuse to incriminate himself. On the other hand, that wrangling also included what is perhaps the most merciless exchange of the entire impeachment proceedings:

> PROSECUTOR: I want to go over some questions again. I don't think you are going to answer them, sir. And so I don't need a lengthy response, just a yes or no. And I understand the basis upon which you are not answering them, but I need them for the record. If Monica Lewinsky says that while you were in the Oval Office area you touched her breasts, would she be lying?
> CLINTON: Let me say something about this—
> PROSECUTOR: All I really need for you, Mr. President—
> CLINTON: I know—
> PROSECUTOR: is to say—
> CLINTON: But you—
> PROSECUTOR: I won't answer under previous grounds, or to answer the question, you see, because we only have four hours and your answers . . . have been lengthy. . . .
> CLINTON: I know that. I'll give you four hours and thirty seconds if you let me say something general about this. I will answer to your satisfaction that I won't – based on my statement, I will not answer. I would like 30 seconds at the end to make a statement, and you can have 30 seconds more on your time, if you'll let me say this to the grand jury and to you. And I don't think it's disrespectful at all. I've had a lot of time to think about this. But go ahead and ask your questions.
> PROSECUTOR: The question is, if Monica Lewinsky says that while you were in the Oval Office area, you touched her breasts, would she be lying?
> CLINTON: That is not my recollection. My recollection is that I did not have sexual relations with Miss Lewinsky, and I'm staying on my former statement about that.
> PROSECUTOR: If she said—
> CLINTON: My, my statement is that I did not have sexual relations as defined by that.

PROSECUTOR: If she says that you kissed her breasts, would she be lying?
CLINTON: I'm going to revert to my former statement.
PROSECUTOR: Okay. If Monica Lewinsky says that while you were in the Oval Office area, you touched her genitalia, would she be lying? And that calls for a yes, no, or reverting to your former statement.
CLINTON: I will revert to my statement on that.
PROSECUTOR: If Monica Lewinsky says that you used a cigar as a sexual aid in the Oval Office area, would she be lying? Yes, no, or won't answer?
CLINTON: I will revert to my former statement.[27]

The Prosecutor's stated intent, to pose questions "for the record" in spite of his belief that Clinton would not answer, was, at the very least, strange for those of us unaccustomed to legalese. It suggested that his interrogation was a lawyerly, procedural one, meant to be reviewed in a future context in which "the record" would stand as a pristine document and allow for an objective evaluation of testimony by objective judges familiar with the conventions of courtroom proceedings. On the other hand, because Clinton's Grand Jury appearance was eventually broadcast to citizens (the transcripts were released to the public one month later by the House Judiciary Committee), it was impossible to delimit how "regular folks" would react to the content of those questions. Given that audiences were promised evidence of perjury, some may have wondered if there were other reasons for this exchange. Perhaps the team of prosecutors organizing this inquiry thought that a verbal "probing" into details of intimate physical contact would exercise due diligence. Maybe they aimed to force Clinton to finally crack and admit what presumably everyone could already see. Or perhaps the prosecutor thought that Clinton would avoid the risk of being ridiculed for maintaining a representation of what happened that seemed to be at odds with the detailed picture that Lewinsky had apparently provided. Presumably, the repetition, the "frank" exposure of sexual terms aimed, *through* their explicitness, to both get to the truth and coerce an honest response from a known equivocator. Meanwhile, that same constellation of devices may have signified to audiences the designs of a too-ardent prosecutor who failed to consider that his version of how to enact a truth-seeking process might raise questions about its legitimacy. And yet, interestingly, many of us who remember the "is is" statement may not have remembered the specifics of this exchange and the ways in which it was contextualized in terms of adhering to representational formalities specifically aligned with the law.

Arguably, the Prosecutor's brutal questioning could be called "neutrally legal" because of a play of appearances. One can appear to be responsible and ethical by adhering to discursive protocol that promises to represent reason and neutral analytical thought. One may deploy such protocol as if doing so is intrinsically responsible and ethical, and use that general regard for linguistic accountability via representational responsibility as a way of providing insidious cover for an abuse of power. Here, we might locate that abuse exactly in the space of an interpretive conversion where a spectacular act of representation in the form of prying questions got read, at least officially, as an enforcement of ruling methodologies and then officially classified as part of a "legal" inquiry. If any momentary surprise at the questions was forgotten and rendered unremarkable, then it is possible to conclude that the prosecutor's adherence to discursive protocol superseded all other ways of reading what was significant to that exchange. (Hence, the commonplaces: "He was only doing his job." "That's what happens in legal proceedings. Lawyers ask tough questions that make witnesses uncomfortable.") The particular viciousness encoded within his cross-examination was masked by the ability to read his purposes as being aligned with community standards. Meanwhile, Clinton's "is is" response was belittled, in part, because it seemed to offer an insincere attempt to participate with community standards.

In an epistemological context that connects proof and evidence to representability, our vigilance requires more than looking at representability through a lens that conflates "bringing to presence" with "being accountable." When evaluating the significance of those representations that appear to act responsibly by engaging with discursive conventions, we can take a cue from Gayatri Spivak, who describes representation as a site of conflict that implicates our responsibility to expose the ideological aims of dominant discourses that claim to be objective. Discourses of reason can perpetuate unjust actions when context and contingency are set aside and "facts" are presented as decontextualized objects within judgments of their significance. In the name of "reason," a discursive exchange like the one between the Prosecutor and Clinton can be characterized as "information-gathering" rather than, say, a "verbal assault." With that orientation in mind, we would note how the Prosecutor's "plain" style functioned ideologically when it seemed to insure the possibility of presenting The Truth through a figurative form that promises to transparently communicate propositional content. Far from being insubstantial, rhetorical style may act in compliance with the dominant ideologies that would naturalize and then reinforce the automatic regard for language practices that already carry cultural authority.

In addition to specific ideological critique, however, is our responsibility to mull over the significance of cultural narratives that would characterize how we go about evaluating what has significance in the first place. Here, the "pragmatic" orientation put forth in rhetorical studies can fail to adequately address how we have been trained to notice significance. The endeavor to "be pragmatic" is an act that requires a narrative of explanation, and often the explanatory narrative is treated as if it fully accounts for what happened as one determined whether rhetorical purposes were met by language uses. Such accounts will have political significance when they contribute to audience estimations of whether a purported purpose is in alignment with the cultural narratives that suggest how to legitimatize and recognize those purposes that serve pragmatic aims. Hence even the phrase "purposeful action" can act to manage judgments by establishing in advance narratives that will influence when a "purpose" gets recognized.[28]

To cut through the tautology of that configuration, we may remember the ambiguity of the aesthetic. Rather than depict aesthetic concerns as being opposite to pragmatic ones, we can notice their mutually constituting influences on whatever "sense" gets made from and through communicative action. In the case of Clinton and the Prosecutor, both could be said to be responding pragmatically—using the languages available in culture to do what was necessary to get through that interpretive situation and hope that audiences would identify with their discursive aims. Yet somehow, that response does not satisfy because it does not address what *else* was at issue during this encounter. It can be difficult to find a way to explain what was disturbing about the Prosecutor's questions and Clinton's responding testimony, and a turn to aesthetics reminds us that the inability to fully represent one's sense of what happened *as* we underwent an experience of interpretation is neither insignificant nor a basis for dismissing those senses that cannot be fully articulated. Any account of how we move from style to substance, from an ephemeral sense of what is going on to a conviction about a speaker's purposes, is itself fleeting and material, not fully explainable but nonetheless consequential both perceptually and materially.

Part of the point here is that, given the tendency to valorize language uses that purposefully *do* something "for the community," it becomes that much more difficult to see the "is is" phrase as other than a trifle, not worthy of more thought, just another instance of meaningless political dissembling. Because it appears to be so deserving of judgments that would ascribe a lack of redemptive qualities, it becomes almost logical to not even consider why so much derision was heaped on Clinton's failure to meet expectations. And certainly, derision is one of the most effective ways of managing conceptions of how we should participate with language. That Clinton's response was regarded as a linguistic evasion and not something else—justified rebelliousness? A celebration of rhetorical abundance? An indication of an exacting, deft and nimble mind?—indicates how judgments tend to be aligned with the idea that the most valuable representations are the ones where robust and beneficial purposes may be clearly identified. Any rhetor unable to produce "robust" signs that clinch ways of reading where a speech aims will be at a disadvantage, especially if audiences agree that the absence of a strong and forceful statement translates into an absence of an inherent force that converts potentiality into an actual presence of meaning and significance.

When we discount the intrinsic contribution of the rhetorical and the aesthetic to political inquiry, we provide a means of systematizing what counts as "taking responsibility" for one's language uses and we develop the habit of downplaying the significance of the dynamic whereby our choices determine how we move from apprehension to judgment. We allow prior explanatory narratives describing how persuasion works to supersede our own discrete decisions. This is doubly so when a sense of satisfaction accompanies responses to narratives that would belittle speakers who fail to clarify purposes in recognizable ways.

Conclusion

Arguably, style killed the impeachment drive. Following the months of inquiry and publicity, rather than feeling enlightened, many citizens felt gross, especially in response to the publication of the voluminous *Starr Report*, the official pro-impeachment document that became notorious for its bad taste.

Like House Republicans, Independent Prosecutor Kenneth Starr attempted to put together a reasonable case for impeachment by collecting evidence and producing a thoroughly articulated account of precisely those acts that "may constitute grounds for impeachment," including (among others): "That Clinton lied five times under oath about his relationship with Lewinsky," that he obstructed justice by concealing evidence about that relationship, that he "made false statements to the American people."[29] In outlining details about the physical relationship between Clinton and Lewinsky, Starr mistakenly believed that truth's dissemination would compel in whatever form it was packaged. Apparently Starr *did* understand that including graphic details about bodies under surveillance might generate controversy, and so he prefaced the report with a cautionary note: "The evidence of the President's perjury cannot be presented without specific, explicit, and possibly offensive descriptions of sexual encounters."[30] The squeamish reluctance to add such information and the apparent need to issue a warning to the reader implied that in other circumstances, it would be possible to present evidence that would not offend, and that Starr understood that something might seem amiss.

But the disclaimer failed to distance Starr from his material descriptions and did not protect his reputation. Given Starr's apparent faith in the self-evidently neutral pursuit and dissemination of truth, it is doubtful that he could have foreseen what would happen next: that because of his narrative, *he* would be made a spectacle, subjected to embarrassing publicity, discredited by the very representational mechanisms that ostensibly enabled him to make his case.

The report borrowed the poetic language of romance novels, complete with overwrought clichés about an ill-fated love that could not be: "The President explained that they had to end their intimate relationship. He said he was attracted to Ms. Lewinsky, considered her a great person, and hoped they would remain friends. . . . The situation, he stressed, was not Ms. Lewinsky's fault. Ms. Lewinsky, weeping, tried to persuade the President not to end the sexual relationship, but he was unyielding."[31]

At other times, the report's language was just blunt. Reporter Diane Sawyer brought this up in a November 1998 interview, just before the vote to impeach, and asked the Special Counsel if he "went too far" with some of his language choices. Referencing descriptions used in a referral that summarized the report and was submitted to the Senate, Sawyer asked about Starr's priorities.

I think there were 62 mentions of the word 'breast,' 23 of 'cigar,' 19 of 'semen.' This has been called demented pornography, pornography for Puritans. Were there mistakes made in including some of this? "Diane," Starr replied, "Don't fault career prosecutors for telling the truth."[32]

For Starr, apparently, context should have no bearing upon judgment and he seemed to be baffled by the idea that anyone would see things differently. "There is no excuse for perjury. Never, never, never. No one is entitled to lie under oath simply because he or she does not like the questions or because he believes the case is frivolous, or that it is financially motivated . . . [P]erjury is [an] extraordinarily serious business . . . Witnesses tell the truth. It doesn't matter what the underlying subject matter is. Once you are in court under oath, you tell the truth."

As Sawyer's interview suggested, that kind of singular perspective came to seem obsessive—too focused, unable to get the picture that encompassed more than an immediate context. Indeed, it seemed that Starr misread how his writing would call attention to itself and what that call would ask the reader to do. And crucially style played a role in how the report was received. When it comes to legal documents, style is expected to be invisible. "Too much" style connotes too much personality and calls attention to the act of writing itself. Within rationalist traditions, *that* call has been depicted as the very site of the feint where one may find a slippage past truth into the realm of seduction, and where one might be accused of taking too much pleasure in the very act of putting forth a representation. Part of Starr's problem was that he seemed to step beyond his putatively neutral role of fact-finder and became too engrossed in his pursuit of Clinton, an assessment that arose because the report failed to adopt the proper protocol for expressing an emotionally neutral commitment to objectivity. Even his supporters questioned his objectivity, at least according to the *New York Times*. "Mr. Starr's defenders admit that he, too, has been blinded by his distaste for Clinton and has committed excesses in his desire to hold the President accountable. . . . The [Starr Report] packed with almost pornographic sexual detail and damning commentary on the President's motives, is the most glaring example of prosecutorial overkill, some of Mr. Starr's associates acknowledge."[33]

The "put it all out there" quality of the report provoked debates about how it should be identified and read. Instead of engendering cool, level-headed responses about the merits of his case, readers questioned what kind of participation it called for. In effect, the report became as scandalous as the charges against Clinton because it seemed unable to establish a proper distance between the reader and the text so as to allow for disengaged scrutiny. Readers began to question the author's motives and purposes.

Clinton's lawyer, David Kendall, accused Starr of harboring such personal vitriol that he purposefully "intended to humiliate, embarrass and politically damage the President. In short, this is personal and not impeachable." An editorial from "America's heartland," the *Des Moines (Iowa) Sunday Register*, concurred. "It's difficult to sort out which is more disgusting—the president's sexual behavior spelled out graphically in the independent counsel's report, or the behavior of the independent counsel in concocting a case that seems primarily calculated to embarrass the president." Many came to the conclusion that the ritualized and public process of humiliation provided enough punishment to Clinton "for his lies." Subsequent media reports concentrated on readers' discomfort with reading the document. Editors ran articles and conducted polls that asked about how much needed to be shown about Clinton's infidelity and whether Starr should have said all that he did. The *Chicago Tribune* reported that "person-on-the-street" reactions to Starr's report were emotional, which came to be regarded as tantamount to a rejection of Starr's conclusions: "Across the Chicago area, people blushed, cringed, snickered and fumed in response to the explicit report . . . many said they were not sure which they found more repulsive—Clinton's conduct or the tawdry nature of Starr's peeping." After its release, a CBS poll reported that two-thirds of Americans believed the report had "too many graphic sexual details" and six out of ten believed "the report was intended mostly to embarrass the president and shouldn't have been released to the public."[34]

The audience's tendency was to disengage, with few likely considering how the material marker of an idea can affect acts of reception, identification and estimation of the idea's value. The emotional reactions produced by *The Starr Report* engendered not a dialogue about its merits, but a breakdown in communication, demonstrating that the philosophic/scientific model of judgment that has been grafted onto the realm of politics leaves us at a loss with how to handle our interpretive encounters when our responses include the felt sense of emotions that offer more than a sentimentalized path back to the realm of the "authentic." The general unease that fueled impressions of prosecutorial overreach contributed to bringing the impeachment proceedings to a halt after several senators reportedly found themselves "horrified" by "pages of pornography," incapable of even viewing the evidence. "'I don't want to look,' sa[id] Virginia Democrat James Moran. 'I feel dirty when I read this stuff. I feel as though when someone walks into the room it's something I should throw under the desk.' South Carolina's Ernest Hollings told fellow Senator Joseph Biden: 'Joe, I can't even talk about this with another man.'"[35]

The Senator's delicate sensibilities notwithstanding, we are left to wonder about these events and what they suggest about how to configure acts of due deliberation otherwise. When noting the distance between the impeachment inquiry and idealized representations of an unbiased and neutral search for truth, we may, as I have already suggested, be tempted to explain this event simply as a failure of reason, leaving intact the possibility that in the next political controversy, reason will finally prevail as audiences come to clarify which issues truly do have merit.

Our stylistic choices can provoke public arguments and there is no automatic way to display reason's signs as an assured antidote to the morass of interpretive entanglements that arise from such provocations. Judgments of how speakers participate with language do not emerge scopically by extracting meaning from form, but through perpetual acts of narrative invention and translation that subsequently will be evaluated for legitimacy, according to whatever values are culturally validated. What we measure in political judgment is rhetorical and in that sense, at least partially illusory: How we think a given re-presentation participates in a cultural context that has staked out how the work of representation should *look*. What seems most basic, direct and recognizable—a "simple" act of substitution that both characterizes and enacts equity—is also most illusory, most dependent upon a non-look at the ephemeral shiftiness of narrative processes that appear to oversee procedures of thought while simultaneously undermining that stability.

The figure of blushing statesmen is both banal and profound in its implications for how to conceive of the political consequences of mandating truth and failing to capture it. In a political context that regards language as an impersonal ground structuring communication, the non-look at Starr's evidence can appear itself as reasonable and neutral, even innocent. But to take such statements at face value is to repeat and reaffirm the legitimacy of a sentimentalizing discourse that characterizes much of the way that political debate gets reported in the U.S. media, allowing for an "aw shucks" sensibility to be associated with Americana itself and a component part of shared attitudes towards representations that purport to be open and free.

The political consequences of valorizing such sentimentalism was evident in 1998 when the "must look away" narrative seemed to legitimate the interpretive result: members of the media mostly stopped talking about this event publicly and stopped weighing its possible social and political significance. (Or, when evaluating this event's significance, journalists tended to offer sentimentalized narratives about the public's common sense ability to make the best judgment about what mattered to the nation.[36]) There was no public reckoning of what the nation had been put through. No one was held accountable for the forty million dollar expenditure that had been made over the years of investigating Clinton to find some malfeasance. No one was held accountable for the psychological and emotional warfare this event visited upon the public, or how traces of that warfare reverberated two years later when the scandal of the 2000 presidential election was put to rest fairly quickly and without much public outcry. Citizens, already fatigued by scandal, barely responded to the possibility that voter fraud paved the way for George Bush to claim the White House. Bush, a man of convictions, a man who many saw as the very opposite of Clinton in character, also sold a preemptive call to war with Iraq by using fake evidence. And yet, ironically, in *that* case, impeachment was, as put by then-Speaker of the House, Nancy Pelosi, "off the table."[37] The message: don't even speculate about that possibility.

If the debates that took place in 1998 demonstrated anything, it was that the presupposed difference between "really" looking and merely pretending to look is steeped in ambiguity, raising a question about whether democratic inquiry should be imagined as the endeavor to distinguish "masked repetitions" from "honest" engagements with form. Discourses about impeaching Clinton put the prevalent model of representation to the test by asking citizens to consider whether a willingness to represent in a particular way—via a resemblance that seeks a return—should continue to exist as the standard for judging whether any given speaker is to be regarded as a virtuous participant in civic life. The impeachment as a discursive event arose in a decade that witnessed a series of publicized disputes over which symbols to promulgate as representative of the nation's spirit.[37] Those disputes were incited by competing visions of social literacies that offered different perspectives on what language use should work towards; specifically, whether to sanction the postmodern-rhetorical work of denaturalizing historically adopted methods of interpretation; whether to perpetuate faith in already-established interpretive conventions and the institutions supporting their practice; and whether to conflate the powers of discernment with nationalism. At the end of the twentieth century, the dawn of a new millennium, citizens in the United States were asked to consider whether to continue to organize political judgment around the endeavor to represent in proper ways—that is, to represent on behalf of the true and the sincere, the philosophical and not the rhetorical. And they were to consider whether to use traditional penalties of expulsion to punish those who do not adopt sanctioned protocols of style to prove membership and good will.

When we judge, we consult a "working ensemble" (Robert Greene phrase 55) of narratives that, when reiterated via dominant media sources, will "stand in" at the space where speculation connects to judgments, a space to which we cannot have real access. We can offer more speculation. When our speculations about that space of conversion uncritically draw upon available narratives, we will rely upon ritualistic ways of seeing, including ways of seeing what has significance in representations that appear to follow a discernible order. We will see insignificance in those that apparently do not. Those evaluations are neither natural nor inevitable, nor even fully justifiable, but we have become accustomed to thinking that the customary response is representative of the common sense response. The same ritualized dynamic influences our "common sense" responses to the ensemble of narratives that pit the "fullness" of actuality against the "emptiness" of speculation.

Rethinking style allows us to change the terms of discussion. We may pose questions about how our sense of a speaker's/writer's purpose connects to our perceptions of the other's attitude about how to use language to achieve that purpose. Accordingly, the criteria for judgment shift. Were we not expected to be beholden to an aesthetics of resemblance that masquerades as a search for truth, then politicized proclamations about how one mode of speech acts more truthfully than another might come to seem nonsensical rather than as intrinsically ethical. In the meantime, an alternative ethics might take shape in connection with the idea that ethics is situated in the changeable, fluid, non-homogenous, ideologically inflected space of interpretive transactions. In this space, interpretation does not look for a reflection of what exists but engages in moment-by-moment acts of aesthetic inventions.

2 THE FORCE OF THE FIT

PART I: RENDERING ATONEMENT

In the summer of 1998, indisputable evidence emerged that proved the existence of an affair between President Clinton and Monica Lewinsky: an unwashed dress left in the bottom of Lewinsky's closet, the incriminating item brought to the public's attention via the illegal wiretapping by Lewinsky's confidant, Linda Tripp. Rumors about the existence of a dress (color: dark blue) had circulated for weeks but seemed too outlandish to be true. Who keeps that kind of souvenir? When the command of a federal subpoena forced Lewinsky to produce it from her private collection of memories, the empirical proof and looming threat of a DNA test made it impossible for Bill Clinton to issue further denials about having had a relationship with her. The presentation of the dress set off a chain reaction of events. By July 30, after months of stonewalling, Lewinsky agreed to cooperate with Starr's investigators by offering an admission of the affair in exchange for a full immunity agreement that would cover her and her parents. Armed with her revised testimony, Starr was able to garner Clinton's cooperation without a subpoena, earning him the dubious distinction of being the first sitting president in the history of the United States to testify before a Grand Jury.

Clinton and Lewinsky were called to the law to offer up clarity and truth. What really happened? This is what the threat of the subpoena and the grand jury appearance asked and promised to answer. And within that promise, one can find an official story about the relationship between evidence and discursive practices, or more specifically, the logic that depicts discursive practices as evidentiary. The endeavor to "out truth" is depicted as an unambiguous moral duty, always imperative and available when animated by proper speech acts.

But therein resides a crucial interpretive exigency. Debates about Clinton's impeachment demonstrated that when it comes to judging political controversies, an audience's sense of whether representations are appropriate can matter as much as revelations of truth. Propriety is a term that rhetoricians use to characterize how audiences determine which statements have value. The power of words rests not in their accuracy but in estimations of whether they seem to fit the occasion of their use. This premise reorients conceptions of how to participate with language by drawing a different kind of attention to the ways in which public discourse steers interpretive negotiations towards existing structures of representations. While we cannot count on language use to reveal what exists, we can consider how language constitutes what we know by establishing "discursive conditions of existence" (Biesecker and Lucaites 5). The emphasis on discursivity is vital. Language does not transmit what is true but what we have *said* about what should matter about how we craft meaning, and this caveat is of considerable importance when assessing the credibility of speakers and political events. Since facts do not automatically signify meaning, any evaluation of their significance and value involves interpretive negotiations undertaken by audiences who decide what to make of whatever evidence is put forth for evaluation. And what audiences will make of that evidence will depend upon *how* it is represented.

This chapter examines how this constellation of ideas might be applied to media discourses disseminated during the year of Clinton's impeachment. The first part of this chapter looks at the national apology that Clinton offered following his Grand Jury testimony, and the anger that it provoked. The second part explores media narratives reporting on the taped conversations between Monica Lewinsky and Linda Tripp that generated the impeachment inquiry. I argue that a rhetorical interest in propriety offers a promising alternative to the Platonic correlation of truth with cognitive insight. It broadens conceptions of judgment by incorporating the idea that because interpretive contexts change, the act of judgment does not proceed by referencing and attempting to mimic static *a priori* forms. But I also maintain that discourses of propriety do not adequately challenge narratives that depict linguistic force as if it has an ontological existence. Indeed, rhetorical theories that link judgments of value to representations of propriety reaffirm the narrative that depicts persuasive force as a traceable presence that may be referenced to resolve political controversies. This premise underwrites the idea that fittingness can be conflated with eloquence, a rhetorical style that promises to activate awareness of when the proper expression has made an appearance.

If persuasion's power is propelled by eloquence (also called coherence), then it would seem to be available to all who engage persuasive techniques. Ethical participation is ascribed to those who are thoughtful when stylizing arguments that appeal. But the open access implied in this formulation of participation naturalizes the idea that certain modes of delivery will be more captivating than others, and says nothing about how discursive histories constitute judgments of which ones. Rhetorical styles mark a place at which embodiment, text, and ideology converge. When discourses of propriety conflate fittingness and eloquence, they help to justify the tendency to dismiss speakers whose words fail to galvanize. Too often, that judgment is regarded as fitting itself.

Saying What Needs to Be Said

Given the sequence of events that led to Clinton's admission of an affair, one might have concluded that Starr's prosecution proved that a reliable representational mechanism exists. Presumably, Starr put forward a rigorous case in which the show of evidence exposed the President's lie and through that act of showing, revealed the proper resolution. Were the impeachment story a Hollywood movie directed by Starr, the final scene might have shown a montage of the dress, its exposure, and then Clinton walking away from the White House, his head hung in shame. Goodbye Imposter! Long Live Morality's Restoration!

This, of course, did not happen. Indeed, when evaluating the issues that were raised during 1998, the call to the law in the form of a methodical documentation of facts proved to be controversial itself. Starr's dedication to "the law" made him a perpetual object of derision, "a modern Inspector Javert, sneeringly derided in one publication as a 'pious lawman,'"[1] too emotionally invested in "The Clinton Capture." If "the reveal" of Lewinsky's dress demonstrated anything, it was that a dogged devotion to truth does not necessarily compel an approving nod from a vigilant audience, especially when truth's capture seems to be motivated by personal animosity. And if truth's search does not automatically signify a moral agenda, then we might rethink our conceptions of what conclusions *a reveal* will allow. These considerations are especially important now that the rise of technologies enhancing public surveillance has met public indifference to being watched.

The turnaround in Clinton's fortunes alludes to the knotted and elusive question about whether it is possible to predict in advance how and whether a given representation will compel a desired response. How to imagine the power part of persuasive action remains, to borrow a phrase, "tantalizingly ambiguous" (Haskins 85), especially when thinking about the critical problem of how to account for audience consent when explaining how representations garner credibility. Rhetorical theorists maintain that persuasive force is conventional rather than transcendent. Its power is dependent upon our willingness to be persuaded. Hence, language is able to constitute meaning not because audiences engage in acts of recognition of what exists but because audiences "gift" speakers and texts with authority, placing the power of logos within the center of the rhetorically forged linguistic community. But there is less clarity about how communities collectively determine what matters. If "meaning" signifies not what is indisputable but, rather, a rhetorical exigence, then we should take a closer look at how rhetoricians theorize the prospect of developing shared perspectives, especially when determining whether a politicized issue deserves public attention.

The evidence of Monica's dress presents a case in point. It provoked any number of embodied responses, from disgust to disappointment to the smugly satisfied, "I knew it!" But as evidence in a legal context its status was strange. It was compelling enough to alter what was *said* about the affair, shifting any tentative response of *maybe* it happened to certainty that it did. That shift, however, did not steer assessments of whether citizens faced a national crisis. Starr may have discovered the facts but his almost literal "digging" into the private lives of the President and his lover did not sit well with those who felt that the search for evidence produced the kind of revelation no citizen should be forced to divulge. Any "call" to the law issued by the presentation of the dress was incriminating, but not in a way that clarified what to do next.

The only thing that did seem clear: the dress, once revealed, constituted a "new" context for Clinton that required him to change his story. For six months, in interviews and at press conferences, Clinton had denied any involvement with Lewinsky and through that denial let stand insinuations about her mental instability—that she was one of *those* women who fantasize about men in power and then fabricate tales of shared intimacies. But once Starr had his hands on the material evidence that literally *was* material, he was able to get the story straight, first by (ironically) vindicating Lewinsky's account and then by compelling Clinton to confess to a lie. The dress, the grand jury appearance, the publicity given to these events produced a discursive exigency in which

Clinton, clearly, had some explaining to do to all citizens, but especially to those who had elected him. Further, he needed to speak directly and not by issuing a statement, or through the White House Staff, or via an interview mediated by a trusted reporter. And, most of all, after six months of dissembling, he needed to forcefully indicate his willingness to "come clean" and "be straight."

But in response to this new situation, what should the President have said? The exigency did not exactly clarify. Unlike the imperative put forth by Starr's command to speak on behalf of the law, when addressing the citizenry in the aftermath of the Grand Jury testimony, no one disputed the facts. There was no need, for example, to enhance knowledge with more information about this wretched situation. Hence in this new "come clean" context, the point of any speech would not be to tell the truth but to indicate that he got it—that he understood that it was wrong to appear before the American people, feign innocence, and through acts of dissembling, let this mess drag on unnecessarily for months. Most of all, he needed to deliver a statement that showed real remorse for all of his bad behavior. He needed, in sum, to issue a clear and resolute statement of atonement in the form of a national apology.

There was, after all, the fleeting chance that a genuine apology might have been forceful enough to put a halt to the impetus to impeach by changing the terms of discussion from the cruel game of "gotcha" to the healing work of reconciliation. A "true" statement "from the heart" just might have fulfilled the positivistic promise made by conventional conceptions of language's call: that it is possible to harness representational power, glide past animosity, heal rifts, and engender reconciliation by prompting citizens to remember their compassion and hear the tender question, could we start again please? Could we put this behind us and move forward?

At least this is one imagined version of the rhetorical situation. In another version, it would not have mattered what Clinton said. The forces against him were relentless and short of a proclamation of world war, the only chance of halting the impetus to impeach would have been for him to try to outfox his nemeses by saying something clever enough to put his political enemies into their own fix. Clinton did neither. Instead, on the evening of August 17, 1998, following his terse exchange with Deputy Independent Counsel Solomon Wisenberg in his Grand Jury appearance (see chapter one), Clinton turned to the airwaves to speak to the nation, an event that was carried live by all the major networks (and is now immortalized on YouTube).

It is impossible to recreate the moments that preceded his delivery wherein millions of Americans sat facing their televisions, ready to listen to one of those familiar yet rare and vaguely anxious events when regular programming is interrupted by a moment of silence, the presentation of the Presidential seal, and the appearance of a somber-looking President seated in the oval office or standing at a podium, about to pronounce something of enormous national importance. Clinton followed this usual protocol, but his statement was brief and the topic of his discussion seemed to be distant from the alarming content typically associated with these occasions. In a total of 4 ½ minutes, he admitted to "having relations" with Lewinsky and then issued a statement that might only charitably be described as apologetic.

> "As you know," he stated, "in a deposition in January, I was asked questions about my relationship with Monica Lewinsky. While my answers were legally accurate, I did not volunteer information. Indeed, I did have a relationship with Miss Lewinsky that was not appropriate. In fact, it was wrong. It constituted a critical lapse in judgment and a personal failure on my part for which I am solely and completely responsible."[2]

Clinton explained that even though he had publicly denied the affair to protect his family from embarrassment, such denials did not encompass unlawful actions such as destroying evidence or tampering with witnesses. "I know that my public comments and my silence about this matter gave a false impression. I misled people, including even my wife. I deeply regret that."

Using relatively short sentences and what might be described as a crisp tone, the president confessed to an act of omission by acknowledging a representational withholding and then a failure to abide by the expectation that one tell the whole truth at all times, not just when mandated by the courts. In effect, Clinton asked that citizens consider how context affected his rhetorical choices, noting that his lack of disclosure arose in response to an act of over-reaching by Special Prosecutor Kenneth Starr.

> "The independent counsel investigation moved on to my staff and friends, then into my private life," Clinton stated. "And now the investigation itself is under investigation. This has gone on

too long, cost too much, and hurt too many innocent people . . . Even presidents have private lives. It is time to stop the pursuit of personal destruction and the prying into private lives and get on with our national life . . . It is past time to move on."

It was, possibly, the most honest statement he ever made to the electorate. But the speech landed with a thud. Given the cultural tendency to conflate showing with a forceful telling, Clinton's confession to an act of omission came to be regarded as one more abdication of a promise to tell the truth. It seemed that so much had not been said during his short delivery and most agreed that there was something wrong with a show of contrition that explained why he withheld information rather than demonstrate his shame and bona fide mortification. Clinton did not utter the right words; he did not take the right tone; he did not issue his own call of sorrow and yearning for forgiveness. He generally failed to adopt the proper "voice of its occasion" (Riley 2) that would deliver its own call to audiences to trust in an unwavering representational apparatus to induce order. And for that failure, his speech was widely condemned:

> From *The Charleston (W.Va.) Daily Mail*: "In a ghastly four-minute session, the president told the nation no more than he had to. It was a calculated, carefully calibrated effort at damage control."
>
> *The Tribune, suburban Phoenix*: "Spare us further insults to our intelligence and to our dignity from the legal maneuvering, semantic gymnastics and televised appeals. The seduction has gone on long enough."
>
> *The Austin (Texas) American-Statement*: "President Clinton's shake-and-bake apology to the American people last night fell far short of what the country deserved after a truly sordid day in U.S. history."
>
> *The Chicago Sun-Times*: "An early confession, no matter how grim, would have been better than the pathetic backtracking extracted Monday. He has only embarrassed those closest to him, disappointed friends and brought critics to new depths of disgust."

The Star-Democrat in Easton, Maryland: "Liar. Sneaky. Insincere. Equivocating. Dishonest. These are not words Americans want to hear associated with the presidency of this nation. Yet all of these words and more such derogatory terms are being used this week to describe our current president . . . His speech to the nation Monday evening was an exercise in insincerity. . . . He never said 'I lied.'"

The Washington Post was no less forgiving. "President Clinton had the opportunity Monday evening to begin the process of putting the Monica Lewinsky scandal legitimately behind him—but that would have required the telling of some unvarnished truth. He passed it up in favor of still another attempt at manipulation—a mostly mock confession in which he made a show of taking responsibility that in fact he once again sought to dodge."[3]

During those four minutes, any hope faded for ending the controversy before impeachment hearings officially began. To Clinton's political opponents, the speech exhibited more evidence of the kind of equivocating that justified a legal inquiry. New Jersey Governor Christine Todd Whitman declared "[Clinton's] disdain for the truth" to be "a national disgrace." Rep. Charles Canady (R-Florida) noted, "the pattern of conduct here constitutes a defilement of the office of the president." Even Clinton's Democratic colleagues added their voices to the chorus of the aggrieved. Rep. Henry Waxman (D-California) described "the mood" of Democrats: "He's an embarrassment to people in his own party." Sen. Joseph Lieberman (at that time, D-Conn) took to the Senate floor to deliver a rousing condemnation of the President's behavior and then subsequently demanded another apology. Lieberman's sentiments, meanwhile, were applauded by Sen. Daniel Patrick Moynihan (D-New York), who reportedly "praised Lieberman for saying 'what needed to be said, and saying it in a manner that gives us hope at a time of profound despond.'"[4]

Evidently, what was most galling: the appearance of having calculated what to say, of offering a statement that was caught in the act of trying to change the terms of discussion by taking attention off the apologist and putting it on the accuser. In effect, Clinton was derided for being rhetorical, and that resounding derision was authorized by the idea that there is a kind of linguistic power—transcendent, ideologically neutral—available to channel the authentic thoughts and feelings of the conscientious interlocutor who, in being authentic, stands as truth's representative. We are expected to have a special antipathy for those speakers who would knowingly channel language's power to play on our emotions and manipulate them for personal gain. But of course that expectation also works to protect emotion—or the *idea* of emotion as a marker of authenticity, as if our experiences of emotional power are impervious to ideological influence. The experience of "true feeling" (Lauren Berlant's phrase) would seem to be representative of that which is most elemental, the locus of rhetorical innocence.

What to do, then, about the possibility of skepticism? For many of us, the declarations of emotional distress that emerged after Clinton botched his apology represented signs of false piety, classifiable under the category "conventional political hypocrisy," potentially even more discreditable than Clinton's non-apology. Here we might note how the urge to renounce political hypocrisy appears to spring from an anterior source that works independently to provoke viscerally satisfying reactions. To be able to definitively declare, "I wash my hands of you! You're all charlatans!" seems to allow the recipient of an assault of sanctimony to push back with a righteous rebuff and resurrect a sense of balance via a restoration of interpretive order. When certain about the propriety of our rejection, we seem to extricate ourselves from manipulative ploys by issuing just the right words to communicate the depth of our animosity, which in this case may have emerged after being called upon to waste the graciousness of a collective good will on a ginned up event. "You're all hypocrites" muttered with a dismissive wave of our hands would seem to supply us with our own discursive evidence of having acted to spurn spurious claims and in the process clear the air, freeing a space for us ("regular Joes") to be unencumbered by them (self-interested political hacks interested in power for its own sake). Accordingly, we're left off the hook, not implicated in that mess in Washington, political innocents just living our lives as best we can. In the meantime, pejorative conceptions of rhetorical strategizing stay intact as does the positive regard for an interpretive technology that promises to enable citizens to see clear differences between pretended feelings and genuine anguish and then decide whether a given testimonial of outrage is real and warranted.

In sum, the logic that depicts discursive practices *as* evidentiary is preserved. While we may endeavor to rely upon an ability to distinguish the genuine from the manufactured expression of distress, we have not resolved the question of how to factor emotion and aesthetics (a felt sense) into conceptions of deliberatory practices. The quandary over how to sort through the significance of sensibility and its relationship to narrative remains intact, particularly when narratives about emotion engender real political outcomes once audiences have appraised the legitimacy of a given expression of emotion. Accordingly, when outrage—especially national outrage—seems warranted, we may feel emboldened to act on it. We may, indeed, feel righteous about our actions, convinced that because we have been provoked by a horrific event, outrage is a justifiable response. Once rendered legitimate, we may then decide upon a course of action to ameliorate that outrage, and to reference the emotional trauma when explaining why a given course of action was taken and is warranted: the death penalty; a call to arms; warrantless wiretapping of U.S. citizens by federal governmental agencies. If emotion is a site of authenticity and if discourse about emotion is unmitigatedly evidentiary, then these diverse political outcomes would appear to be equally defensible, each bolstered by the logic that suggests that having strong feelings expresses a genuine response and the authentic response is an ethical response. This is also the logic that valorizes the state of *having convictions*, the possession of which appears to buttress a moral standing no matter what those convictions might be.

As Lauren Berlant argues, emotions perform politically when regarded as natural, automatic and grounded in the elemental fact of the body (True Feeling 52-53). The representation of true feeling that seems to communicate authenticity is consequently freed from history, context, the weight of ideology; its signs are presumably readable, knowable, reliably available to be referenced, and possibly powerful enough to engender universal audience responses that will also be freed from rhetoric's shady ploys. This kind of logic is entrenched within discourses that correlate the unmediated experience of emotion with the political function of the public apology. Our conceptions of the emotionally honest speech are bound to our conceptions of language's inaugurating power—a power that presumably is strong enough to propel "a people" into a new interpretive space, a power that presumably can be identified when an utterance generates a recognizable action, such as binding citizens in the experience of emotion of "profound despond" conjured by an impeachment or "shock and awe" impelled by exhibitions of U.S. military power or even a general, or national grief spurred by a shared sense of loss.

Conventionally, public concern about failures in speech that do not deliver the requisite emotional intensity seems to follow from legitimate assessments of whether a quality such as contrition has made an appearance. Presumably, any artificial representation of remorse will be critically reviled, and the shared response of chastisement may be referenced to justify the actions taken by members of a given community to dispel the justified outrage.

THE CALL FROM BEYOND

When considering the political consequences of the politics of true feeling, we encounter a question about how to counteract the propagation of sentimental narratives without discounting feelings and indeed, acknowledging them to be a critical resource for political judgment. Platonism lingers within narratives that would respond to that question by depicting representation's power as transcendent, homogeneous and self-sufficient, a power that announces its presence by affecting our very being without producing the interpretive mess that emotional responses can generate. A version of this narrative can be found in one of Plato's most inscrutable dialogues, *Phaedrus*, the subject of much critical debate about whether it offers a coherent message. Among its possible topics: a treatise on the nature of love, rhetoric itself, the role of memory in the service of truth, the relationship between affect and wisdom. Some scholars have read it as presenting a parody of these concerns.[5]

My interest is in how *Phaedrus* represents the parameters of appropriate linguistic comportment and the message it delivers about what speakers should do after they've been caught speaking deceptively, even if that deception is playful. Namely, they are advised to feel shame and then to initiate reparation by delivering a statement of atonement. When remorse is genuine, its earnest intensity should forcefully announce itself to audiences who will feel its presence unreservedly. *Phaedrus* outlines models for proper linguistic comportment and evaluative criteria for assessing whether sincerity has made an appearance.

This lesson occurs right at the onset of the dialogue where the reader finds Socrates and Phaedrus taking a stroll outside of the city, mulling over the question of how to measure verbal virtuosity. An erotic undercurrent accompanies their rendezvous as Phaedrus, a seemingly impressionable young man, expresses his admiration for the renowned sophist, Lysias, who had earlier delivered a thrilling lecture on the nature of love. Socrates reveals a jealous and competitive streak and responds to Phaedrus' admiration with a boast: not only will he immediately compose his own thrilling speech on the nature of love, he will also follow that verbal performance with another—a genuine disposition that will forfeit the superficial thrill of sophistry and replace it with a serious philosophic meditation. But after making this announcement, Socrates' bravado is followed by an odd moment of drama. Rather than launch into his performance, Socrates takes a moment to demur, announcing that he must cover his head as he speaks. "Then I can rush through my speech at top speed without looking at you and breaking down in shame" (237 a. See also Baumlin xi). How to read the meaning and significance of this embodied gesture is open to question. Was Socrates being coy? Can he truly not bear a direct look when commencing his parody of Lysias or is covering his head part of a play of seduction? If so, does the act of looking away signify not modesty but the degree to which seduction and indirection are intrinsic to the endeavor to thrill audiences and get their undivided and admiring attention?

Such questions tend to be downplayed within philosophical traditions that have read this opening scene as a prelude to what the dialogue will eventually reveal—an idealized representation of philosophic love, the kind that is passionate but not consummated; the kind that delineates how an ideal of authenticity can offer an immaterial but inspirational starting point for contemplating the Divine. Eroticism's pedagogic possibilities are not denied but deemed creditable when put in the service of something bigger and nobler than individual desire and embodiment. From this perspective, the dialogue demonstrates how desire and embodiment may serve society at large when properly channeled to direct one's attention towards Pure Spirit.

This lesson, however, is one that may be learned after reading the dialogue, during a time of contemplation. *While* reading the dialogue, other things might occur to the reader. She may, for example, be intrigued by the depiction of a coy Socrates making flirtatious boasts. She may have wanted to see if, in fact, he could deliver that (superficial) sophistic thrill. But just as Socrates is about to make good on his promise, just as he draws the reader in as witness to the occasion of seduction and situates the reader as judge of his bravado, he interrupts himself with a surprise announcement: he has witnessed a "divine" sign that tells him to halt the parody. In that moment of interruption, all personal motives, questionable or not, fall away as Socrates appears to encounter an awe-inspiring restriction that warns him about misusing language's power. The voice of the occasion has come through loud and clear, forbidding Socrates from luring Phaedrus into a state of wonderment and admiration for

Socrates' verbal skills. Socrates confesses that not only must he stop the seduction; he must restart his speech and hang his head in shame.

For those who were waiting to see what Socrates could do—those readers who might have had at least a passing interest in a Socratic show of verbal dexterity—the moment of interruption will likely provoke some kind of response—perhaps surprise or a twinge of disappointment. Once Socrates testifies to witnessing the divine sign, all bets are off and the reader does not get a textual representation of Socrates fulfilling what he promised. Instead, in testifying to hearing the divine call, Socrates also stipulates what the call has told him what to do: atone "for some offense to heaven" (237 a). In effect, Socrates has been shamed for engaging in an improper discursive exchange and the reader who wanted to participate with him is implicated by the chastisement. Indeed, the reading context changes once Socrates is hit by a bolt of remorse. The reading experience is no longer *fun*. What started out as flirtatious banter and the representation of a playful disposition on romance narratives suddenly becomes an earnest and potentially pedantic lesson about all that is essential, commanded, and orderly. But rather than attend to any disappointment engendered by this turn away from a good competition, readers will be expected to approve of this shift by accepting the idea that earnestness is the proper response when summoned by the Divine. Presumably, we will come to agree that being sober when making use of representation's awesome power is the right way to be.

And yet it is critical to note how that lesson is delivered experientially. *Phaedrus* makes a dramatic spectacle of language's call that is memorable and effective because it leads the reader to have an embodied experience of what it depicts. Not only does the text deliver a message about what constitutes proper linguistic comportment. That textual depiction of self-interruption may have also interrupted the reader's anticipated pleasure in being witness to a good Socratic show. Presumably, the "voice" that spoke to Socrates also caused a disturbance in the reader whose anticipated pleasure was suspended once Socrates put a halt to the flirty banter and commenced the austere philosophical disputation. In telling a story about a divine call, the dialogue's textual interruption also offers a representative show of its force. The simultaneity of propositional content about power meeting an embodied experience is mutually reinforcing—story and show come together to confirm the legitimacy of narratives that declare that we will be called by a transcendent power in language and that when it calls, we will know it, and will be obligated to heed its directives.

One's obedience is signified stylistically. The speech that atones should be represented neither as playful, seductive nor coy, but as earnest, sincere, and respectable. The representation of Socrates obeying a voice that calls him to order functions as the origin of the stylistic shift in the dialogue as a whole. A solemn, weighty, and purposeful style is featured throughout the rest of the dialogue, as if to demonstrate the kind of language use that should be adopted by anyone aiming to take the lessons of *Phaedrus* seriously. The stylistic conversion gives the reader a model for how to indicate that he has turned away from sophistry and towards the philosophical as the way to honorably engage representational action. Presumably, the shift from flirt to pedant is representative of the proper mode of speech that rhetors should adopt in general to avoid comporting themselves shamefully.

With this model in mind, it becomes possible to understand why Clinton's apology failed to engender identification and sympathy. What the public ostensibly wanted and what Congressional leaders interested in Authenticity ostensibly demanded was a display of contrition that approximated the Socratic expression of shame, an incarnation of an ostensibly pure gesture of remorse. What the public got instead was yet another performance from Mr. "Slick Willie," the narcissistic verbal trickster. Clinton's meager four-minute utterance offered nothing about transcendence in either word or effect and communicated personal bitterness about the noxious Special Prosecutor rather than asking audiences to look beyond, toward a sublime place of reconciliation. Presumably, Clinton should have delivered a speech of *conviction* using words of apology that would convey the strength of that of conviction.

But, again, we stumble back into narrative even when discussing what would appear to exist beyond narrative and be self-sufficiently present to acts of judgment. Indeed, *Phaedrus* exemplifies the paradox inherent within representations that depict transcendence as the ultimate interpretive goal, and include in that depiction the idea that one of the main purposes of speech is to rise above persuasive ploys. Ostensibly, we can tell when a shamed subject has conveyed real sorrow for having said the wrong thing and for taking pleasure in the speaking act that deviated into shameful territory. But to decide that Clinton failed to truly portray remorse means that there is a preconceived idea of what he should have said instead. This might include, for example, the idea that to speak with conviction, one must have a singular and noble purpose; one should use words to tell the truth by re-presenting its essence with words that aim high, not low; one should feel chagrined about having been tempted to beguile and charm. And specific to the *apology*, key words should be uttered such as "sorry," "irresponsibility," "selfishness," "disappointment about letting down" the citizenry, one's co-workers, a spouse, who should then be depicted as a loving person who did not deserve to share in the experience of shame brought on the family by the apologist's personal selfishness. In other words, an apologist will be expected to channel his apology through preestablished, culturally sanctioned linguistic forms.

These expectations add another wrinkle to any speculations about how representational power achieves its effects because they demonstrate how the act of redemption is accomplished via another speech that presumably differs from the first one, and that that difference is manifested stylistically. In effect, the speaker's show of remorse aims not to configure an essential quality of remorse (which is, after all, invisible even in a Platonic rubric) but culturally approved *signifiers* of remorse. More specifically, the dishonorable speaker may be redeemed (cleansed) through another act of speech that matches prior models of how to indicate sorrow by mimicking the narrative that both renounces the seductive and coy and demonstrates that renunciation stylistically.

Rather than consider how, when displaying our linguistic aims, we are called upon to engage with languages made available in culture, we are encouraged to skip that feature of communication and instead to expect a speaker's language choices to indicate an authentic encounter between a self and a representation of that self's thoughts and feelings. This perspective is affirmed by the idea that the act of witnessing a divine sign will not only inspire an act of atonement, it will (mysteriously) give direction to the speaker about what to say to indicate that one sensed and is endeavoring to obey divine directives. The Platonic depiction of the dramatic interruption and the chagrined shift by the errant speaker to the right path gives expression to an image of virtue embedded within an important interpretive pause wherein one's conscience forces one to stop, crumble, and then begin again by relinquishing questionable personal motives. Accordingly, we will be called from beyond to feel shame when we fail to adhere to ethical obligations of representation—and the effects will be clear to audiences who will recognize a sincere discursive display when they see it.

There is power in the depiction of that moment of interruption and chagrined renewal once the arrogant speaker has been humbled after bearing witness to something greater than himself. Iterations of this scene have appeared in many contexts, especially in old Hollywood films: Claude Raines as Senator Joseph Harrison Paine in *Mr. Smith Goes to Washington*, Paul Newman as a compromised lawyer in *The Verdict*, Tom Cruise as a slick car dealer in *Rainman*. (It is not a coincidence that such scenes typically represent charismatic Caucasian men in crisis, worthy of our attention, earning our desire to witness their redemption.) These images remain powerful because they offer an enticing promise: That speakers can count on being able to hear language's call and that listeners will know if a subsequent speech has answered that call; that we can trust and believe in a guiding order to intervene and assert itself on its own volition to ensure that those who captivate us are doing so for the right reasons and from the right perspective.

Phaedrus, however, can be read to question the parameters of an interpretive model that configures a harmonious conjoining between the act of saying what needs to be said, the power to enact atonement, and the endeavor to judge discursive effects, as if all ride aloft a wave of representational power cresting towards a shore harboring ethics. If a Socratic-inspired act of atonement begins with the recognition of error, it means that the speaker must become self-conscious about having spoken in shameful ways. Accordingly, the wrongdoer must convey not a singularly present self but a self who is conflicted, divided between, on the one hand, the need to step back from the situation to get an overview that allows for recognition of the error in judgment, and on the other hand, the need to be fully present to the delivery of a statement of sorrow for having committed that error, distracted by no other thoughts, and not merely going through the motions of reciting words of remorse without true feeling. The self that recognizes error should indicate that he is conscious of and attentive to the dimension of existence that resides outside of and beyond embodiment, indeed beyond speech. This part of the self should be available to testify to the self's alignment with the divine and universal forms that (presumably) matter more than mere words. Meanwhile, another part of the self must be of this world, present to the moment of the utterance, feeling shame when describing shame to insure that his speech propels the requisite force of feeling. The purpose of the speech of atonement would appear to be to enact restoration of self-unity and then harmony between our experiences in this world and what we know or sense about the one beyond.

For the audience, an act of atonement appears to be delivered when expressions of the contrite self act to re-present the linguistic power that can force harmonious affiliations between the divided self, the idea of remorse and its enactment, the representational display and its reception. When the "story" of an apology (I am announcing to you that I intend to apologize) is also felt *through* the speech that apologizes, that conflation seems to produce an interpretive event that *is* forceful, that truly does act as an authentic re-presentation of contrition in the face of a divine power. The simultaneity of story and show seems to naturally reinforce the validity of the narrative that depicts linguistic action as organic and inevitable. If the force of delivery carries an impact on its own volition, then the arts of seduction are not needed and not welcome. The provenance of the speech that grabs the audience's attention and sensibilities should transcend the worldly, and not emerge from a rhetorical situation.

But given that the act of conversion that would unify the self and the divine is derived from a story that teaches audiences about what to expect in a statement of atonement—including which specific words of sorrow should be uttered—then there has been no escape from narrative. Indeed, not only is the idea of an act of conversion narratively produced, the means for re-presenting it requires knowledge and use of rhetorical techniques. If the speech of remorse is expected to mirror prior versions of representational engagement, then it is also the case that the cultural narratives that establish discursive conditions of existence have influenced how one's representation of emotion will be read. Ambiguity towards rhetoric might be located right there—in the confused regard we have towards the idea that rhetors must be deliberate and purposeful when preparing a display of the putatively "natural" experience of emotion.

The dream of rhetorical innocence is expressed most emphatically in our culture by the continued association of rhetoric with verbal trickery and manipulation as opposed to being intrinsic to any communicative act. The disavowal of the seductive along with the demand that one feel shame for even attempting it describes precisely a cultural confusion about how to account for the dynamic of rhetoric within judgments that we would like to believe emanate from a wholesome felt sense about what a speech and speaker are *doing* (and should do). Emotional appeals can provoke tumultuous responses. We might, then, expect any attempt to express feelings to be messy, difficult, and unique. Given the turbulence of our responses to betrayals that engender the need for an apology, we might also expect the speech of apology to be radically singular in expressing the apologist's particular regret. Presumably, any person's deeply human experience of shame should be one's own, informed by one's recognition of having violated a moral code and sense of duty to others. Having recognized that violation, we might expect mortification to burn and grow, to morph into a sense that language—especially standard tropes—cannot capture. But instead of embracing the ways in which the singularity of these experiences might be variously (and often inadequately) represented and received, we are trained to look for a representation of recognizable signs to be convinced that a (wholesome) show of remorse is on offer.

The means by which audiences determine that sincerity has made an appearance are thoroughly ambiguous, particularly when considering the thin line separating rote repetition of preferred terms from their genuine delivery. We are expected to believe in the speaker who "makes" recognizable terminology his own as a way of indicating obedience to a reigning representational order. How that act of making will get read cannot be predicted. When, for example, a speaker seems over-prepared, his speech may be regarded as a mere show, a false performance, a formulaic repetition of clichés delivered without conviction. No preparation, however, and the speaker risks seeming cavalier, or saying the wrong thing when called upon to do something with words. Rhetoric's retreat from public consciousness is felt most crucially in that bifurcated narrative that aligns spontaneity of action with divine linguistic power while suborning rhetoric's role in how "spontaneity" makes an appearance. The "art" of an apology should not appear to be art-full—a precept that expresses a cultural anxiety about the possibility that it is precisely rhetorical preparation and not the delivery of true feelings that generates linguistic action. We remain reluctant to conceive of linguistic acts as emanating from strategic uses of convention and interpretive habits and instead habitually castigate speakers for engaging in strategic acts of persuasion. (This argument has been influenced by the work of Joe Kelleher.)

Phaedrus both represents and endorses a representational ethic that depicts the act of atonement as forswearing any debt to rhetoric. Indeed, it is the explicit turn away from seduction that dramatizes what constitutes proper linguistic comportment. By making a spectacle of Socrates', whose sensibilities are interrupted but then unified through a representation of reparation, *Phaedrus* depicts and enacts an apparatus for managing the gap between embodied experience and its narrative depiction. The apparently exterior (if not divine) force that is both described and then felt seems to affirm the rightness of the narrative that would claim no association with rhetoric's "mercenary" calculations. Hence, the tendency to read Socrates' atonement speech as a model of ethical linguistic comportment rather than as a literary effect.

Because the Platonic representation of proper linguistic comportment continues to resonate within our own era, it continues to affect current interpretive contexts, including those in which disapproving responses to Clinton's apology were intelligible. The outcry was made possible by an acceptance of the demand for the reenactment of a particular kind of locution that would include, for example, a professed desire for innocence from verbal competition, a rejection of sophistic trickery, the wisdom to know when to put a stop to linguistic play, followed by a genuine show of contrition for having recklessly found pleasure in the endeavor. Accordingly, only a true show of contrition could have paved the way for shared redemption and national healing.

An unexamined rhetoricity, notes Denise Riley, enables linguistic force to be regarded simultaneously as "impersonal" and "indifferent to us" and yet deeply intimate, that which "constitutes the fiber of the personal" (1). Through this impersonal yet personal connection, we craft the idea that our sense of the legitimacy of a given utterance (or written text) may be aligned with what is already present and hence natural, and that the presence of that connection in a given speech occasion will be disclosed. With the promise of that connection, we believe we are able to tell the difference between the formulaic repetition of protocol and the presentation of the familiar that aims beyond mere imitation. We are expected to believe that we can tell the difference between words that are known "by heart" from those that emanate from the heart (J. Kelleher 84) and that we can count on our powers of discernment to let us know if a heartfelt sentiment has been conveyed. *Phaedrus* both describes and activates what might be called the force of the fit—telling a story about a divine performative power that announces itself and forces a feeling of disruption and then a method of reconciliation generated by reverential linguistic comportment. We can find traces of this interpretive model within the analytical frameworks that authorize who is expelled and why an act of expulsion seems just.

Feeling Intertextual

An apology represents more than a speech act that proves that the errant speaker has heard a divine call, felt regret, mortification, and then the urge to display the right sentiment. Apologies, perhaps more than other speech acts, indicate that time, context and audience have a role to play as we determine meaning and judge the significance of another's expressions. One presumably apologizes to someone for a reason, about a prior occasion that hovers in the background but remains present to the moment of judging whether a speaker has made amends. Because these variegated elements, together and individually, do not necessarily emulate whatever narratives have been constructed to describe orderly acts of representation, the most we can say about methods of interpretation is that they involve diverse acts of negotiation rather than a homogenized search for truth's revelation. From a rhetorical perspective, the appeal to emotion is just one of many tactics a rhetor might deploy to help promote acceptance of his or her perspective. The point of making an emotional appeal is not to express true feelings for the sake of honoring and testifying to truth but to get the audience to listen and be affected by one's words. One invokes an emotional appeal to put listeners in a state of receptivity so that communication can occur. This premise modifies the negative connotations that seem to be endemic to the idea that one has offered a fake and calculated emotional response. Instead, rhetoricians have explored how the decision to be strategic about using language to forge connections is itself a virtuous act. The rhetor is ethically obligated to find words that audiences will find acceptable.

To make this case, rhetoricians promote discourses of propriety. Propriety is described as a stylistic virtue and it implicates the judgments we make about whether the words invoked by a rhetor fit the occasion of speech. Propriety helps configure judgments about the *legitimacy* of a given act of representation. Its status, however, can be enigmatic rather than positively construed because our sense of what is proper arises within given rhetorical situations and all of their complexities. For example, after Senator Lieberman took to the Senate floor to publicly rebuke Clinton, audiences may have doubted the sincerity of Senator Moynihan's praise that declared that Lieberman had said "the right thing" at a "time of profound despond." Indeed, audiences may have scoffed precisely at the use of the phrase "profound despond" to describe the emotional life of the citizenry, given that "profundity" and "despondence" were the last things that many felt in connection with the impeachment drive. The rejection of the phrase, then, could be read as emblematic of a general sense of impropriety about the endeavor to impeach. Meanwhile, judgments that deemed pronouncements from national leaders to be ridiculous validated that sense.

Discourses of propriety provide a different lens for thinking about how to participate with language. Rather than attempt to determine who speaks genuinely or with conviction, citizens consider what any speaker's words aim to *do* and whether the purpose and the effect of any given argument seem to be proper, fitting, and justified within a social context rather than a transcendent one. For many rhetoricians, finding the right words to fit the occasion describes rhetoric's central purpose. Hence we will find the word *propriety* adopted by many contemporary rhetorical theorists who aim to delineate a representational ethics that incorporates a conception of a socially conscious interpretive dynamic. To James Baumlin, "propriety" and its cousin "decorum"—both important terms from rhetoric's classical traditions—help rhetoricians outline a conceptual framework that encourages reflexive judgment, especially when refracted through the lens of postmodern theory. Decorum, Baumlin maintains, can be characterized as "a sensitivity toward time, opportunity, and audience, and toward the effect of one's words on an audience" (Decorum 178). The rhetor who aims for decorous speech acknowledges that no single version of truth can be represented as absolutely authoritative. Instead, differences in perspective must be anticipated and can be accommodated. Propriety helps with the work of mediation by offering a stylistic buffer that allows for differences in perspective to be aired without causing offense and with the explicit goal of fostering "harmony among the words and worlds of self and others, dynamically conceived" (Baumlin Decorum 181). By encouraging interlocutors to acknowledge that interpretive resolutions will emerge rhetorically, all will agree that because the circumstances affecting judgments will change, so will potential resolutions. We are less likely to feel alienated by another's perspective if we feel that the rhetor has taken time to consider our various points of view when deciding on how to formulate his or her own.

For other rhetoricians, the concepts of decorum and propriety allow audiences to get control over language's infinite capacity to enact new meanings by providing methods for evaluating the legitimacy of local and specific representational forms presented at specific moments in time. Beth Innocenti Manolescu maintains that formalizing conceptions of propriety allows the concept to act "as a norm for evaluating argumentation from a rhetorical perspective and a method of reconstruction for doing so" (113). Like Baumlin's argument, this exploration of propriety emphasizes how a sense of ethics will be attributed to the rhetor who takes care when stylizing her presentation. She will be valued as someone who considers the audience's sensibilities when forging ahead with an argument that could affect social and civic life. If, during a speech event, all agree to mull over whether a given act of representation is proper to the speech occasion, then it becomes possible to introduce and "maintain an appetite for arguments of integrity" (124) by adopting an interpretive mechanism that prioritizes deliberation about *how* to solicit audience adherence.

Meanwhile, Michael Leff sees decorum as an expansive term that keeps speakers and writers alert to the interpretive complexities inhering within our uses of language while providing an organizing principle able to transform complexity into comprehension and assessment. While decorum commonly connotes "mere" style, it instead demarcates a method for assessing value and significance. These abstract ideas are given tangible expression through the concept of coherence, a stylistic property that not only represents the idea of representational unity but also acts to generate it. Leff believes that our judgments are structured by the endeavor to synthesize component parts of a representational scene into a fitting "whole" and that a teleological impulse underwrites interpretive action and moves it towards the production and apprehension of what fits. The principle of decorum, Leff maintains, "orders the elements of a discourse and rounds them out into a coherent product relevant to the occasion" (Habituation 62). When the rhetor selects language so as to integrate component parts of a rhetorical scene into a representational whole, he or she will be participating in a virtuous way, managing interpretive choices *in order to* facilitate audience identification and interpretive resolutions.

In rhetorical traditions, propriety is represented stylistically *as* coherence.[6] A narrative about how to create interpretive order replaces the Platonic narrative that envisions ethical language uses in terms of correspondences and substitutions of words for referents. Given that coherence is manifested stylistically, style effectively measures ethics; the rhetor who takes time to craft an appealing coherent statement is a rhetor who shows care for the audience's sensibilities. Leff explores this premise in an article with Thomas Rosteck that examines classical definitions of propriety in relation to the theories of Kenneth Burke. The authors characterize propriety as "a guiding principle in ethics" (328), "a principle of local integration—the agency that coordinates what is said with how it is said within some particular context" (328–29). While decorum may be "associated exclusively" with mere style, rhetorical mediations about decorous speech are indicative of a much broader concern with the question of how to imagine the possibility of bringing order about in the face of "a relativistic social universe" (328). The terms decorum and propriety address "cognitive as well as stylistic concerns . . . Artistic skill is neither cosmetic nor deceptive. Instead it reflects the unity of thought and expression necessary for the comprehension and direction of life in the pluralistic space of public experience" (Leff 62). To undertake this act of integration and "uncover order within" is, indeed, to act ethically.

Once propriety is configured as vital to rhetorical negotiations and persuasive success, then it may be summoned within narratives describing proper rhetorical goals: to find proper words, to "integrate culture and eloquence by providing enhancing vocabularies for active social participation" (Mayhew 35). Or, as put by Paul Stob, to "explore how language can solve problems and build communities" (29). Presumably, *propriety* can be found within representations that deliver coherent statements, arguments, and claims. On the other hand, Leff and Rosteck add that the specific look of integration cannot be pinned down. Rather, coherence takes on overtones of the aesthetic in that any particular representation of it cannot be determined in advance. In general, audiences will look to find the connective thread of coherence as they interact with texts and attempt to craft a sense of which ideas properly fit into a "whole" perspective, and the rhetor who consciously aims to facilitate the audience's ability to make such connections will do his part to enhance opportunities for communicative acts to generate social harmony.

Rosteck and Leff make this point to insure that their theorizing of propriety remains flexible. Inflexible representations of "the proper" can transform into pieties, like the kind disseminated in 1998. When one way of organizing perspectives becomes dominant, it can undergo a conversion, no longer standing as a possible way of seeing but as a mandated "orientation, a frame, or a way of organizing" our sense of propriety (Rosteck and Leff 329). Because pieties are not stable or "mere givens," but are "created by human makers as they interact with their fellows and with the world" (329), they may also be "pried apart" by other versions of how to draw connections between elements within a representational scene. Pieties may be converted into new perspectives by what Burke calls "perspective by incongruity" (often experienced as comedy) and also known as a "linguistic impiety" (330).

Here, we might pause and acknowledge that propriety is, indeed, an important concept, very much a part of any sense we have about whether we are "alright" with our worlds—whether our values merge with the contexts we inhabit, whether we have faith in systems of justice or sense when injustices have occurred. When Kenneth Burke connected linguistic strategizing to "the exercise of human propriety" (Counter-Statement 42) he did so by emphasizing that persuasion depends upon an audience's sense of the rightness of a given position. Propriety's relevance to political discourse seems clear. Arguably, propriety influenced citizens' reported rejection of the impeachment drive. It informed disparate responses to the wars in Iraq launched by Bush Sr. in 1991 and then twelve years later by his son. Propriety is central to assessments of any public controversy—from bullying in schools to Stand Your Ground gun laws to voter purges in the "swing" states of Florida, Pennsylvania, and Ohio. And it is immensely helpful to keep in mind that a fragile relationship exists between propriety and piety, and that we can easily slide from one to the other as we take satisfaction in the idea that our perspectives are correct and should be adopted by others.

But theorizing propriety's relationship to representational power presents its own conundrum. The term "propriety" remains strangely insubstantial. It is demure rather than robust, connoting what is decorous and of concern to polite society. Arguably, it bears the taint of the maligned belletristic rhetorical tradition that linked rhetorical studies to the endeavor to teach "the mob" to control linguistic unruliness by developing "good taste"—an appetite for modes of speech sanctioned and approved by the ruling class. In that era, the act of purging speakers and writers of their idiosyncratic styles was depicted as central to rhetoric's civilizing mission, one that endeavored to convince citizens to tamp down unruly passions by learning to esteem representations of linguistic decorum. With this historical conception in mind, the idea of propriety is only vaguely linked to displays of linguistic force that deliver a vigorous blast of intensity. Propriety instead designates a more muted "felt" regard for a given speech or text that keeps everyone from becoming inflamed. But given this connotation of gentleness (gentlemanliness), we might wonder about how propriety's properties get manifested.

This question is especially pertinent to the ways in which we think emotional receptivity factors into the success of a persuasive appeal. In what ways should propriety sway the endeavor to *make* the emotional experience noticed, intelligible, and properly integrated into a representational scene? When we ask, "Do the words fit the occasion?" or "Is this the right thing to say?" we pose questions that speak to an embodied sense about the "rightness" of the words on offer, words that just might move us to see things differently, change our minds, resolve a quandary, return to love. And when we think that the words do fit, we may be satisfied and consider the interpretive transaction to have been worth our time and effort. But when the words do not seem to *work*, does that failure automatically imply a lapse in effort by the speaker to arrange for the kind of representational unity that would unite rhetor, text and audience? And when it comes to mulling over the interpretive contribution of *emotions*, should signs of coherence be championed as the proper representational goal?

"Fittingness" does not characterize a point of view that emerges naturally or through impartial and neutral interpretive transactions generated by an order of representation. Any sense we have of what is fitting will depend upon what has been said to establish an interpretive context that demands a judgment. Feminist rhetoricians who attend to the discursive conditions of experience have explored the ways in which dominant cultural narratives influence embodied responses to representational forms. Discourses train us to have preferences for particular forms and that training will influence judgments about which forms are credible. Lynn Worsham's analysis of ideology and emotion is especially relevant to any discussion about the relationship between political judgment and a sense of whether words fit the occasion of their delivery. Worsham describes the ways in which ideology is mapped onto the level of affect, training us to respond to cultural narratives while veiling precisely that influence by promoting the idea that affective experiences register signs of authenticity. "Ideology binds each individual to the social world through a complex and often contradictory affective life that too often remains, for the most part, just beyond the horizon of semantic availability, and its success depends upon a mystification or misrecognition of this primary work" (Coming 106).[7]

The word *emotion* not only demarcates embodied responses to texts but more importantly, it also signifies the narratives that we have inherited to discuss its meaning. The same applies to the word *propriety*. Emotions are "schooled" (Worsham Going Postal 216) through narratives, and that training is significant to judgments of propriety, constituting the discursive conditions of receptivity while naturalizing culture's contribution to how we judge who is doing what with language. Ideologies work when cathecting emotion to cultural narratives that stake claims on how life should be both perceived and experienced, their messages reinforced when experienced emotionally and somatically. Such observations raise questions about how ideologies intersect with rhetorical narratives that situate propriety as part of an interpretive apparatus guiding political judgments in seemingly ethical ways. When we invoke such terms we are invoking linguistic histories that have characterized how to imagine affect's relationship to judgment. Those histories will influence our sense of what matters to any occasion of speech. If we are trained to prefer coherent representations, to expect to be satisfied by them, to feel at one with the representation of coherence, and to feel unmoored without it, then we encounter a question that is central to democratic political culture about the legitimacy of discursive histories that condition conceptions of which acts of representation should be deemed fitting and then valid and just.

At this point, rhetorical style takes on renewed significance, given that it is an intrinsic part of the dynamic that activates the audience's sense of whether a selection of words fit an occasion. Styles function as the material marker of the dynamic that presumably generates the felt sense of fittingness. *Style* seems to participate in generating the feeling of propriety, as if the power of a coherent form generates the organizing action that brings order to potential interpretive chaos by enabling audiences not only to recognize that ordering action when it appears but also to feel the rightness of the form that emerges as a representational result. But of course styles are not intrinsically forceful. As responses to Clinton's apology suggest, we are culturally trained to see some styles as more valuable or credible than others. When we invoke propriety to judge whether an apologist has managed to say what needs to be said, we demarcate an interpretive space in which the presumably foundational power of aesthetics and persuasion encounters narratives of enculturation that may have influenced judgments of what seems to be fitting, just and right.

Rather than render style as a conduit available to deliver meaning or as the generator of interpretive harmony, style can be described as an *enactment* that designates a reality-making process that implicates the ways in which we have learned to notice and respond to cultural codes. As Worsham's analysis of ideology and emotion suggest, to discover an identifiable speech act, such as a successful or failed apology, is to discover a *narrative* that would explain, codify and organize perceptions of the textual (or oral) "object" under review. The act of identifying whether a given act of representation is proper involves more than looking at how it fits within a prior context of interpretation or how it connects to a history of sayings. Rather, the very act of identifying propriety implicates our (emotional) investments in particular cultural narratives to act as legitimate guideposts for judgment. When, for example, determining whether an apology has made an appearance, we simultaneously will be authorized to denigrate those speech acts that fail to adhere to proper protocol. We are even given permission to belittle those acts of speech that seem to veer too far from sanctioned stylistic markers; when we feel that belittlement is unquestionably justified, we perpetuate an interpretive context in which the pro-forma representational form/delivery may be put forth to stand in for integrity, as if its mere appearance represents/enacts interpretive integrity, even when, as we witnessed in 1998, that may hardly be the case. As long as the experience of emotion is attached to culturally sanctioned comportment (linguistic and otherwise), the rules that govern perceptions of appropriate versus inappropriate ways of participating with language may be referenced as if intrinsically ethical and legitimate.

At this point, we might notice a positivistic logic lurking within the rhetorical call to rhetors to formulate proper expressions. Just as *Phaedrus* made a case for power accrued to the simultaneity of a story and a show of representation, so will the simultaneity of an embodied sense of fittingness provoked by a representation of coherence appear to produce and naturalize an embodied sense of whether a given use of language seems to be *right*. The judgment, meanwhile, will reinforce the validity of whatever narrative is invoked to characterize how proper judgments should be obtained. The narrativization of propriety functions politically to direct judgments about that which will satisfy: the text that meets expectations about how to depict representational forms. So that even though, in a rhetorical framework, the speech act is expected to be spontaneous and free to generate any number of responses, citizens nonetheless will be expected to valorize culture's reproduction.

Rethinking how styles enact emotional responses—including judgments of what seems to be proper—means reconsidering how aesthetic and rhetorical traditions contribute to apprehending the significance of the materiality of the sign in the identification of political formations.

That representations of propriety come to us via conventions and rhetorical strategizing indicates how discussions of "the proper and fitting" are inherently informed by "cultural scripts" (Hesford phrase) and ideologies tied to the languages made available in culture that, as put by James Berlin, name what exists and what is possible. Propriety is one such language that is situated as "both a material and a discursive site of struggle for cultural power" (Hesford Reading 197) that can be located within embodied responses to the "material" of style. The proper style is not merely present to be noticed but also to be evaluated within an interpretive context that branches out into the domain of intertextuality. Our assessment of style's significance engages a constant and irretrievable circulation of textuality—and materiality. Styles make sense to us by a procedure of referencing other texts that have told us what styles mean. For a given style to produce an embodied and authorizing sense of being at one with a text, or person, or an idea, we must forget that we have been taught to *feel* a preference for discursive harmony and to reference that feeling when affiliating with narratives that promote the idea that conceptual unity is both possible and honorable. And we must overlook the interpretive labor it takes to construct a sense of being "in" coherent accord with the words of another, the context that makes those words possible, the narratives that already advise us to find fitting words to be satisfying.

And so, what to *look for* in a speech that endeavors to apologize? Our attachments to narratives that organize conceptions of interpretation can hinder as much as help us to be able to answer that question and hear what the apologist is attempting to do. When we expect to engage in an act of evaluation that will determine whether a given speech act represents properly a preformed version of what an apology should do, we can forget what the apology was ostensibly about. The situation that calls for an apology means that there was some sad, possibly traumatic event that left a lingering trace. When an apology is required, something is off and often that "something" cannot be linguistically captured. The emotions engendered by the rift that preceded the apology exist as a kind of transitory intensity—as subtle or perhaps hardened feelings of dashed hopes, lost faith in someone we admired or loved, the suck of disappointment, of not wanting to have to be apologized to, of wishing to be able to go back to the time before the apology seemed necessary. All of these feelings may flicker through our minds. They may be noticed, veiled, buried. But they are not regularizable and not necessarily presentable.

Style's effects are "always only fleeting, for not only is intensity ultimately indeterminate, it is always on the move" (T. R. Johnson *Writing* 274). The stylized apology, meanwhile, acts as an offering, a tonic to hopefully inaugurate healing, an act of restoration, a return to a time of "before" connections were broken. These are terms that gesture towards movement, an ephemeral energy that will elude our attempts to describe it. The styles of representation that we would use to initiate such movements speak as much to tenderness and fragility as they do to a robust persuasive force that clearly positions the response that "fits."

What flashed through the minds of viewers who watched the President deliver a national apology, having been compelled to place himself before the public by engaging in a monumental representation of remorse fueled by shame? The passing sense of awfulness when bearing witness to that kind of event is precisely the kind of experience that tends to be suppressed once the moment has passed, once the election season gets going, once narratives of "what happened" have been accepted and then filed within memories and some new issue is brought before the public's attention. Meanwhile, during that moment of witness, we may have had other responses to the terseness of his delivery than those that expressed disappointment about his failure to indicate remorse in proper ways. Clinton's utterance might have been read otherwise, perhaps as an indicator of his unwillingness to perform contrition on demand, especially after being subjected that day to a legal proceeding (the Grand Jury appearance) that had all the appearances of being proper yet somehow felt devastatingly inappropriate. To those of us who judged the impeachment drive to be an abuse of power, Clinton's failure to comply with a demand for a proper performance of contrition was the right thing to do. From this perspective, his out of order apology was a show of strength.

And yet even that description of an alternative response to the event of watching Clinton "apologize" does not adequately convey all that might have been experienced if one felt defensive on the President's behalf or more generally concerned with Congressional overreach. Whatever we might say about possible reactions to Clinton's confession of an affair, we will not be able to encapsulate the subtle, complex interconnected relationships between the given situation and the words used to describe it, our embodied responses to those words, our own sense of ethics, and the range of emotions we might be feeling as we engage with the narratives about political life presented for our review.

Part II: Transitory Materiality

Does a turn to propriety help sort through those fleeting senses we might have about whether a given representation is itself just and fair? How to theorize the encounter between fleeting potentiality and material presence when assessing what has value and importance? The events of 1998, wherein politics, propriety and stylized representations converged, can help us consider how to answer these questions, particularly as they applied to public representations of Monica Lewinsky and Linda Tripp, the women associated with Clinton's impeachment who were also deemed to be notoriously irrelevant.

By the summer of 1998, it was common knowledge that Tripp had been Lewinsky's trusted associate. Citizens learned that the two women met at work and became friends and that the rules of friendship were violated once Tripp taped telephone conversations of Lewinsky's love struck confessionals about her affair with the President. During those phone chats, Lewinsky spoke openly and at length about her aching heart, unaware the recordings would be delivered to a Special Prosecutor with ties to the opposing political party. Tripp was subsequently recruited by Starr to conduct a covert sting. Wired with an approved recording device, she met Lewinsky at a bar in Virginia and under the guise of another consultation of friendship, attempted to goad Lewinsky into revealing evidence of a Clinton cover-up about their affair.

Once these tactics were made public, they did not sit well with the citizenry. There was even a movement to have Tripp arrested for the initial act of taping a conversation without the knowledge of the other speaker. (This went nowhere.) But regardless of whether the taping was legally sanctioned, Linda Tripp came to be, according to ABC news anchor Diane Sawyer, "the most hated woman in America" and that feeling was given expression through narratives that denigrated her physical appearance. Tripp was characterized as the meddling gossip—the quintessential old hag—frizzy bleached hair, tired eyes, crooked teeth. Her stylized look "inspired" commentary, especially from merciless comedians: "Linda Tripp just spent $30,000 on plastic surgery. That is one expensive veterinarian." "Linda Tripp told Monica Lewinsky in one of their phone conversations that she hadn't had sex in seven years! Oh, yeah. Like it's her choice! That means at some point, some guy got drunker than any man in history!" The press unleashed name-calling, seemingly triggered by her shameful conduct: "Friend from Hell" (*Time*), "a hideous creature" (*salon.com*), "a specimen" who "gained fame when scientists cited her as proof of the falsity of the theory of evolution" (*Kansas City Star*).[8]

What to make of the regularized negativity that was both comprehensible, permissible, and given its regularity, presumably regarded as proper, at least to some? I would like to think about these questions in connection with Wendy Hesford's discussion of *kairos*, another rhetorical term that, like propriety, highlights the ways in which representations are rhetorically situated. Hesford defines *kairos* as "a multidimensional term that refers to a situated understanding of space and/or time and the material circumstances—namely the cultural climate—of rhetorical situations" (*Kairos* 148). *Kairos* speaks to a linguistic balancing act, typically imagined in terms akin to propriety, wherein the rhetor considers the urgency of the situation and thinks about potentially disparate perspectives as he or she endeavors to find the right words that will restore balance by conjoining perspectives into a harmonious whole. "Balance," Hesford adds, "is achieved and sustained to the extent that *kairos* can anticipate the needs and values of imagined or intended audiences" (148).

Hesford goes on to critique this notion of balance but before turning to that part of her argument, I would like to think through the implications of linking phrases such as "the right words" and "restoring balance" to those public locutions inserted into impeachment discourses that shamed Tripp. Presumably, those linkages were persuasive at the time because they met the needs and values of the intended audience, which in this case might be described as the television viewing public that had been subjected to an onslaught of media spectacles involving breathless discussions by "experts" dissecting what had been said under oath about the president's sex life. In this cultural climate, mockery and a healthy dose of cynicism may have seemed like the perfect way to respond. Given that the entire debacle had been brought before the public because of the actions of Linda Tripp, her sorry person was regarded as emblematic of all that was wrong with the proceedings in general. The drive to impeach Clinton had a most inauspicious beginning, surfacing not from the reveal of a dramatic betrayal involving, say, misleading the people into a war by disseminating false information about an imminent threat to national security. Rather, the impeachment emerged from a context that most would likely agree lacked drama and cultural significance: Tripp's grim face, Monica Lewinsky's ample body, queasy methods of evidence gathering, girlfriend gossip.

If *kairos* suggests urgency, what this event seemed to represent was its absence—at least to the majority of citizens who repeated in poll after poll that they were sick of impeachment talk. By October 1998, just as congressional leaders were meeting to decide whether to move forward with an inquiry, a majority of polled citizens said they just wanted the issue to go away.[9] Indeed, in response to a lack of urgency, in response to being called to attend to an event that, for many, summoned neither the awesomeness of a divine call, nor reason's order, nor even a sentimental sadness about a scene of ruined domesticity, many journalists adopted a rhetorical style that seemed most fitting: the language of irony, expressed via "witty" double entrendres directed especially to Tripp and Lewinsky. "Papa Bill, Mama Linda, Baby Monica: The dysfunctional family at the heart of the scandal," headlined a *Time* magazine article summarizing the case, which also described Lewinsky as "a typical child of divorce—skilled, as many such children are, in secrecy, guilt tripping and seduction" (20). "Monica Lewinsky trying to pare down her body, her fame" announced a headline on the "Allpolitics" section of CNN's website. "Does Monica's hair make the cut?" asked the *Detroit News* in anticipation of one of her first public appearances. "Hasta la vista, baby—Monica needs to shed weight of notoriety" ran a headline for a column by Leonard Pitts Jr. who wrote about wanting to take back his previous praise of Lewinsky, initially granted after she failed to sign an autograph. That act, wrote Pitts, led him to mistakenly conclude that Lewinsky properly understood "the difference between fame and its unsavory cousin, notoriety" (15).[10] After she published a book and went on a speaking tour, she indicated a lack of understanding of what should have been her proper response—to not speak at all.

Like any rhetorical style, the ironic mode of delivery implies an intended audience who will understand what the tone conveys and why it has been adopted. Rhetoric's attention to language as a site of audience participation is especially relevant here because it underscores how styles work in conjunction with our willingness to be persuaded. While we tend to conceive of language use in terms of individuals making choices about how to represent ideas, the rhetorical tradition envisions the rhetor's relation to discourse as a social activity—a domain that implicates audience preferences, desires, sense of what is permissible and why. And in this domain, the question of who speaks and in what way also matters. Accordingly, any response that has been deemed "fitting" does not emerge simply because the rhetor is naturally eloquent or has made the right choices. Rather, the capacity to use language to compel audiences will depend upon whether audiences want to affiliate with the mode of speech up for review.

As Kenneth Burke argues, styles convey attitudes. A choice of words shapes a way of seeing by indicating what has significance and, more elusively, of what kind. Audiences are discursively constructed to the extent that we "enter" into a mode of delivery and embrace the "we" that would want to share in whatever stylistic attitude a given representation conveys. We become a particular *kind* of "we" through our interactions with stylized discourses, a premise that reconstitutes the singular and homogeneous "voice of the occasion" into a historically contingent site of materiality. From this perspective, "the voice of the occasion" says less about truth and more about our allegiance not only to social conventions but also to the desire for social conventions to tell us what to hear and how to process it.

The attitude of derisive irony invoked within media narratives reporting on Tripp and Lewinsky invited readers to take a skeptical look at the people under review and then at the larger topics implicated by their representations—the impeachment, national sentiment, friendships between women, and hypocritical calls for a return to life's "basics." Styles convey cultural attitudes about whether a given representation of a person is worth our time, attention, energy, and emotional investment. Styles act as repositories of the histories of affect with which they have come to be associated, and as such, they allow for explorations of how those histories may animate judgments of what matters to us.

In other words, there is no intrinsic link between being ethical and finding the right words for the occasion. Narratives that champion propriety institute an orderly formulation in which an embodied sense of fittingness seems to structure and facilitate a judgment about what has authority, credibility and legitimacy. If, however, we think of styles as actions that take form as attitudes, then we can develop a rhetorical awareness of how we think we engage with cultural constructs that would give expression to sensibilities engendered by particular rhetorical situations. In the process of developing this awareness, we may dislodge the commonplace that suggests that people have a "common sense" or an innate compass that will guide their judgments of what seems to matter—as if the element of mattering will present itself forcefully for all to see and acknowledge.

In what follows, I will explore how style can be read to disrupt the idea that we can consult an embodied sense of propriety to determine whether an utterance fits an occasion. As I have suggested, this idea bears traces of that Socratic scene of the call that arrests the listener's attention. Because the authority underwriting "the fit" is, in principle, not too far removed from the Platonically conceived divine call to order, it sets up expectations about how representations should look, and more elusively what they should *do*. While the source of authority may differ—while it may be located in the idea of consensus rather than a divine command—both the Platonic and the rhetorical versions of how to instigate representational power teach citizens to see particular representations of that power as having legitimacy. By designating a type of representational artifact as legitimate, the priority of the fit contributes to retaining the authority of an interpretive order that has historically been associated with the culturally loaded term "masculine" set against its perceived opposite, "feminine." And while the word "masculinist" may at this point seem dusty and old-school, I will argue that conventional political discourses remain beholden to patriarchal norms that subordinate matter to mind and effectively place "masculinist" demands on interlocutors who wish to be recognized as having value and significance.

Freedom to Choose

Presumably, everyone understood how to read those verbal assaults lodged against Tripp and understood that on some level of reality, they did not matter. This was not explicitly stated. Everyone presumably knew that any endeavor to humiliate her was a joke—the mere appearance of an expulsion, a symbolic disqualification that did not translate into actual physical banishment.

That kind of knowledge introduces us to one more key rhetorical term that pertains to discussions of propriety, the inference. To infer is to select from propositions attached to a rhetorical situation and reference them when rendering a verdict about which conclusion or course of action is warranted. The dynamic of inferring seems to ensue as facts get examined and then applied to the situation at hand. But when assembling those facts into a coherent "whole" (a judgment), we will close any interpretive gaps that might arise as we traverse from proposition to judgment by drawing upon what remains invisible, what we might call a *connecting logic*. The connections we make to close interpretive gaps will appear to be logical, coherent, and even reasonable, when we recognize and identify with whatever judgment has been delivered.

But if those connections are drawn from prior *premises*, then when we infer, we reference narratives to determine what matters to our various judgments. We summon not logic but discursive conditions of experience that will influence our embodied sense and cognitive perceptions of what appears to be logical. With its status tied to narrative, the inference might be better described as an interpretive locus where cultural training is transformed into felt sense. Knowledge driven by inferences is precisely not based upon sight or citation but by what is left out. If the inference provides the means of crafting coherence, then persuasive power emerges not from an assured grip on what is true or forceful but from socially cultivated perspectives that direct visions of how component parts of a rhetorical scene should be made to fit into a contextual "whole." When we overlook what is entailed in that act of assembling a fit, the question of how we infer, how we "fill out" context to craft coherence, drops away as we attend instead to the representable "result" of our interpretive transactions—the judgment, the dismissal, the embrace of the speaker whose words appeal.

The dynamic of inference is a key component within discourses of propriety and *kairos* because it is through the act of inference that we render judgments about the putative motives propelling speech acts, including judgments about whether we think a speaker or writer desires to comply with linguistic protocols that oversee our sense of propriety. Inferences are made whenever we decide if a given representation fits with our internal sense of what should be. Typically, when this work is ascribed to logic or reason, it seems to be manifested stylistically, and then to be empowered to organize the deductions that are gleaned from an act of representation including, for example, a sense of cause and effect, a way of reading material evidence, a way of connecting perceptions of the evidentiary to an overarching explanatory narrative.

But when it comes to the question of how to link representations to perceptions of sexism, whether *logic* oversees and directs this interpretive dynamic is open to question. Presumably, we could infer that the motives of the comedians and journalists mocking Tripp were not overtly hostile. They were just part of a rhetorical scene in which we allow for freedom of expression, for irony, and for the sometimes uncomfortable give and take of expressions that will never please everyone at the same time. Of interest here is how casual we can be about how we draw conclusions after encountering a rhetorical scene, and how we tend to believe that a general order of representation will oversee the inferences that audiences make when responding to anyone's specific locution. Presumably, we know how to travel between invisible and represented interpretive domains because that movement proceeds in a systematic way. Hence, if we all knew the invisible purposes of those verbal assaults—that they were made in jest or even if meant—we may conclude that they merely delivered stylistic trifles, not physical threats. And then we might infer that we need not take the locutions too seriously. Unlike other insults that *do* seem to act as provocations to physical violence, the taunts directed towards Tripp were conventionally regarded as pretense, the derogatory comments like effervescent medicinal tablets that pop, fizz and fade when plopped into liquids.

A presumed faith in the work of inference guides many public discussions about how to contend with languages that cause controversy, especially the language of the joke. A more recent example arose in July of 2012 after a comedian named Daniel Tosh delivered a joke about rape while performing his act at a Los Angeles comedy club. After a subsequent public outcry, Tosh issued a "tepid" apology over Twitter. As reported in the *LA Times*, during his stand-up routine, Tosh made a pointed remark about a woman in the audience who apparently felt offended when the comedian observed that he found humor in some rape jokes. The patron "interrupted his show, yelling, 'Actually, rape jokes are never funny!'" He responded when he "singled her out [saying] . . . 'Wouldn't it be funny if that girl got raped by like, five guys right now? Like right now? What if a bunch of guys just raped her?'"[11]

Once the incident went public, questions were raised in the press and on blogs about whether any subject should ever be off limits to comedians, most of whom came to Tosh's defense, including the female hosts of the television talk show "The View," who agreed with moderator Whoopi Goldberg that if a joke works, "then it's okay." Nothing is off limits, according to this perspective, because the point of humor *is* to sometimes cross the line and challenge the status quo. Further, because this is a nation that prioritizes freedom of expression and that is founded on the idea that people are free to make choices about how to represent life, one should never draw a line demarcating what can be said and what cannot. Other comedians concurred. "If you don't want to hear an edgy joke, don't listen" was the title of a column written by comedian Gilbert Gottfried and posted on *cnn.com*.[12]

And yes, of course. Many of us might agree with the idea that the most reasonable response is the one that is congenial with rhetorical traditions that recognize that contexts influence acts of reception and that understands that people will have different points of view, that would never support any legislation that would regulate language use, and that would instead hand over authority to the audience's good sense of what to embrace. The testimonial to keeping a democratic spirit alive that is encoded within the responses from Gottfried and Goldberg seems especially promising. It's the people who decide what has significance, not a divine order removed from the life of the everyday.

But the idea that all is fair in the land of verbal taunts is made possible by the idea that all may reference a linguistic order that is equitable—that offers equal resources to all speakers to use its properties and empower themselves, especially once they think strategically (rhetorically) about how to craft a stylistic impact. Audiences, meanwhile, are perfectly capable of determining the parameters of permissibility because we all occupy similar places within language's equitable terrain. Ostensibly, then, there are equal changes to change someone's mind—equal chances to use language to galvanize an audience, to speak urgently and convey urgency to listeners. We are free to respond in kind—to issue a retort that will attempt to outperform the initial edgy joke, as did female comics responding to the Tosh incident, including "Lilith" who tweeted, "If you're a comedian who can't be funny without making rape jokes, you're a really s—comedian," or Miss O'Kistic who also tweeted, "How dare you call out Daniel Tosh. This is AMERICA, where rape jokes are free speech but condemning them is censorship by humorless bitches." Clearly, anyone subjected to ridicule is free to use language to devise a fortified and fitting comeback.[13]

When we say, "If the audience accepts it, then it's ok," we effectively throw judgment out into the "open market" of ideas. We let ideas "compete" to see what audiences will buy. Or, to use Burke's rhetorical metaphor, the potentially offensive joke becomes part of an on-going conversation in which all speakers may join and vie for attention and audience identification. An imagined symmetry between the triangulated elements within a rhetorical scene (text, audience, rhetor as well as context) inheres within the suggestion that equal opportunities exist for all to participate in whatever discursive exchange is taking place. Presumably, then, acts of interpretive negotiation adhere to a general order.

Generalized narratives about majority experiences may be regarded as representative of individual experiences with acts of interpretation.

But while we may accept, indeed embrace, the nod to agency implied in that formulation, when it comes to sexism, the generic recognition of propriety's pertinence to judgment may not yet satisfy, especially given the ways in which sexism's legacy lingers in subterranean spaces, shaping perceptions of what is permissible, or apparently humorous, in the first place. The very fact that sexist cultural narratives are both available and continue to be viable is reason enough to wonder about whether the rhetoric of propriety adequately addresses what is at stake in rhetorical conceptions of our discriminatory competencies.

Rhetorical investments in discourses of propriety do not question the provenance of that dynamic of symmetry organizing how to draw connections between the vectors of the rhetorical triangle and how they get attached to imagined contexts. The idea that "all things are equal" within acts of interpretive negotiation effectively imposes a diffused narrative of generality over the specific points of contact between narratives and embodiment. An apparent self-sufficient force would seem to initiate and then structure acts of reception. In general, we might say, the work of identification will proceed when the words on offer meet audience desires and expectations. Specifically, however, each point of contact can engender its own dizzying dynamic of judgments about what matters when attempting to settle perceptions of what is visible, inferred, permissible, stylistically recognizable, indefensible, etc.

When getting a sense of *kairos* and propriety, preexisting narratives depicting what is proper will ensnare us and influence the inferences we make as we engage our sensibilities with existing cultural narratives. Those narratives will influence one's felt sense of what seems to be urgent, fitting, a trifle, or even worth attention. Lynn Worsham's study of how political orientations are mapped on the level of affect pertains: Any sense of *orientation* involves an emotional connection between self and other that "runs deeper than a cognitive understanding" (Coming 105). Ideological appeals work on the level of emotion and that includes the ideologies that train us to orient our sense of what fits to the reproduction of sanctioned cultural forms. Through our embodied responses to terminologies and rhetorical styles, we make inferences that can predispose us to "feel" significance and value in culturally sanctioned ways. We are inevitably caught within webs of discursivity, our bodies discursively identified, those discourses subsequently affirmed through practices of embodied interpretive acts.

A putatively homogeneous (and wholesome) interpretive dynamic seems to enable us to integrate component parts of a representational scene into singular and conclusive judgments about what, finally, matters in that scene. A cultural regard for the image of a homogeneous dynamic of interpretation is simultaneously substantial and fleeting—substantially important to what we think we do as we judge; fleeting in its ability to deliver on the promise to actually provide an orderly method able to finalize judgments. That specific duality tends to be overlooked as we move from the openness of apprehension to the satisfaction of an evaluative conclusion. When interpretive practices appear to actualize idealized representations, we have a tendency to see those idealizations as real events and to treat persuasive power as existing on its own accord. Consequently, we may be predisposed to make changes in attitude when there appears to be an urgent need. When that embodied sense of urgency is absent, the need for change does not seem to be compelling. These premises imply that the compulsive force will make an appearance and be noticed and then acted upon. And they also imply the opposite: with no sense of a need to act, then no action needs to be taken.

In the case of Tripp, we can note that negative portraits were made permissible by an obvious source—a history of sexism that continues to exert influence over how women are judged *as* physical beings. Jokes about Tripp's lack of beauty merely repeated what we have become accustomed to. And as Worsham's analysis of ideology and emotion suggest, recognizing the significance of this history, and even bemoaning its continued impact, will not necessarily compel anyone to change attitudes about whether sexist narratives are acceptable or even funny. Indeed, attention to pervasive sexism can produce boredom. Statements that denigrate or sexualize women's appearances are so familiar as to be tedious and as such, not *that* serious. Here, a lack of urgency seems to authorize the yawn and a decision to, in effect, do nothing to change attitudes or provoke audiences to ponder why a persuasive, albeit subtle sexism, continues to shape public perceptions of gender identities. And with no vigorous (or transcendent) call to adjust linguistic behavior, then the significance of women's "feelings" about such representations would hardly register and fail to act as an urgent catalyst for altering perceptions about whether sexist barbs matter or should be deemed improper.

The political significance of the materiality of the sign becomes apparent when considering whether responses to "The Tripp Story" would have changed had Tripp looked, for example, like Fawn Hall, another woman brought to the public's attention during a controversial political event. Hall was a key player during the Iran-Contra Affair in the 1980s, in which officials from President Ronald Reagan's administration authorized the covert sale of arms to a hostile Iranian government in support of militant contra rebels in Nicaragua, end-running an explicit directive from Congress to not do so. Hall, long blond hair, tall, thin, angular face, the picture of model-like elegance, confessed to destroying documents that may have proven Reagan's complicity. But that was not represented as the main story. The story of Fawn Hall was told as a tale about a glamorous defendant whose testimony included the sexy fact that she smuggled those documents out by placing them in her leather boots. Not only was she not mocked, she and her handsome boss, the uniform-wearing military officer Oliver North, were treated as celebrities and the seriousness of the act of covert sales became less urgent by comparison. Here is a partial summary of a profile of Hall from Brown University's website, *Understanding the Iran Contra Affairs*:

> 'Near-hysterical excitement' greeted Fawn Hall at a time when "a pretty, appealing witness was desperately needed," wrote the *Washington Post*. The former secretary to Lt. Col. Oliver North failed to disappoint, with details of North's shredding of document "the most dramatic presentation" so far in the hearings, according to The *New York Times*. Hall simultaneously came across as an innocent, loyal aide to her boss and as a duplicitous government employee fully aware of what she was doing" when "her simple typing mistake . . . caused [a] $10 million donation to end up in the wrong Swiss bank account. Later she stated that she did not question the actions of her boss. "Sometimes," she declared, "you have to go above the written law."[14]

The material matters to judgments about which issues have what kind of urgency. The question is how and what to do about it.

I would like to situate this question within the elusive connections we make between the fleeting potentiality of the unsaid and the material presence of representational styles that presumably may be properly organized to depict credible representations. What *about* materiality matters to the work of inference that seems to allow audiences to make connections between perceptions and judgments, to consult the nebulous realm of the unsaid and find alliances with stylistic, material markers of representation? When we presume symmetry between elements of the rhetorical triangle, then we will expect particular kinds of inferences to be made and executed in orderly ways. But when it comes to the look of rhetorical styles—to their visible features—we may wonder about what precisely should get inferred (referenced) to determine whether a style compels our attention, will have an impact, and be judged fitting.

In asking if one's physical appearance influences judgments about one's person, we may begin to address what else matters to judgment besides, for example, the sexism that informed the specific way in which a woman like Tripp could be relentlessly denigrated. This is not to say that those sexist barbs were insignificant. For many of us, those kinds of locutions continue to matter, particularly given their sustained viability. If reasonable arguments and appeals to fairness will not alter the seemingly visceral and "natural" response that presumably validates sexism's perpetuation (especially when all is said to be said in jest), then rather than try to legislate what can and cannot be put out there for public review, it may be worthwhile to rethink the relationship between the visceral and political life. Clearly, sexist "humor" satisfies some sort of need, especially for audiences who issue sounds like "woo hoo!" in response to someone making a joke about, for example, how nice it would be if women would "shut the fuck up," as put by comedian Louis CK when discussing the Tosh incident on *The Daily Show*.[15] Those of us who are not amused by the repetition of that kind of phrase, who wonder why it continues to elicit fervent support from, presumably, men who seem to be compelled to emit whooping noises to indicate that they've just about had enough with all of that prattle from women who continue to go on and on about things that don't matter, will be caught in that narrative bind in which our failure to either shut up or see humor in the suggestion that we do indicates that we must be humor-less, our own annoyance acting as evidence to support the premise. (The whole dynamic is immensely irritating.).

The visceral response is akin to what seems to be elementally present, a "substantial" quality that seems to exist in a self-sufficient and physical way. When we react to the wit or absurdity of a joke, or to an object that conveys signs of beauty, our embodied experiences might suggest that a material heft is encoded within the object. Like testimonials of emotion that produce responses of sympathy, or like discursive eloquence that engenders audience approval, the objectified content of beauty would seem to have an inherent power that drives both the expression and reception of those qualities. Strangely, this power would also apply to "inverse" phenomenon—to those representations deemed to be opposite of what pleases us. The absence of beauty, of mirth, of eloquence, would seem to work naturally to repulse us, the response induced by a power that works on its own, without any assistance from narratives that would tell us how to see them. From this perspective, beauty and its lack are placed on a seemingly equitable terrain, occupying opposite contexts but similarly empowered to produce audience responses.

The same principle applies to conceptions of how rhetorical styles convey effectiveness. We tend to think of style's power in monolithic terms—as functioning like the call that arrested Socrates and led him to change the style of his delivery. The force of style, after all, would seem to account for the beauty and power of eloquence itself, acting as a component part of the dynamic that creates opportune moments for acts of identification once words fit the occasion of their delivery.

Because stylistic appeals to the visceral can be put to sentimental and/or contemptible political uses, because the visceral response so often expresses our worst impulses, our first tendency might be the habituated one that would try to discount the influence of the material by transcending it, by rejecting the idea that the physical responses engendered by representations have any value to political judgment. But this response would forego what discourses of propriety offer—an affirmation of embodiment as an important and significant component to interpretative action. Given that styles (and categories classified as feminine) are already subordinated to propositional content within dominant systems of representation, downplaying the significance of the power of the material would change nothing in our outlook about how to conceive of an ethics of linguistic participation.

We may instead think differently about our capacity to be moved by beauty, eloquence, wit, clarity, and alternatively repulsed by perceptions of their absence. And that means looking at the material realm in ways that would disrupt the presumed symmetry that organizes our understanding of how a vision of a material referent meets the act of drawing upon (invisible) "logic" to make sense of what one sees. We can think about, for example, the significance of having become accustomed to sexist narratives and how that cultural training might affect our embodied sensibilities about what is humorous and seemingly fitting. In the interest of ethics, we may also be prompted to consider what specifically has been put together to enable a sense of a fit to be made. And we might further consider *how* we justify the choices that we've made about what to notice and what to overlook once we're satisfied by the judgments we've rendered. What discursive histories may have influenced how we render judgments about which speech acts seem proper? And is there something in particular about the rhetorics of propriety that give an assist to the sexist attitudes encoded within public responses to women who go public?

Evaluating Proper Significance

Classical rhetorical traditions suggest that "the opportune moment" of speech will be captured when words grab our attention. Stylistically, *kairos* is aligned with propriety's goal of arresting time by devising the right thing to say and letting its persuasive power settle disputes. The context of *kairos*, then, presumes a dispute, followed by a rendering of the valuable utterance able to generate interpretive resolutions. The principle of singularity and stasis invoked by this image is reconceived by Hesford, who advocates a "critical methodology" that situates *kairos* within "identity claims" that are not static and monolithic but "dynamic moments of action that are at once rhetorical and material, individual and social, local and global" (*Kairos* 163). If styles are sites for audience participation, then our consent to their forcefulness will be affected by that training that conditions embodied responses to material forms.

Take, for example, the style of speech identified as gossip, a type of discourse that, in the contemporary cultural milieu, ranks as one of the least significant of all forms of discourse, precisely opposite of noble speech acts and therefore not a proper genesis for arguments about the fate of the nation. Citizens are expected to take a dim view of gossip, to regard it as a depraved mode of linguistic participation, as far removed from all that is consequential as possible. Because gossip was central to bringing about the impeachment itself, it could be characterized as being at least partially responsible for the failure of the drive to oust Clinton.

"Gossip, innuendo, and hearsay are being passed off as fact. Allegations by unnamed sources are claimed to be credible," declared Bob Bennett, Clinton's personal attorney, in a motion filed in January, 1998 to expedite the Paula Jones trial.[16] This quote framed a CNN.com report that posed the question: "Facts—What do we Know?" when "Keeping Score in the Lewinsky Matter." Presumably, we did not know much given that so much about this event emanated from gossip. And yet, much of the gossip turned out to be true. But being true is not the same as being significant. Here, an inherited vocabulary of classifications will influence assessments of significance. Gossip tends to be disparaged because it seems to encourage a kind of bad participation that is configured as the opposite of that which is proper and respectable. Rather than submit premises to the light of reason, gossip's purview is dark, mysterious, and slippery–precisely unlike the muscular image of the good man fulfilling his civic duty to speak publicly in measured tones about a suitable course of action. Gossip instead works by innuendo and does not extend a democratic call to everyone. Its membership is by invitation only. One is choosy about whom to trust with gossip because the gossip risks being exposed for maliciousness. Most crucially, gossip works by making inferences, precisely by *not* assuming that language bears a transparent relation to the object world. Gossips relish ambiguity and speech acts that engage in speculation, that appreciate the drama of artifice and in so doing, highlight the mysterious ways in which we make sense by connecting what is represented to what is left unsaid. When we gossip, we are allowed to mull over what *else* is implied by any seemingly respectable and upright message. We need not support judgments by demonstrating how they follow from a socially redeemable logic of cause and effect. Gossip also is chiefly and significantly associated with women and their relationships with other women.

Because discourse identified as reasonable is privileged within U.S. political cultures, any discursive practice that represents differently may be depicted as unfounded, unreflective, based on selective experience, and too emotional. In sum, wrongly motivated. Ignoble discursive practices seem to move audiences away from preferred realms of critical reflection and intellectual freedom, where one is not trapped by embodied experiences of emotion and materiality. Rather than deploy terms that would drive home a singularly forceful point, *stylistically*, gossip offers a narrative equivalent of a variety of possible identifications. If making a singular point is prioritized, then offering anything less may be regarded as flimsy, enfeebled—engendering a felt sense that legitimizes the dismissive response.

The hierarchies established by this binary logic make an appearance by enacting exclusions and designating preferred categories as well as modes of representation. Feminist theorists such as Irit Rogoff challenge this logic by examining the conceptual apparatus that oversees how categorical distinctions get made and rendered legitimate. Rogoff analyzes the cultural disregard for gossip in order to question how narrative structures produce categorical differences that *appear* to add a sense of order to interpretive negotiations by adhering to predetermined evaluations of what has significance. Her goal is not to "cleanse gossip of its negative associations (of distinctly feminized communicative activity) and turn it into an acceptable cultural artifact" (269), an aim that would keep the organizing binary structure intact. Rather, Rogoff looks to narratives about gossip to chart the ways in which judgments are driven by our cultural and emotional investments in available hierarchies of value.

This kind of analysis is pertinent to judgments made about what mattered to the impeachment, especially given that all of the collected information devolved back to speech acts exchanged between two "silly" women. Indeed, plenty of judgments about the insignificance of this national event were made once the House Judiciary Committee released "the Lewinsky-Tripp Tapes" in November of 1998, an act that was itself controversial. These were the tapes that Tripp secretly made when listening to Lewinsky pour out her heart about romance miseries. According to a CNN poll, citizens did not want the tapes to be released by a margin of three to one, but that did not stop the Judiciary committee from disseminating them.[17] Nor did public reports about the public's lack of desire to hear the tapes prevent members of the media from broadcasting and analyzing their content. The tapes transported listeners to a domain of intimacy both in terms of what was discussed and through the means of dissemination, which involved a public act of eavesdropping on voices engaged in a putatively private conversation.

The general view seemed to be that because the tapes involved two women talking about domestic and personal issues, they had no importance or urgency, and because there was no urgency, the women engaged in the conversations deserved to be disparaged. Interestingly, the ridicule centered on a seemingly material source—their voices. While transcripts of the tapes had been available since October, included as part of "The Starr Report," the experience of hearing the women actually talk to each other provided an additional element to the mix of interpretive negotiations, one that was not welcome and that effectively sealed in the judgment of the women and their issues being colossally insignificant. Headlines conveyed this response.

"Just Out: Lewinsky, Tripp on Tape. The Voices, Alas, Ordinary." "Wake Us When It's, Like, Over. The Tripp-Lewinsky Whine-A-thon." "Monica, Linda, Yada, Yada, Yada," where the reporter noted that "hearing the two women talk and knowing the ending adds context to the excruciating banality." A syndicated column by Richard Roeper put things directly: "The Lewinsky-Tripp Tapes were Simply Pathetic." In his column, Roeper explained why the tapes did not matter. "Who has time for restraint or thoughtful contemplation when you're flooding the airways with the endless gabbing of two of the more unpleasant women to grab the spotlight in recent memory? 'I never expected to feel this way!' Monica wails at one point. That makes two of us, dear."[18]

Of interest here is the repeated vehement proclamation of a lack of interest that presumably justified the collective derision directed towards Tripp and Lewinsky. The demeaning designation does more than generate a perception. It will carry a material effect that can affect the kind of embodied response the designation seems to provoke. (On this point, see Nathan Stormer.) When a marginalized status is incorporated into the very definition of the marginalized term, then the embodied response of dismissal may be said to be fitting. To think of this in terms of material rhetorics, we might note that if we are preconditioned to reject gossip categorically, then the definition of gossip will materially affect our reactions, influencing the stance we take to the "gossipy" representation, including whether we will even pay attention. The very word "gossip" is expected to activate both a cognitive and visceral rejection that is often physically expressed with the dismissive eye roll, the drop of shoulders no longer on alert, the drift in attention that might precede an act of listening—*oh yeah, this is not going to matter much.* We infer that gossip is illegitimate, attach that inference to a judgment about the legitimacy of what is up for review, and then dismiss significance and regard that judgment as valid if not inevitable, our conditioned body responses influencing what we see and how we see it. We will likely not feel a need to consider how such judgments come to be situated when categories appear to be put in their place.

This is what happened on a national scale once the tapes were released. Inferences about their insignificance were presented as facts, as legitimate conclusions based upon the evidence, which in this case was the materiality of culturally constructed definitions of "the female," a categorical type that seemed to generate impatience. "In her own words, Monica Lewinsky sounds like a vixen, and other times like a miserable little girl. Sometimes she sounds petulant, sometimes warm and winning," concluded an AP report by Anne Gearan published on *CNN.com*. According to the writer from the *New York Daily News*, "the adenoidal Lewinsky comes off as what she is: a lovesick post-adolescent, at turns frightened, vengeful and confused. Tripp emerges as the Wicked Witch, coolly monotone, luring the younger woman into a web of betrayal as she offers a mini-lesson on gathering DNA evidence with q-tips."[19]

In devoting an entire column to express how insignificant he found the tapes to be, syndicated writer Roeper offered precise descriptions of what annoyed him. "The somewhat shrill Monica sounded like a needy Valley Girl. ('I mean, like, you don't understand.')" Tripp was "husky-voiced," a "stereotypical man-resenting, middle-aged, couch-potato—watching TV, gobbling down food and scolding the dog while gossiping on the phone with her young friend . . . These two clucking hens set back the women's movement ten years with their inane boy-crazy girl talk." Or, as depicted in *Time* magazine, "the vengeful woman, an insecure gossip who had become embittered about the opposite sex because of a philandering father and her own failed marriage" (64).[20]

The responses from media commentators were not only arch and ironic, they also were presumptively personal. Television personality Deborah Norville appearing on the CNN program *Larry King Live* positioned herself as a disapproving parent. "A lot of folks have said, what would you want to ask Monica Lewinsky? My tendency is, I would want to turn her over my knee, spank her, cut up her credit cards and take away her phone privileges." A front page *Washington Post* article collected comments from people on the street who, after hearing the tapes, also apparently felt comfortable making pejorative assessments about Lewinsky's person.

> Like Harpo Marx, J.D. Salinger and a generation of silent film actors, Lewinsky existed until yesterday as a mute celebrity, an empty vessel into which millions could pour their fantasies and theories. The voice provided a dose of deflating reality. "A little girl, a teeny-bopper," concluded insurance man Dale Davies as he listened to Lewinsky on TV replays of the tapes at a K Street bar. "I mean, as a professional person, you'd never date somebody who sounds like that. People would look at you funny." Over at Burger King, lunchtime customers described the Lewinsky they heard for the first time as "a small, anxious voice" and "a dumb girl." "I always knew she wasn't so smart," said

office assistant Tonya Willis. "But you have to hear her to see how dumb she really is." There were derisive comments about Lewinsky's "Valley Girl" inflection, her sentences that rise like questions, her coos and tee-hees. . . Rep. Louise M. Slaughter (D-NY) dismissed the tapes as nothing more than "two ditsy ladies talking about stupid things." [21]

These responses offer a "highly contextualized" act of "positioning" Tripp and Lewinsky as subjects who deserved to be ridiculed. The articulations of how people responded to the sound of their voices "mobilized" "normative identity narratives, cultural myths, and rhetorical commonplaces" (Hesford *Kairos* 157) to enact judgments and then situate them as inevitable and legitimated by an organizing force that seems to carry its own authenticating power.

The idea that a self-sufficient linguistic power will automatically alert us to what has significance is evident within the attitudes we are expected to have about which issues should be taken seriously, including, for example, global issues involving "hard" military hawkishness versus the "soft" issues of domesticity; work habits vs. habits of the heart; the "masculine" impulse to deliver the potentially offensive joke versus the flimsy whine of the feminist complaint. The convention that suggests that such power signals what is worth our time contributed to making it possible for a newspaper employee like Roeper to give a patronizing sigh of forbearance and expect to be understood, if not affirmed. Because the release of the Tripp-Lewinsky tapes seemed to unleash dimensions of superficiality, they were referenced as if they lent automatic support to the choices made about what could be said, as if the genesis of this event in gossip gave way to an expansive context of conjecture by journalists who decided, well, since we were dealing with sex and gossip anyway, why not just speculate—at length—about the people involved?

Undocumented speculation began as soon as the story broke months before the tapes were released. One of the earliest reports appeared in February of 1998, by *Newsweek* reporters Michael Isikoff and Evan Thomas. The magazine cover featured a front page with Lewinsky's picture and the title "Monica's Story"; the story has since been filed on the WashingtonPost.com website under a heading called "Impeachment: Special Report," archived as a memorial to the investigative journalism that garnered respect and praise and helped bolster Isikoff's reputation in particular. Indeed, as of 2013, Isikoff regularly appears on cable news programs as an "insider" expert on national issues of import. He earned his reputation as a serious reporter in part for breaking news about the Lewinsky affair in 1998 in a co-written report that included the following "revelations":

> At the heart of the story is a young woman's craving for recognition and attention. Monica Lewinsky grew up pampered but possibly emotionally neglected in Beverly Hills, Calif. . . . Last week Monica's classmates at Beverly Hills High remembered her unkindly as a girl who had "gone to a fat farm" and strived to be popular. . . . The real estate agent who showed the house Lewinsky was renting described her as "cold" and her house as "filthy." Lewinsky "kept a container with about a dozen new condoms by her bed on a table," said the agent, Bob Elston. She was "very flirtatious, also a bit emotional, young and somewhat immature, and she talked a lot," said classmate Steve Enghouse, who spoke to reporters because of his suspicion that Lewinsky had concocted an imaginary romance with President Clinton in order to attract attention. Enghouse told reporters, "I don't think anyone who really knew her would put it past her to have made this up."[22]

Up until that time, the public knew little about Monica Lewinsky. The *Newsweek* profile was one of the first to convert the "mystery" of "that woman" into a narrative that incorporated assessments from two men that rendered her in familiar terms: Spoiled. Loose. That crazy chick who obsesses over men and then tells fantastic stories about her significance as the object of desire.

Like the responses to sexist jokes, it was possible to publish these kinds of assessments and expect them to be recognizable and legitimate because derived from an immediate, seemingly self-validating embodied response. "It's shrill," suggests that the respondent has come across a tonal quality that alienates on its own accord. This conflation is made possible when "an ideational space" (Gunn Public 4) is presumed to be "homologous" (4) to a quasi-material referent. In the case of the Tripp tapes, vocal quality was treated as material evidence and seemed to offer knowledge about who was speaking while providing an "object" that could be referenced to render judgments about that speaker's character. The conflation here seemed to follow an order that correlated the intangible voice to the character of the person being evaluated, while also connecting the intangible judgment to a felt sense of repulsion.

Speech patterns seem to imbue style with a "material" substance that may be objectively evaluated. The idea that voice (or delivery, or style) bespeaks personhood seems to offer critics a concrete object to scrutinize and then methodologically situate within an analytical rubric capable of explaining the relationship between a cause and an effect—in this case, the tonal quality determining judgments of who deserves merit and respect, and who, if their voice grates, does not. But as Joshua Gunn observes in an article about sexism and voice, when referencing voice, "we encounter the pickle of sonorous re-presentation" in which no matter how "sophisticated" our terminology, we will fail to linguistically "capture what one senses when listening" (Public 13) to tonal qualities, moods, personalities. "It seems impossible to describe what Roland Barthes terms 'the grain of the voice,' that pure sound of expressive vocality that doesn't simply carry meaning, but also bodies forth the *body in feeling* in a manner that cannot be signified" (13—original emphasis).

Because "the grain of the voice" defies a full linguistic rendering, our only recourse is to invoke adjectives, "'the poorest of the linguistic categories'" (Barthes qtd. in Gunn 13) that aim to stand firmly and represent what is transient and on the move, including our own embodied responses to a quality that we hear, feel, and judge. Gunn notes that any adjectives that get invoked can be analyzed so as to "locate the (re)establishment of a binary and the movement of ideology" (14). And we can find a binary logic reestablished by the adjectives used in reactions to listening to the Tripp-Lewinsky tapes, where masculinist norms were reasserted with a vigorous certainty, as if the denigrating responses emerged naturally, as part of *a priori* ideologically innocent response patterns. But once the embodied response is attached to a judgment about quality, we're no longer enacting an equitable exchange between an initial encounter and an act of reception. If the material presence of the voice matters to judgment, then an additional component has been added that will disrupt the presumed symmetry and natural order directing apprehension, assessment, and then explanation. This additional element involves the act of borrowing from cultural norms to organize the inferences that will connect a presumptive cause of judgment with an effect.

Every regularized portrayal of the banality of "the gossip" rearticulated the long-standing idea that *femininity* and *being marginalized* share intrinsic and interrelated qualities. Because ubiquitous, this set of associated ideas helped to normalize the particular kind of denigration directed to those two women speaking on tape. Arguably, the familiarity of the specific kind of denouncement of Tripp and Lewinsky, the ways in which it has been sustained, the ways in which its cultural availability prompts audiences to feel that they are allowed to take pleasure in its repetition, is one material site in which expressions of sexism lingers and remains culturally viable. Sexism lingers in the exuberant consent audiences have and are expected to have towards particular representations of women and corresponding judgments about the insignificance of those representations. Not only were the representations of these women dismissible, presumably so was their role in this historical event. In this context, the repetition of pejorative and insulting commentary seemed warranted, if not anticipated. Marginalized women using a marginalized discursive style, repeatedly and summarily dismissed by most media outlets, the repeated trope seeming to offer discursive evidence of a natural cognitive-sensuous response that would justifiably disparage gossipy women. When the constitutive force of language that establishes a sense of social reality is regarded as self-sufficient, then the interpretive result seems to emerge on its own volition. Accordingly, the absence of a sense of urgency about the need to defend "the gossip" may be regarded as a bona fide indicator of her inconsequentiality.

But given narrative's influence on judgment, the question for rhetoricians is whether and how the rhetorics of propriety facilitate the conversion of an aestheticized collection of sense impressions into an organizing premise that carries weight. If inferences are the point of contact between narrative and embodiment, then we can see a putative conversion of metaphor to "reality" in the very idea that we link sentences together to find a fit between a set of utterances and a given rhetorical situation. The point of contact between narrative and experience can only be imagined but the call to find that fit in each interpretive encounter is presented as if that call goes beyond description to designate a reality in which selected signifiers truly enact a coherent and fitting sign of identity. When repeated, this enactment begins to *matter*. But not because it carries a noticeably coherent and forceful impact. Rather, because it reproduces a relation of premises and inferences that have already been deemed acceptable/proper. Finding a fit, meanwhile, comes to be anticipated before the next interpretive encounter, the anticipation marking the effect of the narrative on our bodies, and indeed, becoming a point of reference itself when we judge.

Louis Althusser called this interpellation (175). Styles assist in interpellating us when they appear to demarcate a site of intimate contact between the embodied text and the embodied feelings that result once we encounter language practices. Like voice, styles can only be described through adjectives, their essence finally elusive even as their effect on audience reception can be palpable. When style's potential provocations get treated as both methods of representation as well as evaluative standards, we lose sight of style's aesthetic/rhetorical moments—those that demarcate differences between narratives that depict sensibility and the emotions they presumably describe and generate. When the story of an embodied response seems to cohere with the felt sense of an embodied response, then what exists as a possibility seems to materialize into a common (sense) interpretive experience that reaffirms the validity of interpretive habits. As critical theorists have argued, we need not regard the pull of interpellation as inevitable once we remember that responses to styles involve choices about *whether* to engage with a speaker's mode of participation. To not engage with marginalized representations because they seem to lack urgency is a choice, not an inevitability. (For more discussion about interpellation and individual agency, see Butler's *Excitable Speech*.)

Styles mobilize a fleeting materiality that can have significant political consequences, and this means that when it comes to considering style's significance, we are called upon to do more than follow the advice to devise and look for statements that fit the occasion of their use. Adopting a democratic aesthetics to orient a representational ethics will remind us that because interpretive frameworks are narratives, we can choose how to conceive of the interpretive labor that follows their lead. It is possible to alter conceptions of how we arrive at the hierarchies of value that organize our judgments of what to notice, overlook, infer, and affiliate with when determining whose words count and seem deserving of attention.

As Rogoff's analysis of gossip suggests, combating sexism will take more than a direct assault on cultural narratives and practices. Outraged denouncements of sexism—while absolutely necessary—may not persuade. Meanwhile, such denouncements may challenge the interpretive result but leave the organizing logic intact, reincorporating it and all its interpretive entanglements in ways that leave culturally constructed hierarchies of value intact. While rhetorical discourses of propriety endeavor to change minds about what matters to judgment, they can fall short of the goal of helping us reconceive the dynamic of interpretive action.

THE WILL TO MATTER

The repetition of negative portrayals of Tripp had at least two material consequences on judgments, one already mentioned—name-calling became normative. More importantly, the unflattering portraits also affected audience responses to Tripp's endeavor to represent herself. Like any other rhetor, she was put in a situation of trying to find the right words to fit the occasion. But given the discursive context that preceded her, it was not clear that any words would have been powerful enough to generate audience identification. Could Tripp have inaugurated a linguistic force strong enough to wipe out old associations and rehabilitate her image? Her very act of speaking was figured as superfluous and dispensable and hence her example raises a question about whether the concept of propriety is an equal-opportunity resource available to anyone under any circumstance who takes care when crafting representations.

Initially, Tripp did not respond to the relentless name-calling and, in the words of one journalist, remained "shadowy and reclusive."[23] That ended in the summer of 1998, when she came into the light and spoke publicly about her actions. Following her ninth grand jury appearance, Tripp decided to break her silence because, noted her counsel Philip Coughter, "we understand that there is some interest in hearing from Linda today."[24] By this time, she had literally changed her face via plastic surgery that was remarkably effective to audiences that have come to associate a youthful appearance with a person's value. The jowls were eliminated and in place of the perpetual fatigue that settles upon many of us in middle age, her skin recovered a dewy glow. Standing on the courthouse steps, she spoke in a putatively decorous tone: respectful, forthright, and seemingly sincere about speaking truly. She was also visibly nervous about going public. Tripp trembled as she noted that she was not a practiced speaker but art-less and in need of consulting her notes. Her motives for taping Lewinsky, she explained, stemmed from her belief that Clinton and his followers were dangerous and would stop at nothing to save his reputation, even if it meant doing her harm. The investigation that followed from her actions, she added, "has never been quote 'just about sex'" but stemmed from her very real fears about the "legions of paid prevaricators" whose job it was to find new and "cruel" ways to malign her.

Like Clinton, Tripp made a conspicuous attempt to change public perceptions of her person. And, like the president, she not only failed to win over audiences, she also delivered a speech that was memorable for generating vehement rancor. Indeed, the failure of her courthouse speech ranks with Clinton's apology as one of the most infamous utterances during the year of the impeachment:

> I understand that there has been a great deal of speculation about just who I am and how I got here. Well, the answer is simple. I'm you. I'm just like you. I'm an average American who found herself in a situation not of her own making. I'm a suburban mom, who was a military wife for 20 years, and a faithful government employee for 18 years. I never, ever asked to be placed in this position. Because I am just like you, I ask you to imagine how you would feel if someone you thought was a friend urged you to commit a felony that could jeopardize your job, potentially put you in jail and endanger the well being of your children. Imagine how you would feel if your boss's attorney called you a liar in front of the whole country. And imagine if that boss was the President of the United States. Imagine how you would feel if your employer illegally released your confidential records to the media, then demoted you and cast you aside for daring to tell the truth. Imagine how it would feel to see the pain in your children's eyes when they hear a seemingly endless barrage of lies about their mother, a mother who is not going out to defend herself.[25]

Tripp's call for sympathetic identification was clear and straightforward. It followed normative protocol that directs speakers to deliver "controlled reasons" to explain a situation and how it should be perceived. Her statement was coherent, outlined causes that led to effects, and asked audiences to put themselves into her situation—to get an overview and to see beyond the immediate issue of taping a friend to the larger issue of the nation as ruled by law.

Arguably, Tripp spoke genuinely about her fears. The appeal was rejected, the response visceral. But unlike reactions to Clinton's apology, what appeared most galling to spectators was not that she was rhetorical, but that she attempted to appear to be sincere. "Who could forget Tripp's whiny, self-justifying comments as she tried to tell us, 'I'm just like you'" wrote *CBS*'s Rita Braver in an on-line column a year after the impeachment. "'No!' We recoiled in horror, shouting back at our television sets. No, No, impossible! We would never tape a friend and rat on her." A similar sentiment was published in an *LA Times* op-ed essay entitled, "An Average Mom? Hardly; Linda Tripp: Her Plea to Americans for Sympathy comes a Little Late in Scandal of Her Own Making" wherein the writer's rejection of Tripp entailed rejecting the very idea of a resemblance. "I don't know about you but I looked in the mirror. Linda Tripp is not just like me. . . . The simple fact is Linda Tripp is an angry, frustrated, political loser."[26]

In subsequent interviews, Tripp reiterated claims of feeling threatened by Clinton factions. Appearing in an interview *The Today Show* after the Senate acquittal in 1999, Tripp said that she "watched what the administration did to people who tried to disclose the truth. No one's happy about that. I least of all. I was honored to be at the White House. I came from a military—20-year military—background. I am an army wife and an army employee. . . .I can promise you, the words duty, honor, country mean something." She repeated her unwillingness to perjure herself to Larry King: "Friends don't ask friends to commit a crime . . . the notion that I would bastardize my values, my sense of integrity for a young woman with whom I had worked for a year and a half and commit a crime was not ever an option."[27]

People refused to make the connection between sanctioned identify categories (dutiful citizen, patriot, suburban mom) and Tripp. Her attempt to attach her identity to categories that *matter* provoked scorn rather than commiseration. Whatever call she issued "worked through" recipients by compelling an intimate and dramatic rejection.

Rhetorical theories of propriety help explain why her words failed to generate the desired cognitive-embodied responses of recognition and affiliation. Arguably, her use of valorized signifiers could be judged as pious in Leff's and Rosteck's sense of the word, invoking formulaic sentiments in a bald attempt to win over audiences, prompting them to effectively "pry apart" those words and sentiments and unearth the strategic ploy. Like Clinton's "apology," Tripp's courthouse statement called attention to itself as an act of representation and hence it did not seem to emerge authentically. She seemed to be trying too hard to forge community, and in the process, seemed to be performing an identity rather than occupying one. Meanwhile, her call to normalcy did not seem to fit with her actions. Who tapes their friends? Her attempt to be read as a "commoner" could, then, be characterized as a failure of common sense, enabling the rejection of her plea for unity to be depicted itself as reasonable, if not inevitable.

It might seem plausible, then, to deduce that her claims of shared identity were counterfeit. Not just misguided, but a misrepresentation. And with that judgment in place, it seemed possible to infer her motives when she stood before the microphone on that day in July, shaking, explaining, looking for affirmation. Once it became public that she was a cohort of Lucianne Goldberg, a known enemy of Clinton who had made a point of finding ways to remove him from office, Tripp's identity hardly seemed *average*. Goldberg reportedly encouraged Tripp to make the tapes, which was not only an awful suggestion in general, it also revealed that Tripp was calculating and strategic when befriending Lewinsky. Indeed, it was Tripp who explicitly encouraged the unwitting Monica to keep the blue dress that clinched Starr's case and led to Clinton's impeachment. On this point, the tapes revealed Tripp's deviousness as she seduced Monica by talking to her with an understanding tone, as if truly concerned about Monica's embattled heart, giving Monica the support she wanted to hear, and then going in for the kill.

Tripp: Don't be upset right this moment with him.

Lewinsky: I know, I try not to with him, I just—he's so [inaudible] and he's so [inaudible] and nobody takes a [inaudible].

Tripp: I know.

Lewinsky: And it's so hard.

Tripp: The navy blue dress. Now, all I would say to you is, I know how you feel today, and I know why you feel the way you do today. But you have a very long life ahead of you and I don't know what's going to happen to you. Neither do you. I don't know anything and you don't know anything. I mean the future is a blank slate. I don't know what will happen. I would rather that you had that in your possession if you need it years from now. That's all I'm going to say.[28]

Given her role in making Clinton's prosecution possible, those "I don't know" statements seem particularly Machiavellian. As far as "the public" was concerned, Tripp deserved whatever rancorous reaction she received, especially since her alienation followed from her actions—her own decision to deviate from the norms of female friendship and then attempt to fashion a "redo" with a self-serving and seemingly disingenuous call for sympathetic identification and unity. The shared acrimony seemed to affirm its own validity.

Given this context, it would seem that the reason Tripp could not inaugurate the power to shift perspectives was because there simply were no right words to convince "the public" that she credibly possessed admirable qualities. Audiences instead saw a looming gulf between her version of herself and their perceptions of her reality. Beneath this version of what happened, however, is that training that audiences receive about how to put pieces of a representational scene together to determine "what goes with what" to "round things out" (Burke qtd. in Rosteck and Leff 329). If coherence is intrinsic to propriety, then feeling the force of the fit would seem to be co-extensive with the delivery of the right form and proper amount of stylistic intensity working to activate the formation of a collective view of a given issue and its merits.

But as I have been arguing, the social "reality" of the fit that seems to be secured by this simultaneity gives us permission to overlook how the political is waged over how to "fill in" gaps in meaning with reference to entrenched narratives that allow us to justify our choices. In Tripp's case, several unspoken inferences might account for the visceral reactions her words prompted. There was, of course, the matter of her face and body, ridiculed, mocked, repeatedly discussed and referenced within cultural narratives that both fetishize the female form and render matters of the body as less significant than those of the mind. Platonic influences are felt most keenly when we align the ethical and the moral with the endeavor to transcend matter and rhetorical exigencies. Accordingly, Tripp's look should not matter to judgment, and any suggestion that it did would appear to be a shallow one. But the vehemence of proclamations of her insignificance suggests that we rethink what "mattering" means—that we rethink how *not* mattering does, indeed, matter. It's not just that Tripp's argument was rejected. Public responses effectively said: I want nothing to do with *that* face; *that* way of being.

The seemingly self-evident validity of her expulsion, and more precisely the sense of its satisfactory fittingness, requires a rhetorical review that considers how feeling the force of the fit will have been influenced by narratives that have taught us to reject representations that fail to engage our sympathies. When the extra component of aesthetic sensuousness in judgments of legitimacy and value is recuperated into discourses of propriety, then we are off the hook, not called upon to consider how we're imagining power working on its own to direct ways of reading signs while simultaneously viscerally feeling their effects.

The equity promise inhering within rhetorics of propriety falters when it implies that the various vectors within the rhetorical triangle are somehow equivalent to each other, equally situating encounters between bodies, texts, and judgments, neutrally calling upon the lived body that has become acclimated to cultural narratives that condition bodies to respond to representative objects in culturally sanctioned ways. The choices we make when crafting coherence involve more than determining whether an utterance packs a recognizable punch that can be made to fit our sense of what is right or fair or balanced. Arguably, to find a fit is to create a match that appears to fill in a gap between an idealized narrative and the situation at hand—the match instantiating that embodied sense that the fit has been found. Any reconciling dynamic seems to work forcefully when a felt sense gets linked to an ideological imperative to feel a particular way—to feel for a fit in the first place, as a way of organizing and then justifying a judgment.

In moving past satisfaction to analysis, we may consider the political consequences of a seemingly self-evident rejection of another's words. Tripp's enfeebled call to fellow citizens articulated a desire to become part of the national community, to convince all to agree that her life did, in fact, matter. A community did form in response to her call, but deemed her message to be strident and desperate. "Linda Tripp"—the person and the idea—provided "material" for the formation of a group identity forged through a shared and ritualized dismissal of her national significance. Tripp's expulsion enacted an aesthetics of dehumanization, one that has become ritualized in public discourse that relishes a particular kind of public mockery. That pleasure is itself validated when representations such as the signifier "Linda Tripp" get emptied of particular meaning and converted into a familiar trope, then squarely and forcefully planted within the domain of the trivial. "Linda Tripp" became a phrase that participated in creating a rhetorical context in which *she* was rendered less significant than the cultural sport of denigrating her person and her desire to matter. Meanwhile, Tripp was publicly shamed in a specifically material way, through the invocation of signifiers that were visually recognizable and experientially familiar. Media narratives about the women associated with Clinton's impeachment deployed the category of "woman" as a public site of readerly identification, illuminating "the ways in which patriarchal authority reenters the national body through the rhetorical construction of the female body" (Barnes 11). The shared rejection of her particular desire to matter became a leitmotif in the impeachment as audiences were apparently willing to be constituted as a collective by relishing the denigration of a woman who presented herself as a citizen up for public review.

When this energetic dismissal is "pried apart" we will find the legacy of cultural training that would ask us to be seriously suspicious and disapproving of material bodies that stray too far from the ideal rhetorical subject. Once identified as a specific kind of female form, Tripp could be rendered as the very opposite of the form that we are expected to valorize—the abstract citizen of virtue, typically configured as a "disembodied" masculine subject (Socrates) and most certainly not the woman credibly occupying the identity category of the gossip. The repetition of such hierarchies of value function as points of reference to organize conceptions of the political work of the strong emotional rejection, including the work that rejection appears to accomplish on behalf of community formation.

Narratives that denigrated Tripp (and Lewinsky) helped to articulate a particular vision of virtuous judgment in which the seemingly visceral response functioned as shorthand for an interpretive outlook that would situate emotion as an elemental category of experience and then a resource for drawing the fitting conclusion. Emotion's putative force seemed to illuminate a clear path to interpretive reconciliation by immediately prompting shared acts of antipathy. When the kind of strong feelings generated in response to Tripp's speech get ratified as normative and valid, then *having the same feelings* seemed to offer an affirmation of a judgment that seemed to be inevitable and fitting. Left out of that depiction of ethics is a consideration of the significance of the materialist premise: *the "lived in" body is both the condition and the consequence of rhetoric* (See Greene 44). The lived in body is the provenance of persuasive performative force. Subjects are taught lessons in how to regard the "coercive" effect of the call of emotion and to determine when the call matters. This lesson is delivered in a participatory way. If we don't feel a strong connection, then its absence seems to indicate a lack of significance. The one perception seems to logically follow the other.

Rhetorics of propriety reiterate these precepts by failing to address their own contribution to valorizing and naturalizing conceptions of the performative power of coherence. When it comes to delineating what matters to judgment, the contribution of affect and sensibility tangle with the rhetorical effects of the materiality of the sign. Rhetorics of propriety do not encourage us to think about the enigmatic space between embodiment and narrative that will not necessarily be translatable into recognizable forms. When we're on the lookout for coherence, we need not question how we have been trained to make decisions about which linguistic effects are worth attending to—i.e., those that are singularly awesome, that seem to fit our sense of what is reasonable, or that seem to carry their own force. The validity of such narratives is itself established most forcefully when a felt sense gets linked to an ideological imperative to look for the forceful and compelling show and then to be satisfied when we find what we were looking for. We are expected to consent to that forceful feeling and not consider how it might also push us to disregard the significance of our responses to speakers like Tripp who fail to compel. In the process, we were—and continue to be—encouraged to overlook the role of narrative (of aesthetics and rhetoric) in establishing expectations about how language should exert a persuasive force.

How then, to regard Tripp's failure to persuade? The lack of identification with her person can prompt not a dismissal but the sense that more could be said about why she was regarded as *so* objectionable—even though she may have not earned unwavering sympathy, there was something unjust and significant about the ways in which she was symbolically disqualified and virtually expelled. Indeed, there was something compelling about her melancholic attempt to redefine herself when confronted by a relentless media harangue. What *would* we do if a friend urged us to cover for them during a court proceeding? How much more alarming for us would that question be if this appeal was made in connection with a court case that implicated a public official, let alone the President? And while the taping of private conversations seems especially venomous, indeed approximating entrapment, it is also the case that, as Tripp maintained, the dress she advised Lewinsky to save did indeed save the young intern from an ordeal even worse than the one she experienced. "Without that dress," Tripp said during a February 1999 interview with ABC, "where would she be today? Would she be en route to London on an extensive book tour, being heralded by pipers at Harrods? Or would she be branded a stalker or worse? This was all coming. I feel that blue dress served as Monica's insurance policy, much as my documents served as my insurance policy."[29]

Not only was she right about Monica Lewinsky's reputation, some of us may also have been amused by a style peppered with phrases like "being heralded by pipers at Harrods." And for all the platitudinous piety encoded into Tripp's self-representation, there also something poignant about her attempt to summon familiar terms to make herself matter—using "regular" identity categories to try to give expression to the agony of alienation; earnestly "following the rules" when addressing the public with a clear, indeed, blunt, form of address that claimed "I'm just like you." And in a subsequent interview, when she said with a rueful laugh that she regretted making that claim, one might have found her to be especially vulnerable when attempting to appear light-hearted.[30]

My guarded sympathy for Tripp offers an example of a "hard to explain" space of judgment wherein meanings emerge through inferences and a phantasmal act of drawing linkages between premises. The "proper" expression will emerge from a dynamic process of judgment, a "latticework of interconnected movements" (T.R. Johnson qtd. in Loewe 245) that, were we to give them their due, would alert us to the often incoherent tumble of responses we may have to public representations of issues and people. The act of bringing order to that disarray is not representable and will be lost in translation once a bona fide perspective is put forth for review.

The "between" space that marks the point of contact between text and body, visible and invisible, attitudes and realities, is also the place where cultural conditioning and personal predilections emerge. When the dynamic of intertextuality is applied to discourses of propriety, we open a conceptual space for inspecting the ways in which material circumstances and ideological formations (See Hesford Spectacular 190-95) give shape to an imaginary experience of identification, with the understanding that the imaginary is not the same as fake. Rather, it underscores the idea that a real but tentative and provisional relationship between narrative and embodiment will underwrite our sense of the force of the fit. Propriety might be redefined as a culturally trained yet personally embodied sense of how another's choice of figurative language shapes perceptions that generate a social dynamic of communication and participation. If the force that provokes that shaping is regarded as provisional, then we may revise our conceptions of what constitutes interpretive connections. Rather than signify interpretation's resolution, they may be viewed as an invitation to further review of how we choose to respond to the words of another—perhaps to reaffirm a judgment; perhaps to rethink an embodied reaction to a texts.

3 The Politics of Ethos

On January 31, 2007, Senator Joseph Biden (D-Del.) found himself "burned" by his own language, having to explain the meaning of a comment attributed to him that day in *The New York Observer*. Biden was in the midst of a run for the presidency, his second try and the second time his language choices presented an obstacle to his success, his first candidacy having ended in 1988 after he was accused of plagiarism, effectively disqualified for stealing someone else's words. This time, Biden's mistake was one of boorishness. When asked to evaluate other Democratic contenders for the office of the presidency, Biden said of Barack Obama, "I mean you got the first mainstream African American who is articulate and bright and clean and a nice-looking guy. I mean that's a storybook, man."[1]

At the time, Biden's comment engendered criticism and "scrutiny," as put by a CNN.com headline.[2] Did he mean to belittle Obama? What did "first mainstream African American" imply about the prior candidacies of other African Americans? For his part, Obama brushed the remark aside, responding in a written statement. "I didn't take Senator Biden's comments personally." He did correct the historical record: "But obviously they were historically inaccurate. African American presidential candidates like Jesse Jackson, Shirley Chisholm, Carol Moseley Braun and Al Sharpton gave a voice to many important issues through their campaigns, and no one would call them inarticulate."[3] And in a gesture that showed that he truly did not take it personally, Obama selected the bumbling Biden to run as Vice President.

This was an interesting move, particularly for what it suggested about Obama's attitudes about public discourse and race. Did it matter that a rival for the office of the president was able to invoke and attach the word "storybook" to Obama's campaign—a trope that would come to haunt Obama's main rival, Hillary Clinton, after her husband was accused of denigrating Obama's efforts by likening his primary victories to a "fairy tale"? Did it matter that the story included a condescending observation about the specific attributes of being "articulate" and "clean"? But if the person who is the object of the seemingly derisive utterance says, "I did not take it personally," shouldn't the rest of us let it go and move on?

Indeed, Biden's comment is of interest not for what it says about Biden, but about the electorate's view of Obama, who went on to win the race for the White House and who is generally acknowledged to be a gifted orator as well as a remarkable person notwithstanding the cultural stereotypes imposed upon men read as black. Not only is he articulate, to many he presents the ideal rhetorical subject—a man of integrity who has sought public office for altruistic reasons. His Biden response helped to fashion this impression. "Don't worry," it seemed to say. "I know what you meant. I trust that you did not mean me harm." Indeed, we might characterize Obama's reply to Biden's blunder as one of his first presidential acts. It aimed to seek a higher ground and not wallow in the metaphors of violence typically ascribed to candidates by a corporate media that depicts elections as sporting events. Instead, we got a glimpse of the man who, one year later, would come more fully into focus when called upon to deliver a speech on race, a speech remarkable for its call to community and for suggesting that his own mixed heritage embodies the very promise of democratic reconciliation.

Arguably, Obama's words enabled him to craft a strong and appealing ethos. This chapter explores how the term *ethos* has been deployed by rhetoricians to theorize connections between acts of representation and judgments of a speaker's character. We are not merely persuaded by arguments. Our sense of the speaker's/writer's character will also affect our willingness to listen to his or her message. More specifically, ethos describes perceptions of character in relation to a speaker's language choices and whether a speaker's mode of speech generates audience receptivity, both intellectually and emotionally. Hence ethos describes character as a discursive formation and this means that ethos is the site of political struggle as audiences evaluate whether a speaker's language choices indicate acceptable motives. In delineating this nuanced formulation of how credibility gets determined, theories of ethos set forth a reflexive conception of a pliant interchange between rhetors, texts, audience predilections and the ways all are situated within historical contexts. With an emphasis placed on a transactional dynamic between these elements, ethos construes judgments of character to implicate the audience's social responsibilities.

I am interested in charting the ways in which this seemingly capacious rhetorical terminology is impelled by an endeavor to tame linguistic unruliness. Rhetorical theories of ethos supply metacritical discourses that promise to explain one component of persuasive power and that do so by incorporating a civic-minded preference for normative language uses. This stance reiterates the one explored in the last chapter. The responsible rhetor is the person who demonstrates an aim to further the prospects of communication and understanding by stylizing utterances in ways that audiences will recognize. Once a preference for community-enhancing language uses becomes customary, indeed, taken as a given, then theories of ethos operate as technologies of evaluation that accomplish two ends: they establish the terms for determining what kind of speech should carry cultural authority; they render portraits of a lively and democratic reflexive dynamic activated *by* sanctioned modes of representation.

An analysis of media representations of Barack Obama in 2008 helps to expose the ideological and emotional commitments audiences are expected to have to sanctioned modes of representation when judging whose speech shows evidence of "good character." When theories of ethos treat style as a signifier of character, then style-as-ethos functions in a literary way—as part of a text to be read within an exegetical analysis. Not only is ethos characterized as an interpretive *result*, rhetorical theories of ethos often reference a history of textuality when organizing conceptions of what constitutes socially responsible language uses to generate audience adherence. By taking recourse in an imagined *a priori* textual order, audiences seem to have a way to ground and understand which kinds of language uses should earn their intellectual and emotional allegiance. A "trust in texts," to quote Susan Miller, seems to anchor evaluations of character to a stable transcendent order and insure that any judgment of another's character will itself be participating with language in ethical ways.

Textual standards seem to offer a neutral mechanism for mediating the sometimes bitter disagreements that can arise over how to read the character of those seeking public office. I analyze how a textual trust was featured within media representations of Barack Obama as he campaigned for president in 2008 and established that he was that ideal rhetorical subject—the good man speaking well, able to earn citizen approval by adhering to stylistic protocols that acted in accord with certain socially determined criteria endemic to judgments of legitimacy and credibility. Specifically, Obama adopted a rhetorical style that indicated that he is a person in control of medium and message. Journalists embraced the image of Obama as a responsible orator, and referenced that image to affirm the validity of a cultural narrative that emphasizes that responsibility lies in personal consciousness rather than social action.

But Obama's example also demonstrates the ways in which narratives of mediation can function as management, especially when the trust in text orientation is applied to interpretive situations wherein rhetorical style is attached to racial identities. The stories told about Obama's striking and yet temperate rhetorical style were made possible by a dynamic of expulsion involving a comparison between Obama's mode of delivery and the oratory of his pastor, the Reverend Jeremiah Wright, who was depicted in the mainstream press as an overzealous provocateur of dangerous emotions. Besides reviewing the ways in which media portraits set up this comparison, I argue that rhetorical theories of ethos help to establish an interpretive context that makes the hierarchies within that comparison seem credible. A look at mainstream media portraits exposes how rhetorical theories of ethos participate in enabling acts of displacement by affirming the legitimacy of styles that promise to stabilize and regulate language's potential emotional power. The presupposed cultural preference for a specific manifestation of interpretive order affirms the idea that to *be* responsible and authoritative, speakers should adopt rhetorical styles that appear to be chaste and moderate—as if the installation of one version of order will overcome any generalized apprehension audiences might have towards strangers who ask to be heard. From this perspective, ethos functions as a technology that facilitates access by habitualizing exclusions.

Styles of Affect

When applying a rhetorical lens to Obama's reaction to Biden, we might say that Obama said the right thing at the right time. In response to a tasteless and inappropriate comment, he offered an eloquent reply that guided audiences into but then out of the controversy, enabling all to turn their attention to issues of more import. "Don't worry" stood in for a cluster of ideas that promised that the nation has progressed beyond a divisive history of painful, race-based exclusions. It implied the possibility of imagining a future not rattled by debates about identity politics that shook the nation during the 1990s, in which citizens were asked to think about which specific bodies and which bodies of speech could claim to act as representatives of the collective (engendering disputes that, arguably, culminated in a presidential impeachment). By 2008, those questions appeared to be settled. An equal playing field was open, occupied by a viable African American male candidate and a Caucasian female candidate, both of whom had huge support from citizens who, through that support, demonstrated a national commitment to the idea that equality for all should be a reality.

And Obama's comment also offered the kind of generous response that, arguably, citizens wanted to hear. The nation was on the brink of an economic crisis, still fighting two wars, and unhappy with the current president, George W. Bush. Indeed, it was into this context that Barack Obama, a man not only marked by race but also bearing the "ominous" middle name of "Hussein"—the same name of the nation's sworn enemy—placed himself into the hands of the electorate, effectively trusting citizens to look past superficial measurements of character, while reassuring them that they need not add the fraught topic of racial discord to public conversations about how to select the nation's next chief representative.[4]

By asking for that trust, Barack Obama earned respect and admiration, both of which solidified his overwhelming victory over challenger Senator John McCain (R-AZ) (53-to-45.7 percent). According to a UPI report, Obama received the most votes of any candidate in U.S. election history, even though a relative newcomer on the national political scene. He effectively crossed that yawning divide that separates public from private, past from present, race from non-raced, to convince an overwhelming majority that he was both the generator and representative of needed change. And more than that, he was (and remains) a charismatic speaker. During the 2008 campaign, citizens swarmed stadiums to hear him speak, the show of support deemed to be newsworthy itself.[5]

Of course the infatuation faded. While much of this has to do with the difference between the fantasy of campaigning and the reality of governing, we can attribute at least some of the public responses to the effects of his language choices. Notably, Obama's approval ratings have risen and fallen along with public speculations about the quality of his oratory and whether his mode of delivery has interfered with his message. In the years after the election, articles tracking the popularity of the president and his policies have noted that "Obama Lost the Narrative" and that he needs to "get a clear message."[6] Indeed, he has been depicted as "too professorial," "an intellectual," "an elitist," "patronizing" and "too removed," particularly when compared with his predecessor Bush, the man you could likely sit down with and share a beer and a burger. Obama, instead, eats arugula.[7] The conversion of public "hope" to wariness was perhaps most definitively expressed by MSNBC's Chris Matthews who, during the 2008 primary campaign, confessed to feeling "a thrill going up [his] leg" whenever he heard Obama speak, but by 2010 declared his former hero to be "too cool."[8]

All of which meant that his 2012 bid for reelection was not guaranteed. Media commentators offered advice about what Obama needed to do to make up for lost ground, including the *Washington Post*'s Chris Cillizza, who argued that political candidates vying for the office of President should think about how to use language to construct a pleasing public persona:

> Obama is, at heart, a college professor in his approach to politics—clinically, not emotionally, studying all sides of an issue. It's no accident that when Obama is at his best, he's personalizing his politics. . . . The challenge before Obama . . . is to find ways to play into the populist sentiment coursing through the country without appearing inauthentic. (The only thing worse than a politician who doesn't understand "the little guy" is a politician who fakes like he understands the little guy).[9]

The advice, to strategically appear to speak naturally by seeming to identify with "the common man" even if one is, in one's heart, something *else* (in this case "professorial"), effectively argues that audiences recognize that there is a conceptual separation between speakers and their language choices. It is of interest because it diverges from the commonplaces that conflate authenticity with truth. Cillizza offered the same advice to Obama's 2012 rival, Mitt Romney, whose seemingly "stiff" exterior was the subject of any number of news reports during the Spring campaign season, perhaps most desperately (and somewhat poignantly) given expression in another *Washington Post* article titled, "Romney Camp Says Candidate is a Prankster."[10] What could be more awkward than having to ask one's aides to make this kind of declaration public and official? From this perspective, the contest between Obama and Romney included the question of which candidate would be most capable of "faking" it—most able to appear as a personable politician when, *in reality*, both just wanted to get down to business.

In effect, candidates are counseled to adopt a "casual" (vernacular) language of the personal in the *right* way because audiences will make use of such disclosures to gauge the candidate's credibility and electability. Divulge one's private person in public as a way of convincing voters to see goodness in one's person. But make sure to cultivate "private" disclosures that appear to be effortless and natural.

As will be discussed later, this advice repeats precisely what rhetoricians have counseled since antiquity. What is of interest at the moment, however, is how the advice to Obama to ditch the dry speech of logic is paired with the presumed alternative: the language of "the personal" and its capacity to produce collective public sentiment. Presumably, persuasive representations promote emotional connections that compel audiences by earning their trust and then their votes. Emotional power seems to fuel persuasive power and that relationship would seem to account for the ways in which audiences render judgments about a candidate's legitimacy.

Here we might note how Cillizza's advice exposes the paradoxes within the reigning conceptual frameworks that explain how we determine who to believe and believe *in*. Those paradoxes become especially apparent when considering how the 2012 media narratives about Obama differed from those of 2008, where Obama was mostly depicted as a masterful speaker able to tap into reservoirs of emotional strength and move audiences to feel strong connections to his aim to become the nation's chief representative. Indeed, instead of prompting advice from journalists about how to engage audience sensibilities, in 2008, Obama's words were represented as being so intrinsically powerful that many were swept away by them, even the most stoic of individuals.

"Colin Powell did not dance for joy over Obama's victory; he wept," wrote *New York Times* columnist Judith Warner in the aftermath of Obama's election night victory. "'Look what we did. Look what we did,' (Powell) said, puffy-faced, red-eyed, fighting back more tears on CNN. 'He's won. It's over.'" Warner noted that during that election victory speech, Obama "resisted giddy gladness" but "proclaim[ed] an end to the world as we've known it for far too long," telling the audience who cheered his victory, "'This is our moment. This is our time.' The glory of Barack Obama is that there are so many different kinds of us who can claim a piece of that 'our.'" (And, in another example of fading infatuation, by 2012, Powell decided to endorse neither Romney nor Obama.)[11]

Narratives describing voter support for Obama in 2008 went beyond the conventional accolades accorded to a victor. Many voters regarded Obama's victory as an apolitical signifier of moral progress itself, as if his very candidacy was able to transcend the rituals of political campaigning and testify to a national healing from previous racial discord. Obama, the unmarked/raced man, seemed to have truly overcome a history of discursive and real alienation to make a historically significant and successful run for the nation's most powerful elected position. The emotional satisfaction engendered by this version of events seemed to validate its legitimacy. But given that his incredible power to unite the nation apparently faded, we are left to wonder about what happened in the wake of its (presumed) disappearance. Did Obama change? Did he, as media reports suggested, lose a quality that he at one time possessed? Did audiences change? How do narratives of loss implicate the reality of those narratives that depicted Obama as a master orator able to compel audiences to recognize the coming of a better future?

The shift in attitudes about what Obama is able to do with words indicates a need to consider more carefully the question of how to conceive of the relationship between language use and emotional connectivity, an aspect of political experience that since the Enlightenment has been characterized as uncivilized, given to extremes and most crucially, unresponsive to reason's formal structures. As I have been exploring in this book, emotion's contribution to political judgment has been rehabilitated within media portraits that acknowledge that emotions will play a significant role in how we determine who and what to believe. But those portraits offer inadequate sentimentalizing representations of emotion as a site of interpretive authenticity. The previous chapter explored how, in the current political milieu, the felt sense is treated as evidence of the authentic and morally grounded interpretive experience. This chapter builds upon that exploration to consider the ways in which affect seems to drive judgments of character. Because affective responses seem to register something real, they appear to exist beyond ideology and to offer both a justification for why a given person is embraced or reviled and then explanatory evidence for the consequences of such assessments. As Obama's example shows, emotions were referenced to demonstrate the essence of an authentic happening—i.e., "true progress"—a happening that seemed to be real and hence available to reference within explanations of why emotions ran high, and more importantly, what Obama's victory meant to the nation. Narratives about Obama's victory in 2008 offer another example of public discourse that represents feelings as arhetorical signifiers of what is genuine and dependable. Feelings appear to guide interpretive processes and instigate ethical political participation by registering a righteous starting point for judgments of which representations should impel a sense of national community precisely because they seem to bypass ideology's influences. In this iteration of political authenticity, the presence of feelings is regarded itself as evidentiary of a "true" interpretive experience occurring independently of representational processes, an experience that appears to be unimpeded by any questions about whether what is *felt* should be subjected to critique. *How* feelings are represented is precisely not of interest because presumably "authenticity trumps ideology, truths cannot be concealed, and communication feels intimate, face-to-face" (Berlant *Cruel* 223).

But the dissonance between portraits of Obama in 2008 and 2012 speak to the ways in which we remain confounded by the relationship between fantasy and reality, as well as the cultivated and the natural, when conceiving of emotion as an embodied/cultural experience generated by representational action, and then credibly generating political judgment. Commonplace narratives about the relationship between feelings and judgments do not reveal how these phenomena truly connect but a desire to be able to identify how orderly connections are made. Rather than delineate *how* emotions figure into judgments about political candidates, the 2008 media narratives that testified to the distinctive emotional power of Obama's candidacy gave voice to that desire and what it promises: that we can indeed gauge political legitimacy in terms of the seemingly forceful and clarifying power of affect. This apparently is preferable to mulling over the interpretive complexities embedded within conceptions of how emotions integrate with modes of representation to provoke acts of identification. It just seems *cleaner* to be able to treat a speaker's language choices as if they signify something true about the speaker's personality, including whether they are *personable* (aka—pleasant, friendly, amenable—qualities we presumably want in our national leaders).

Perhaps this is why every election cycle we find ourselves mired in the language of "the personal"—from media reports, from the candidates themselves, from voters who often pose impertinent questions during public debates (New Hampshire teenager to John McCain in 2008: "Are you too decrepit to be president?"[12])—and then we watch speeches as spectacles, unclear about what to do with the information such disclosures seem to provide, often looking for a gaffe that seems to offer a glimpse of the real person, their unrehearsed locutions serving as a point of comparison to any practiced talking point, seeming to provide a way of testing whether the "inner" person matches a scripted persona.

The tendency to view speech as a lens of true character might explain the desperate push in 2011 to get New Jersey Governor Chris Christie to join the crowded field of Republican candidates running for president when it seemed clear that Romney could not generate love. Christie was regarded as Romney's opposite: aggressive, in-your-face direct, insulting, and for his fans, brutally honest. "His humorous and tough-talking style has brought him fans and 2012 speculation" read a sub-headline in a September 2011 *Washington Post* article that asked, "Why Do So Many Republicans Love Chris Christie?"[13] In the article, "long time Republican strategist" Curt Anderson explained that Christie appeals because he breaks discursive taboos. "'He is not politically correct. Political consultants would say you can't argue in public with a teacher [as did Christie] . . . Christie just throws caution to the wind.'"

For his supporters, that stylistic brutality conveys something desirable about Christie's character—a man who, for all of his brusqueness, gets right to the issue and refuses to play it safe by regurgitating pre-approved clichés. His stylistic choices appear to convey a strength of character that can withstand public ridicule when enacting cutthroat policies. Many, apparently, found such traits to be redeemable, if not presidential. "Please run," implored a woman during a question and answer session after Christie spoke at the Ronald Reagan Presidential Library on September 27, 2011. "I mean this with all my heart. We can't wait another four years, to 2016. I really implore you as a citizen of this country to please, sir, to reconsider. We need you. Your country needs you to run for president."[14] Presumably, this was a plea for the authentic expression as well as for the authentic person because authenticity is, without question, an ethical base for moral leadership.

Once again, we can see how rhetorical style remains an undertheorized site upon which sociability and public intimacy appear to be grounded. Style provides the mechanism—the action—through which "affect worlds" (Berlant Cruel 226) get created. When we overlook the significance of style, we lose sight of the ways in which style serves a constitutive function to craft responses that appear to be in accord with contemporary demands for public intimacy and the experience of "true feeling." And by overlooking style, we turn attention away from precisely that dynamic of connectivity—the place where the cultural training we receive about how to regard acts of representation influences ways of seeing what has significance and value.

Believing Ethos

Rhetorical traditions have acknowledged that emotion has an important role within judgments of a speaker's character. Gerard Hauser, for example, draws upon the classical tradition when defining emotions not as "things or states" but as "expressions of self-involving judgments," defined as "experiences of seeing oneself as the type of person who exhibits certain behavior when confronted by an object of a specific sort" (Rhetoric 177). The rhetor's emotional comportment is rendered an object to be judged within a persuasive appeal. It communicates to audiences how the rhetor has decided to participate with language, whether, for example, to deploy an emotional appeal to accomplish a noble aim like engendering the sentiments of confidence and hope. What remains slippery and ideologically suspect, however, is determining what kind of linguistic comportment should account for that kind of inspiration. Or, more precisely, what explanations of discursive processes seem to authoritatively account for the ability of words to mesmerize audiences by invoking spellbinding styles in *responsible* ways?

Ethos offers one such discourse. It names the dynamic wherein audience estimations of one's character affect judgments of whether one is credible or, in common parlance, "for real." As Michael Hyde notes, ethos "takes form as a result of the orator's abilities to argue and to deliberate and thereby to inspire trust in an audience" (xvi). Ethos depicts speech as conduct. The rhetor indicates a mode of comportment by choosing language that will encourage audiences to "'take something to heart' . . . so that they might be moved to thoughtful action" (xviii). In Hyde's reading of Martin Heidegger, the rhetor crafts a sense of character by putting forth representations that move passions in ways that allow for "collaborative and moral deliberation" (xviii). In this view, rhetorical style is a choice made by the rhetor within a rhetorical situation that asks audiences to assess if that choice makes use of the constitutive action that facilitates the formation of shared perspectives about what has significance and value. Styles communicate whether the rhetor has good will towards his audience and an interest in how its members see issues. Ethics, then, is tied to visions of language as the instigator of a cooperative transactional dynamic where meaning is negotiated rather than discovered. Indeed, the rhetor's ethos tends to be commended when he or she engages audience emotions via styles that indicate a concern *for* the audience's sensibilities.

This nuanced attention to the relationship between style, choice, enactment, and participation is at variance with conventional conceptions of ethos as a persuasive appeal impelled by the strength of the speaker's character. Conventionally, readings of the rhetor's character are said to generate audience estimations of his/her credibility, a formulation that suggests that audiences reference a life *lived* rather than stylized acts of representation when judging merit. This conception presupposes a unified and true self that preexists language uses and makes an appearance within ethos-based appeals. In *Rhetoric: A User's Guide*, for example, John D. Ramage notes that "the quality of any act" of persuasion "is tied to the perceived quality of the act's agent, his or her ethos. Are they trustworthy people? Do they have the appropriate credentials and experience to speak to the issue? What is their 'history' on the issue?" (91). These questions tend to generate positivistic responses wherein ethos is not depicted as a component part of a rhetorical transaction but as a personal attribute possessed by the speaker who can encapsulate his good character in language and draw upon its power to captivate listeners. In its conventional usage then, ethos is regarded as a discernible trait put on display and available for review, functioning like other familiar terms that would name individuals—persona, identity, agent, voice, reputation—terms, as noted by Jan Swearingen, that are informed by a post-Romantic conception of "the self" as "inward-looking, reflective . . . a derivative of the Cartesian subject" (115). The *true self*, a lá Oprah Winfrey.

Because judgments of a speaker's character seem to emanate from a straightforward reading of the speaker's personal power, the speaker who has an intact character should be able to convey it to audiences who are equipped to see it. The hierarchy of values encoded within this formulation prescribes how to decide who deserves to be heard—namely, speakers able to captivate audiences with their charisma. Those who cannot should probably not bother with running for public office, at least on a national level. We expect public speakers to say things that move us, using exhortations that are demonstrably invigorating. Further, we expect to come to know who that speaker *is* given that word choice would seem to reveal true character. Discourses that align ethos with personal character help to craft a political context in which voters expect candidates to provide access to their privacy. We apparently want to know who is *in* there—who is the "real" person so we can judge if we like what we see. "Likeability" has been coined as a term to characterize speculation about whether any given individual is electable. In 2012 Romney's aspirations to be president seemed to be hindered by the question of whether voters could connect to someone who came off as wooden and not especially appealing. "Likeability a Problem for Romney," reported a Boston affiliate of CBS in March 2012. "Gender gap and likeability keep Obama over Romney" reported a CNN poll. "It's called the likeability gap" read a similar story in *The Washington Post*. "It's a real thing and a potential problem for Mitt Romney as he seeks to make his case against President Obama."[15]

The concept of "likeability" reaffirms the priority of authenticity. "Who is the Real Candidate X?" is a common headline in every election season that plays off of the idea that the act of revealing one's true self is imbued with integrity. Any deviance from that goal is regarded as noteworthy and dubious. Mitt Romney's advisor made the mistake of admitting that the candidate would transform his persona after he officially garnered the Republican presidential nomination. During the primary season, the popularity of rival candidates Rick Santorum and Newt Gingrich "forced" Romney to embrace conservative social policies when laying out his platform. Reporters wondered if that kind of hard-line positioning might hurt him during the general election. In response to these concerns, Romney's senior adviser, Eric Fehrnstrom, told a CNN interviewer, "I think you hit a reset button for the fall campaign. Everything changes. It's almost like an etch-a-sketch—you can kind of shake it up and we start all over again." The comment was generally regarded as a major misstep and would soon be used against Romney within political ads. Following Romney's defeat, it was commonly reported that the Republican Party needed to take a long hard look at its identity, or ethos, a look that was characterized by news outlets as "soul searching."[16]

In contrast to Romney's 2012 etch-a-sketch configuration, in 2008, Obama appeared to be a man of true character, regarded by many journalists as an individual who possesses that mysterious "it" factor. Allusions to John F. Kennedy—that other national icon of charisma—abounded as reporters took note of Obama's magnetism, including the following observation from a commentator for the *Christian Science Monitor*. "Among this season's presidential candidates, Barack Obama has clearly had the edge when it comes to that magical quality known as charisma . . . After meeting him even the most jaded political reporters have been known to report that he is something special and rare." A similar view was expressed in *U.S. News and World Reports.* "FDR had it, as did JFK and Ronald Reagan. Barack Obama has it too—charisma, that rare and elusive quality that enables a leader to excite and motivate voters and capture the popular imagination. One of the most discussed aspects of Obama's presidential campaign, in fact, has been his ability to create a sort of political rapture in his followers, especially young people."[17]

Charisma is treated as a possession that one can lose. ("Has Obama's Charisma Deserted Him?" asked a blog in *The Telegraph* in Nov. 2009; "Obama loses his campaign Charisma" ran a headline that same month in the *Washington Times.*[18]) Positivistic conceptions of personal power set up the conditions for audience reception and an organizing interpretive framework that depicts political speakers as texts themselves, available to be read. Such responses indicate the tendency to mobilize the concept of ethos in contexts that define linguistic action as a disclosure of a true self through languages that properly captivate and persuade audiences to see an element of personal strength that is already present. Indeed, the nation's political fortunes would seem to be actualized when citizens are capable of perceiving whatever greatness exists in impressive individual leaders. The reverse is also possible. We can expect to be disillusioned when such greatness fails to make an appearance.

The question is whether a turn to rhetorical studies of ethos can help to arrest the logic that seems to propel this kind of mobilization. At first glance they do, especially given Hyde's richly nuanced reading of Heidegger. Depicting ethos as an interpretive transaction rather than the result of a unidirectional act of exegesis disrupts the tendency to look for correspondences between true selves and self-representations. Indeed, rhetorical studies of ethos put the idea of a constructed self at the center of the interpretive dynamic that forges connections between audiences, rhetors, and texts.

James S. Baumlin clarifies this point by observing, "ethos concerns the problematic relation between human character and discourse; more specifically it raises questions concerning the inclusion of a speaker's character *as an aspect of* discourse, the representation of that character in discourse, and the role of that character in persuasion" (xvii). That relation is problematic because speech and character are not the same entities, notwithstanding the inclination to conflate them. Indeed, rhetoricians as far back as Aristotle have noted the difference between one's self and one's self-representation, and then offered advice about how to compose the kind of self that will provoke audience identification. Speakers are understood to use language not to reflect personal qualities but to invent a persona and establish a reputation for being able to speak well. Consequently, when we judge the speaker's character, we are judging the speaker's attempt to exhibit admirable qualities by demonstrating a capacity to make wise language choices. As noted by Eugene Garner, "'the ethos which the audience trusts . . . is the artificial [artistic or 'artful'] ethos identified with argument. It is not some real ethos the speaker may or may not possesses . . . but ethos as exercised in some particular argument'" (qtd. in Hyde xvi). The rhetor's ability to summon language practices that audiences will embrace constitutes a good ethos.

In other words, the idea of "a self" is just that—an idea, a linguistic construction, a rhetorical marker for a concept that is believed to serve a useful social purpose, one that has emerged within historical contexts and then is entangled in all of the complexities that affect any representation, including the need to consider which ideas about selfhood and styles for delivering them will activate an audience's emotional receptivity. Hence Aristotle's advice: try to *seem* natural when presenting a speech that has been constructed. (A premise that, as noted earlier in this chapter, recalls the advice given by the *Washington Post*'s Chris Cillizza to Obama and Romney.) People generally don't like speeches that appear to be artificially produced. Try to seem spontaneous because audiences will more likely be willing to embrace what you have to say.

Given that artistic invention/fabrication is intrinsic to the rhetoric of ethos, then it might seem that audiences are at the mercy of speakers and can only hope that they are not smitten by false promises from political hacks. Indeed, part of what makes theorizing persuasive power so complex is that it must address what audiences should *do* with the idea that ethos describes an artistic assemblage of words and images drawn from contexts that influence how a speaker's persona will be read. The rhetorical response is to advise the rhetor to trust audiences to understand that invention and fabrication are intrinsic to rhetorical communication.

But here is a place to pause to consider the ways in which we are trained to embrace certain acts of composing as being "of good character" as they endeavor to predispose us to be amenable to persuasion's influence. As discussed in the previous chapter, when evaluating how the interplay between emotion and persuasion affects and effects judgments of how a rhetor uses language, there is a tendency to minimize the significance of cultural training on our conceptions of emotions as well as how they are represented. Lynn Worsham's concept of "pedagogies of emotion" remains pertinent in this regard because it does not treat emotion as a site of an authentic experience but as a term that signifies a "tight braid of affect and judgment that is socially and historically constructed and bodily lived, through which the symbolic takes hold of and binds the individual in complex and contradictory ways, to the social order and its structure of meanings" (Postal 216). Emotions represent not true experiences but troubled sites of identification that can become part of a disciplinary apparatus that educates citizens in how to regard those words that seem able to represent virtuous personal qualities and linguistic modes of comportment.

The rhetorical word for this training is *paideia*, the enculturated narratives we internalize that direct our regard for common language practices and shape expectations of how rhetors should participate with representational power. According to Susan Miller, the ancient rhetorical use of paideia described "a formal curriculum in liberal arts" that offered "the standard example of a broadly conceived emotional education that is woven from shared sessions of rigorous attention to oral and written texts" (Trust 21). Paideia, she adds, act as a "civilizing force" by providing

> a conceptual frame around the lessons it teaches its elite recipients about a shared emotional code. It bonds them as a class demarcated because it shares the emotional range demonstrated in the texts its members have . . . taken as models for their compositions. They hereby also share this education's ideas about standards of credible behavior, a mobile judgment of fitting responses to specific situations and appropriate ways of talking about them (22).

The word *paideia* is a useful term for mulling over how cultural narratives influence ways of reading the dynamic of connectivity that seems to enable audiences to merge estimations of public speech acts with judgments of a speaker's inner life. Rather than signify an unmediated path to knowledge about who is credible and of good character, the powerful emotional response to a political leader can be read as an indicator of precisely the ways in which we get trained to adopt enculturated perspectives when seeing connections between public words and private selves. If we agree that ethos is an aspect of discourse, then taking account of the ruling paideia means considering how we learn to read representational modes or styles *as* signs of character. The ruling paideia will inform judgments of "standards of credible behavior" that often go unquestioned, and that, when unquestioned, naturalize those emotional responses that then seem like validations of judgments.

Rhetoricians often offer a matter-of-fact acknowledgment of this dynamic, particularly when theorizing the relationship between "being" and "seeming to be." Hence, in Hauser's reading of ethos, because desirable moral habits will be projected onto speakers who seem to exhibit qualities we have been taught to hold in high esteem (courage, temperance, generosity, prudence, magnanimity, magnificence. See Rhetoric 155-56), then the rhetor who desires to persuade should devise styles that seem to convey those qualities. Doing so is called *being pragmatic*. It incorporates an Aristotelian orientation that effectively counsels, to make a good impression, exhibit traits that audiences recognize and value. This rhetorical advice is not meant to be mercenary. Instead, the very ethos of rhetorical studies is rehabilitated via narratives that describe how a concern with audience sensibilities is central to a pragmatic rhetorical ethics. Not any language practice will do, and certainly not those that manipulate by playing on audience sensibilities. Rather, a rhetor's concern with exhibiting qualities held in high esteem may be read as evidence of his or her civic concern with using language to craft community. The "good rhetor" is the one who uses language purposefully to accomplish defensible goals, such as exhorting audiences to change for the better.

Such premises, oddly, lead us back to a Platonically inflected realm of interpretation, wherein representations get examined to provoke speculations about where the representation aims. This concern with "the aims of speech" situates ethos within the domain of the "ontological," according to Craig R. Smith, "because (ethos) is a moral enterprise; practical wisdom, virtue, and good will . . . aim toward a moral end (a telos) . . . The teleological dimensions of ethos lead the speaker toward a higher potential, one capable of advancing a cause, uplifting an audience and guiding a society aright" (15–16).

In other words, personas may be invented but we need not worry about the potential for deception when we can count on the good rhetor to invent a persona that aspires to be moral. And when determining whether a given fabricated self aims in the right direction, rhetorical style takes on renewed significance. When Edward P. J. Corbett, for example, rescues classical rhetorical texts and the concepts they advance (such as ethos), he underscores style's role by noting that the ancients believed that studies in style were "interwoven with discovering ideas and creating textual choices" (Pace 12). We not only look to style to tell us about whether moral qualities have made an appearance, the endeavor to judge where a speaker's language aims can appear itself to be imbued with morality, particularly when such judgments are made in situations that affect a collective like a nation. Style protocols appear as conduits that connect component parts of the rhetorical triangle, helping to facilitate the interpretive interplay between rhetors, texts, and audiences in ways that may be morally assessed, enabling audiences to determine whether the style on offer does, indeed, facilitate social interactions that lead them to reach "higher potentials" as they labor to negotiate meaning. Arguably, then, styles offer tangible sites for analyzing the kind of affect that is produced, and how that production connects to the social dynamic of garnering access to power and authority. We see, once again, a version of the rhetorical idea that styles should assist in communicating not just ideas; they should help the speaker indicate what remains invisible: one's goals, purposes, motives for seeking an audience. The influence of a ruling paideia echoes within these premises. When it comes to the aesthetic elements of representational action, ideologies influence judgments of which stylized fabrication seems to (truly) move audiences towards preferred aims. Ethos can be described as a disciplinary space that gives expression to how one's constructed identity is positioned within a social structure that prioritizes the reproduction of normative language practices as a way of regulating interpretive complexities. The idea that the man of good character aims to accommodate audience preferences will be converted itself from pragmatic advice into a legitimating mandate.

Orders of Emotion

How the conversion from advice to mandate occurs is subtle but significant to estimations of who has good character. It is informed by the idea that acts of interpretation are duty-bound to reproduce orders of textuality. The ruling paideia that trains us to conflate morality with order also trains us to value the appearance of seemingly orderly, "text based" representations of emotion. This training can be traced to those Belletristic models of rhetoric that were concerned with finding ways to tame emotions through language uses that would instruct audiences not only to aspire to "be civilized" when using language but also to want to do so.

The Belletristic tradition that introduced the phrase *faculty psychology* explicitly charted pathways for connecting acts of representation to experiences of emotion and then to judgments of character. Belletrism endorsed a conceptual framework that prompted an "inward" look at selfhood and the self's relationship to universal linguistic structures. This way of looking led to the creation of a taxonomy of mental faculties along with proposed rules for their responsible engagement. "The faculties," notes Roger Thompson, were believed to exhibit "general properties that could be explicated and then generalized to rules of expression" (264).

A technology of evaluation developed from these premises that gave rhetorical style renewed significance, casting it as an explicit sign of the speaker's sense of ethics. The conscientious speaker used styles that reproduced a pre-established order to insure order's harmonious reproduction. Adam Smith, for example, "fused" style to character by effectively depicting ethics *as* a concern with style. According to Vincent Bevilaqua, for Smith, "good style" promotes civility because "style is an effect of certain native powers of the mind" (564). If style "itself is founded on mental powers common to human nature" (564), then it should be possible to devise stylistic protocols able to communicate the kind of courteous character that can compel civilized subjects to want to affiliate with representations of that character. As put by Michael Carter, one's "character was the primary determinant of his style. . . . Style was considered as good only insofar as it was a true reflection of character" (11).

The tendency to conflate style with character has not disappeared and its traces are evident within public discourses that explore how audiences read the personalities of political candidates by evaluating their language practices. An October 2012 Gallop Poll, for example, asked registered voters "to put aside their voting preferences in naming the 'greatest strength' of each candidate." Romney's greatest strength was listed as his "economic experience, including being a good businessman" while Obama's greatest strength was listed as his personal character "led by excellent speaking and communication skills." According to Gallup's news release, "In total, 47% of respondents named some aspect of Obama's character as his top strength, compared with 23% naming a *character* trait for Romney."[19]

Belletristic correspondences between innate psychology, representative rhetorical styles, and morality prepared the way for drawing connections between a sense of a speaker's character and a sense of how he participates with language when representing his ideas. As put by Susan Miller, this model "embeds consciousness in discursive practices" (107), as if the two are inherently, inevitably, and systematically intertwined. If consciousness is bound to language practices, then determining which kind of practice will affect what kind of consciousness will seem necessary and reasonable, as will the idea that regulating language practices (and then consciousness) can serve a social need. In the Belletristic era, narratives of nationalism were disseminated in an effort to convince publics to identify as national subjects and to reflect that act of identification by adopting uniform styles of delivery, both oral and textual. (See also Bender and Wellbery.) The aim to standardize language practices was deemed to be a moral aim because it promoted civility and helped to "personify a normative moral character" (T. Kelleher 81).

At the same time, as critics of Belletrism have noted, the act of standardizing the English language also promoted "cultural hegemony and social assimilation" (T. Kelleher 81). Not only were citizens trained to regard standardized language uses as signs of good character, as Belletristic models disseminated the idea that language could unproblematically reflect the consciousness of the writer, they also disseminated the idea that appropriate emotions could be cultivated in readers to benefit the state (Harrington 254). Reader reception was targeted to induce an "introspective" mind (Harrington 253) within citizens who were (ostensibly) free to participate in democratic culture in whatever way they saw fit. One effect of the drive to civilize the citizenry via instruction in "good" linguistic participation: the instigation of an interpretive framework that correlated ethical political participation with a political passivity of reception rather than, for example, one that encouraged citizens to activate a good ethos by producing their own versions of what is and what should be.

This cultural training not only put boundaries around perceptions of which styles should be valorized, it also worked to install a cultural preference for a kind of orderliness that can be textually represented. Seeing correspondences between consciousness and textuality helped to install the logic that links the production of a specific version of *representational order* to morality's very enactment. Susan Miller traces how these linkages coincided with the Belletristic era of influence and merged historically in connection with the rise of the printing press in the West. Print technologies regularized the dissemination of disembodied acts of communication and that development had a profound effect on conceptions of how language uses seem to enforce orders of reception. Once print replaced the body—the scribe's hand that copied the text, a person's spoken avowal of a statement's origin—then the idea that consciousness is embedded within discursive practices took on new meaning. Narratives were needed to explain how the anonymous, disembodied text could claim to represent the individual who was no longer present when the words were received. Eventually, Miller explains, "the phenomenology of texts as a material realm" began to be envisioned as running "parallel to consciousness: a differently materialized *published* textuality that locates trust in media, not as conveyers of messages but for their own sake" (107—original emphasis). Over time, expectations arose around the idea that the speaker should imitate the discursive practices associated with textual publication and to perceive that correspondence as an enactment of anonymous neutrality. While "disseminated publication regularly compromises [the] conception of presence itself" (107), publicity via publication gave form to the legitimizing power of neutral anonymity. The rise of the printing press paradoxically concretized an abstract conception of how to instantiate orderly interpretive negotiations. Print, once formalized, also established a provenance for such conceptions that seemed real and not aesthetically constructed.[20]

Contemporary theories of ethos have abandoned the pedagogies in taste promoted by the study of Belles Lettres, but in treating ethos as an aspect of discourse, style's value continues to be aligned with a representational obedience to textual protocol. This orientation is given expression in two ways: through the affirmation of a principle of anonymity mobilizing ethical action and through a concern with "form, structure, and the internal movements in discourse" (Short 367) that effectively tamps down regard for perceived linguistic unruliness. Theorists tend to favor narratives about ethos and style that promote orderly methodologies that promise to navigate the politically difficult problem of distinguishing "seeming" from "being." In effect, the orderly style not only seems to be reasonable, it gets treated as if it is reason's representative. Undergirding this treatment is "an ideology of style rooted in a social text of neutrality" (Patricia Williams qtd. in Flannery 57) that affirms the text-based idea that an anonymous and neutral force propels rhetorical action. Audiences are effectively trained to look for evidence of that anonymity when judging whether a (textual or oral) representation of emotion is credible.

Consider, for example, the response of Michael Hyde to the interpretive question of how to evaluate the legitimacy of ethos and style. Building upon Richard McKeon's influential idea that the artful speaker be "architectonic" (see xxi), Hyde observes that "the call of human being, of conscience, calls on us to be rhetorical architects whose symbolic constructions both create and invite others into a place where they can dwell and feel at home while thinking about and discussing the truth of some matter that the rhetor/architect has already attempted to disclose and show forth (*epi-deixis*) in a specific way with his or her work of art" (xxi). The metaphor of architecture positions the authority of speech within a pre-existing structural order that apparently may be referenced to assist audiences when judging the validity of any specific self-construct. To invoke architecture within conceptual models of ethos is to place confidence in the existence of a formal order that may be referenced to sort through whatever representational ambiguities arise when we stop and think about *what* styles communicate about the person who engages them. (Here we might recall the meditations of Elizabeth Grosz, discussed in chapter one, who questions whether a conceptual bridge can be forged between the material practices of architecture and the practice of organizing conceptions of acts of interpretation.)

The metaphor of architecture reinstalls a vision of rhetoric as *techne*—the art of producing a text for imagined audiences. But the implications of the rhetor-architect narrative extend beyond a call to use "solid" discursive techniques and materials when constructing a dwelling place for a discourse community to inhabit. Indeed, invoking architecture and the metaphor that describes language as a "living space" may be thematically connected to the concept of "community" in the sense identified by Benedict Anderson. Anderson coined the phrase *imagined communities* when considering how it is possible for strangers to feel that they are connected both to each other and to container categories such as "the public" or "the nation." The word "community" is itself a container category that demarcates not a physical location but the subject's imaginary relations to signifiers that would stand in for the idea of a phenomenon that (apparently) collects people into shared spaces and establishes a sense of belonging to each other as inhabitants of that metaphorical place.

Crucially, the subject's imaginary attachments to any particular version of a linguistic community would seem to be forged by a systematic execution of rhetorical action that produces the shared interpretive experiences that bind subjects to each other through the reading of fixed texts. Persuasion's force is ascribed to an equitable anonymity that would seem to inhere within transactional dynamics rather than to any cultural training that generates conceptions of what constitutes procedural action. So, for example, Anderson describes how the production of daily newspapers provided a material method that encouraged citizens to imagine themselves as belonging to a larger collective of like-minded readers. The print technologies that arose during the industrial revolution fostered a mechanical production of texts while providing a material basis for envisioning a metaphorical interpretive "togetherness." As a result, the very idea of community—a seemingly intimate and personal domain that would collect real bodies in space—could be attached to the *image* of shared of acts of reading and interpretation. This *text based* generator of acts of sharing (that was in a sense real but also imaginary) came to be incorporated into the narratives that would describe the parameters of interpretive action—that of a general, anonymous and repeatable process, structurally sound, and always available to direct how bodies encounter written texts and to what ends.

In elaborating this point, Marc Redfield develops Anderson's observation about how "'community in anonymity [is] the hallmark of modern nations'" (qtd. In Redfield 63), an anonymity that seems to penetrate the processes by which the subject is incorporated and conjoined to the imaginary realm of "the public body." Appealing to a structural anonymity as foundational to (and a foundation *for*) nation-building comprises an "aesthetic-pedagogic project" that "exploits the same processes of technical reproduction that make the imagining of a nation possible in the first place" (69). Subjects are interpellated as citizens through the imaginary act of *joining* others within an aestheticized space of anonymity, an idealized construct that comes to seem *real* when reproduced experientially, creating a material consequence in which "anonymity becomes familiarity" (71). The sensuous experience of aestheticized anonymity not only becomes familiar, it begins to take on the overtones of an ethical moral stance, held out as a perceivable point of entry to the deliberatory acts that both exercise and express one's commitment to a national interpretive framework that equates anonymity with moral neutralitry. The idea that there is a structural method available to direct evaluations of representations and those who produce them allows for an imagined sameness in everyone's ways of participating with language. Printed discourse creates an imagined space of a shared context; it seems to establish a unified domain (i.e., *to house something*) to contain the production and reception of language.

This chain of ideas is embedded within the architectonic metaphor that Hyde invokes to anchor readings of ethos. The metaphor similarly references a structural anonymity as a method for understanding how speakers, rhetorical styles, and content interconnect to generate judgments of what is credible and has merit. "Ethos" functions as a method of suture—a way of establishing the "cement" that would connect shared experiences of participation with language uses within a consolidated political-cultural domain. Once the connotations of "fixed" spaces, stable foundations, and solid building blocks that inhabit the architectonic metaphor get ascribed to ethos, then there appears to be a way to ground reflexive interactions between audiences, texts and rhetors to account for how speakers are able to create desirable, virtuous effects with words. If a constructed persona should aim to establish a dwelling place, then the aims of discourse and ways of reading character as an aspect of discourse are given a discernible direction. Meanwhile, the conceptual apparatus that offers methods for reaching identified aims will likely be regarded as itself valuable, enabling it to quietly shape expectations about the kinds of character one may legitimately construct. Once so regarded, that conceptual apparatus will appear to truly enact sensible and sound judgments about any persona being evaluated.

Crucially, however, the building blocks of the dwelling place will be comprised of linguistic forms aligned with culturally respected rhetorical styles. Here, we might hear echoes of the Belletristic valorization of linguistic "establishments" as the moral ground underwriting judgments of whether a speaker aims well. The rhetorical correlation between representational order and the use of particular language practices will effectively reign in ways of reading which styles count as solid signs of "good character." The building blocks of, for example, vernacular speech, perspicuity (Hugh Blair's old word for clarity and intelligibility), discourses of reason, and signs of coherence will continue to get invoked as stylistic markers of speakers who mean well, who seem to have a strong moral character, and who seem to aim to be inclusive—to invite audiences to participate in the dwelling places crafted by their way of participating with language. Not only will the goal of using language to enact persuasion continue to be treated as inevitably valid and the very point of studying rhetoric, those narratives that integrate emotional appeals with responsible aims will affirm the legitimacy of an interpretive apparatus that favors text-based versions of discursive discipline.

Paradigm Ethos

When it comes to determining whose words offer inhabitable dwelling places for voters, citizens often convey a desire to support political leaders whose language uses appear to be ordinary and familiar and expressive of a personal character that is reliable and predictable. On the other hand, we also want to be captivated by speakers able to mesmerize with innovative plans and proposals. Indeed, we might say that a paradoxical desire for recognizable "newness" prevails in many election cycles, particularly when citizens are in the mood to rid Washington of hypocritical charlatans.

Such was the mood in 2008. Obama's hard-won primary victory over Hillary Clinton was achieved in part from the idea that as a former first lady, she represented "the old" while Obama, a relative unknown Senator from Illinois, represented something unique and remarkable. But as a person without a national reputation, Obama had to demonstrate that he could be trusted with the presidency. While the idea of newness may have intoxicated some citizens, it is equally the case that Obama's mixed race and international heritage was read as foreign (literally and metaphorically) to others who, with the help of the compliant mainstream media, managed to perpetuate a running dialogue on the question of whether Obama's aspiration to be president was legitimate.[21]

Obama had to contend with the question of how to use language to negotiate the boundary between strangeness and familiarity, distinctiveness and resemblance. This negotiation was especially interesting given his decision to craft a persona who stood for change, delivering stump speeches that included statements such as, "It's time to move beyond the politics of yesterday, because we're a party of tomorrow. We're going forward." Slogans in political ads reiterated this theme. "Tired of the same old politics? Vote for change we can believe in."[22]

The public and the press quickly embraced the narrative depicting Obama as the embodiment of innovation and hope. What constituted the element of newness, however, was unspecified, but at least one component of Obama's "fresh" appeal was his ability to enthrall audiences with rousing speeches that seemed to exercise a broad-based appeal. When taking stock of Obama's victory over Hillary Clinton for the Democratic nomination, *Newsweek*'s Howard Fineman attributed that success to a charisma powerful enough to alter a sedimented and somber historical narrative.

> On that sunny February day in 2007, Obama seemed to radiate uplift and glorious possibility. He was making a statement: that his candidacy would be the exclamation point at the end of our four-century-long argument over the role of African Americans in our society. By electing a mixed-race man of evident brilliance, moderate mien and welcoming smile, we would finally cease seeing each other through color-coded eyes.[23]

As Obama rode the wave of popularity to victory, a majority appeared to be emotionally receptive to the idea that it was time for the people of the United States to enter a new era in which they could finally put to rest a racist past and give up the habit of disqualifying candidates simply because of the color of their skin.

Nonetheless a problem was raised when it came to the question of what, exactly, accounted for Obama's popularity. Did race play a role in establishing Obama's distinctiveness and help to constitute a sense of what was new? Should the category of race be treated as insignificant? Geraldine Ferraro stumbled over this question when she suggested that Obama's success did indeed derive from his atypical identity, arguing, in effect, that because of his race, Obama was getting a free ride by "the liberal media," and receiving undo positive coverage that almost sanctified him. In March 2008, the former Congresswoman, first female Democratic vice-presidential candidate (1984), and supporter of Hillary Clinton, ignited a controversy when she said, during an interview with a local California newspaper, "If Obama was a white man he would not be in this position. And if he was a woman of any color, he would not be in this position. He happens to be very lucky to be who he is. And the country is caught up in the concept."[24] The unspoken implication: there was nothing extraordinary about him, nothing intrinsically powerful about his person to account for his popularity. Ferraro effectively argued that people were in love with a *narrative* about equity. Within a week of making those comments and refusing to retract them, Ferraro stepped down from Clinton's campaign.

The Clinton campaign became further entangled in the complexity of discourses about race after Bill Clinton, normally so adept at pleasing audiences, made his own gaffe when campaigning for his wife in New Hampshire. Clinton reportedly said of Obama's bid to be president, "Give me a break. This whole thing is the biggest fairy tale I've ever seen," a statement that audiences interpreted as a reiteration of Biden's problematic observation—that a man "of color" winning a presidential election was a fantasy. Whatever credibility Clinton had had as the "nation's first black president" (an observation attributed to the esteemed writer Toni Morrison) seemed to evaporate. Umbrage followed the implication that the former President had committed an act of rhetorical violence by questioning Obama's legitimacy. Clinton's comment apparently galvanized voters who might otherwise have backed Hillary Clinton's campaign. In the months following this public fiasco, defections by former Hillary supporters to Obama's camp followed, including, most notoriously, New Mexico Governor Bill Richardson who until his defection, had been an ardent Clinton supporter. Rep. James Clyburn of South Carolina, the highest-ranking African-American in Congress and a former Clinton ally, told the *New York Times* that he was thinking of ending his neutrality in his state's January 26 primary "out of disappointment at comments by Bill and Hillary Rodham Clinton that he saw as diminishing the historic role of civil rights activists."[25]

As Obama endeavored to establish a good ethos with the American public in the spring of 2008, the question of what to do about racial identity—whether to address it at all, whether doing so was in some way racist—infused public discussion, as if the very topic presented an inevitable dilemma. Once votes in state primaries began to tally in Obama's favor, it became clear that he was a genuine and formidable contender, but public statements about his identity continued to directly and indirectly question whether and how to attach significance to his mixed-race heritage. Reporters often floundered when contending with this question, as countless headlines in the mainstream media reflected the apparent difficulty of both asking this question and considering its legitimacy. "Does Race Matter?" "Are We beyond Race?" "Can Obama Capture the White Vote?" were among the questions specifically posed in articles advertised on national magazine covers. These were accompanied by the attempt to "be responsible" by objectively examining whether racism is an intrinsic emotional response, one that voters (read white) will naturally confront as they make political choices. *The New Republic*, for example, addressed the issue in an article that looked at Obama's candidacy through the lens of psychology: "The Big Race. Obama and the Psychology of the Color Barrier." *Time* magazine, instead, went for biology: "Race and the Brain" read the headline of an article that ran three weeks before the November election, followed by the subheading, "We're hardwired to react suspiciously to other races. But we also have the tools to overcome it." The article also included an illustration of a brain that identified the sections that respond with "reflexive fear."[26]

Arguably, in 2008, the signifier "race" functioned as an important "keyword in defining national identity and culture in the United States" (Behdad 220). Underwriting this dynamic was the question of whether an orderly representational logic may be referenced to help citizens sort through the complex emotions engendered by public narratives that described the presumably fraught topic of race and its significance to democratic culture. The media reports that fumbled when giving publicity to this issue exposed conceptual limitations within the idea that a structural anonymity may be referenced to direct representational procedures and then evaluations of what a given representation accomplishes. Theories of ethos are implicated. Indeed, at the center of a democratic ethos is the putative anonymity of force underwriting the presumed act that conjoins the phrase, "we're all equal," to the phrase, "because we're all the same." Because we tend to believe that structure *means* anonymous equity, this premise would seem to be demonstrably valid, proven via that structural organizing force. In other words, we would seem to have interpretive methods for determining whether the idea of race should be relevant to "The Big National Race." We should be able to consult language's equitable anonymity and expect it to move us beyond any local discord to get an overview about what should generally matter to all citizens. And clearly, in a democratic state that values equity, anyone's racial identity should not matter, especially when judging ethos. Presumably, audiences will know this is so when structured interpretive methods get referenced to resolve whatever tensions are produced by competing narratives about what has significance within contexts that require judgment. Indeed, most media reports suggested that while explicit coverage of the topic of race was required, questions about the significance of Obama's race should be set aside, especially as his campaign gained momentum. The implied logic: voter support for Obama demonstrated that race did not matter to discussions of his campaign and indicated instead the emergence of an ethically improved "post-race" reality.

Hence, while most would agree with the premise that one's race should not matter to who is elected to public office, the passionate support of Obama's candidacy seemed to convey more than a neutral endorsement of his specific candidacy. It was also regarded as making a statement about the nation's very ethos, suggesting that at least in this case, the category of race did have political significance after all. Indeed, citizen support for

Obama's candidacy seemed to signify a public commitment to proving that the phrase "all are equal" is more than an imaginary ideal. Arguably, the seemingly contradictory perspective that situated race as both significant and insignificant need not be read as conflicting with the premise that honors interpretive neutrality. Presumably, it is precisely the availability of a neutral interpretive methodology that enables citizens to weigh both the general significance of identifying what counts as national progress along with the question of whether the category of race implicates a specific historical event like an election. But precisely *how* those distinctions get delineated and then weighed is left vague, underscoring the ways in which any conception of "equity" is fused to how we think we should participate with stylistic protocols. The actual work of assessment seems to bypass social training when judgment latches onto the structural neutrality ascribed to linguistic processes. But as I have been arguing throughout this book, conceptions of language's equitable action will be informed by stylized narratives that contribute to establishing the very faith we are expected to have in the authority of textuality. Such narratives function as textual precursors, markers within a history of textuality that loses its textual status and comes to be regarded as a real descriptor of a bona fide interpretive dynamic that, for example, acts to get an "overview" of a situation, situate one's perspective in a context of neutrality, reference that context when rendering judgments that aim to be coherent and fair. When considering how to address the significance of race in a political context in which discourses about race provoke emotional reactions, we are effectively being asked to evaluate and have faith in the ethos of such dominant interpretive methodologies.

Whether it is possible to actually engage language uses and transcend "discord" by implementing neutrality gets convoluted, especially when that action implicates the question of how to read the significance of diverse discursive practices, including styles. The "rise above" metaphor privileges representations that appear to be neutrally structured themselves. In 2008, this privilege was translated into a preference for representations that appeared to be racially "unmarked." The representation that is specifically not marked by race seems to generate those acts of interpretation that could be identified as equitable, fair, and ethical. But if those acts of identification are perceived as outgrowths of a ruling paideia, then what they convey is neither neutrality nor fairness but an enculturated point of view about how to reflect a benevolent aim within an order of signification. This becomes evident when discourses of neutrality are invoked to measure the legitimacy of vernacular language practices. Instead of summoning an unbiased and objective perspective, the "rise above" metaphor effectively calls attention to acts of representation that signify differently, that neither model nor aim to model discursive styles that have been identified in dominant cultures as signifiers of an anonymous structural equity. In effect, when discursive practices *do* mark difference—including those that mark different racial identities—it seems fair to critique them for refusing to leave off the stylistic characteristics that specify *that* they are distinctive rather than representative of the anonymous everyman.

All of this played out in 2008 once reports about Obama's minister, the Reverend Jeremiah Wright, were introduced into the national conversations about the election. Throughout the primary season, *Fox News* had been playing clips of sermons that Wright had delivered over the previous decade. *Fox* commentators depicted Wright's rhetorical delivery as contentious and divisive and maintained that giving it public attention enabled them to bolster the ethos of their own news organization, which they represent as the noble savior of American values. *Fox* commentators effectively argued that Wright practiced reverse racism when he depicted U.S. policies as a form of white supremacy and delivered that message within sermons that, per *Fox's* media celebrities, were stylistically shocking. For several weeks, public attention to the Reverend was largely overlooked by other press organizations. That changed in March 2008 when an *ABC* news program, *Good Morning America*, picked up the story and reiterated the perspective presented by conservative commentators: that the minister associated with Obama's family was a provocateur whose preaching style was combative and unpatriotic. Once clips of Wright's sermons from 2001 and 2003 aired on *ABC*, the story became part of the mainstream news cycle and began to receive coverage on all networks. Before long, it became common to refer to Wright as Obama's "Pastor Problem."[27] The pastor was a problem because not only had Obama been a regular member of his church, Obama had declared that the two of them celebrated a special bond. He had borrowed one of Wright's phrases (the audacity of hope) for a book title and composed a dedication to this influential man, who performed Obama's marriage to Michelle and baptized their daughters, Sasha and Malia. Wright was the head pastor at Trinity Church in Chicago, the church that Obama regularly attended and used as evidence of his conversion to Christianity. (Obama explained that he became a Christian "later in life" after spending his youth with no religious affiliation).

In the aftermath of this publicity, it seemed that the momentum of Obama's campaign stalled. Most interesting in this development was the crossover effect. Obama's ethos took a hit not because of his language choices, but because of those from his pastor. Somehow, Wright's mode of speech was believed to reflect something about Obama's character. Articles that focused on both the content of Wright's sermons as well as on the style of his delivery insinuated that Obama's approval of Wright's perspective should raise doubts about the man who aspired to act as the nation's representative. *Time* magazine, for example, ran an article that attempted to explain what was at issue and why Obama had "a pastor problem" by publicizing photos of Wright preaching, and placing those photos above a sidebar that transcribed "some provocative sound bites" made by Wright that had been circulating on television. That line appeared in red ink, the color apparently assisting in identifying what was "biting." Each quote also included the date when Wright gave voice to the controversial utterances:

> *"About 9/11"*: "We bombed Hiroshima, we bombed Nagasaki, and we nuked far more than the thousands in New York and the Pentagon, and we never batted an eye. We have supported state terrorism against the Palestinians and black South Africans, and now we are indignant because the stuff we have done overseas is now brought right back to our own front yards. America's chickens are coming home to roost" (Sept. 16, 2001).
>
> *"About patriotism and race"*: "The government . . . wants us to sing God Bless America. No, no, no. God damn America; that's in the Bible, for killing innocent people. God damn America for treating our citizens as less than human" (2003).
>
> *"About the Clintons"*: "Hillary is married to Bill, and Bill has been good to us. No, he ain't! Bill did us, just like he did Monica Lewinsky. He was riding dirty" (Jan. 13, 2008).
>
> *"About the U.S."*: "The United States of White America" (July 22, 2007).[28]

Following the broadcast of the *ABC* news report, there was a groundswell of commentary from pundits, especially, and again, on *Fox News*, including Bill O'Reilly, who delivered his typical brand of reductive thinking: "Because Barack Obama is running on his judgment, a big question pops up. How can you be close to a man who hates America that much?" His colleague, Sean Hannity, concurred. "If you can't disown Reverend Wright, you're not qualified to be president of the United States. I don't even think you're qualified to be Senator." *The Weekly Standard*'s Joseph Loconte used the Wright controversy to question Obama's integrity. "What Obama does now to distance himself from Wright is less important than what he failed to do over the last 20 years. Why didn't Obama leave this church when he learned that its senior pastor was committed to ideas that are 'contrary to my own life and beliefs'? . . . All of this suggests a weakness in Obama's character, a shrinking back from principled decisions if they seem too costly. . . . Obama couldn't find the moxy to stop attending the church of a minister who makes anti-Americanism an indispensable doctrine of his faith."[29]

Such responses took advantage of the cultural narratives that train audiences to judge ethos in a positivistic way by devising straightforward connections between speakers and their linguistic comportment. A presupposed positivistic logic underwrites such perceptions and made it possible to extract excerpts from Wright's sermons and read them as representative of a generalized attitude that one would expect audiences to find objectionable. It was also possible to draw upon the logic of narratives that posit the existence of an equitable organizing representational order when crafting connections between Wright's utterances and Obama's character, an action that would seem to be ratified by the presupposed teleology inscribed within those interpretive technologies that ascertain where representations aim. Accordingly, the dissemination of snippets from Wright's sermons could be treated as decontextualized "facts" (he uttered those words after all) that proved that Wright harbored a renegade/unpatriotic point of view and then a bad character that then rendered Obama similarly "guilty" by association. Accordingly, mobilizing public opinion through public pronouncements that denigrated Wright's sermons could be itself characterized as a responsible and ethical act.

Ostensibly, a rhetorical perspective would challenge this positivistic methodology by investigating the social and political frameworks that sustain conceptions of interpretive practices to reveal the ways in which interpretations are culturally constituted. (More on this in the next section.) Yet notwithstanding rhetorical resistance to epistemological assumptions underwriting positivistic ways of seeing, discourses that connect ethos to the attempt to craft a linguistic "home" reanimate the logic of positivism as the means for judging a speaker's attitude about what representations should do. If we expect speakers to construct dwelling places that are built in accordance with audience preferences, then the question of which audiences and which stylistic preferences is paramount. If ethos is an aspect of discourse and if "most" regard a given use of language to be offensive, then those who concluded that Wright's language choices expressed "ill will" would seem to have adopted a legitimate and indeed sensible perspective—rather than, say a perspective invested in pushing a conservative agenda at all costs. The rhetorical shift away from the explicit promotion of a positivistic outlook to a discourse of ethos that recognizes interpretive flexibility can have, in effect, little consequence on judgments of which acts of speech show good character, especially if we believe that a neutral architectural structure may be referenced when judging discursive aims. The presupposed neutrality of the organizing metaphor, along with that seemingly benevolent goal of creating an interpretive space for sharing, can act to disqualify those who hope to do something else with language, such as trigger discomfort by challenging hegemonic norms.

Anyone who judged Wright's words differently, who identified with his message or was mesmerized by the stylistic vehemence and persuaded by his perspective, may have felt a sense of interpretive dissonance when encountering the iterations of outrage disseminated by the mainstream press. The self-righteous and vigorous public condemnation of Reverend Wright can be analyzed to extricate the insidious underside to prevailing interpretive technologies, especially those that seem to benevolently promote fairness and community and yet invoke a representational order that ostracizes. To unravel this complexity we can consider the ethos of journalists reporting on this story who, presumably, relied upon prevailing discursive technologies to engage respectable aims, such as neutrally conveying information. Hence the *Time* article that included the snippets from Wright's sermons could be characterized as engaging in an act of clarifying the issue by showing audiences what Wright said. This act of exposure could be called objective, reasonable and fair when situated within a context that connects the act of exposure (publicity) to the laudable goal of informing the public and thereby advancing the public's *right to know*. Ostensibly, the neutrality of this motive is itself describable and recognizable. (Hence, positivism returns.) But when mulling over whether we can know where discourse aims, we must ask about how we have been trained to look at style as a socially constituted credentialing practice.[30] Qualities like "fairness" are aesthetically constructed but we tend to forget that aspect of linguistic production when drawing upon stylistic conventions to help us interpret representational goals.

So, for example, not all mainstream journalists berated Wright. Some endeavored to "be balanced" by engaging in acts of representation that would textually reproduce the ideal of neutrality by "showing both sides"—that is, that would give publicity to the idea that Wright's statements were credible and authoritative to his supporters. With this approach, journalists in the mainstream press could be said to use language to construct a responsible ethos, that of an unbiased observer who aimed to look dispassionately at this controversy and retain a sense of objectivity when representing controversial issues. Giving full attention to "opposing perspectives" promised to offer needed information in the form of structured summaries that would allow audiences to evaluate the legitimacy of Wright's discursive conduct and its possible significance to Obama's campaign. But the very fact that this "story" was given publicity implied that there was something inherently disturbing about Wright's sermons that needed redress. From this perspective, the act of "showing both sides" actually meant showing to the putative shocked audience that there was another side, one in which Wright's perspective was defended.

The *Time* article that published sound bites from Wright's sermons, for example, also included a description of various responses from multiple audiences. "Much of white America," noted *Time* authors, "is unfamiliar with the milieu of the black church. When clips . . . began circulating, many whites heard divisive, angry, unpatriotic pronouncements on race, class and country."[31] In an attempt to be fair and balanced, *Time* reporters endeavored to explain why Wright spoke as he did by contextualizing Wright's rhetorical choices within a narrative about the history of the African American church. "The Reverend Terri Owens, Dean of Students at the University of Chicago Divinity School, says the black church tradition has it roots in the era of slavery, when African Americans held services under trees, far from their white masters. 'Churches have always been the place where black people could speak freely,' she says."

This history matters and I will return to it in the next chapter. But in the context of this *Time* article, giving publicity to that history by calling attention to modes of speech connected to racial identity marginalized as it appeared to enfranchise. The *Time* authors noted that "many blacks" listening to Wright "heard something more familiar: righteous anger about oppression and deliberate hyperbole in laying blame, which are common in sermons delivered in black churches every Sunday." A subtle "othering" accompanied the aim to show "both sides," especially because the act of giving publicity to "another" side was not treated as if it would impel audiences to question how connections are made between representations and judgments of their validity. Rather, the act of representing "the other side" reaffirmed the idea that there is a nondiscriminatory norm at the center of interpretive transactions, and that alternatives may be positioned as deviations.

Indeed, the story about Wright's significance to Obama's campaign was deemed to be newsworthy *because* Wright's statements diverged from "the customary"—in this case, the discursive conventions associated with the white audience attending Sunday services who would not expect a pastor, of all people, to fiercely pronounce indelicacies. The clip of Wright's sermon delivered in the aftermath of the September eleventh attacks seemed to be especially scandalous, given the ways in which Wright broke with the convention that conflated quiet mourning with acts of patriotism, accompanied by an absolute refusal to speculate on U.S. culpability. The "show both sides" method treats the fact of representation as neutral and universally available for democracy's grand conversation, working to enable all perspectives to be heard. Presumably, if one's position has merit, it will be persuasive. But the "show both sides" coverage does not automatically institute equity if one side is constructed *as* a side because it differs from a putative norm. In this case, then, giving publicity to an "other" side effectively converted a complex interpretive site into an orderly representation of opposing perspectives, as if doing so systematically created the conditions that would allow for a just and fair consideration of which side should be chosen.

Discourses that conflate representational action with a presumed preexisting textual order effectively position preformed narratives as baseline standards and then ethical points of reference in judgments of representational controversies. The very act of giving publicity to this story seemed to provide the means for resolving its tensions while supporting commonplace calls to action, such as "rise above divisiveness." Indeed the acts connected to commonplace descriptors of interpretive action are presumably executed no matter how they are described. But as Wright's example shows, a component part of acting to reconcile interpretive dissonance includes overlooking how the narrative of equity can reproduce conditions that generate inequitable outcomes. Instead of considering how representations execute sites of conflict and contest (see Spivak), the fact of representation is treated as an ethical manifestation of inquiry that can be identified as democratic.

Inequities of value inform ways of reading "normative" styles of representation and this was evident in a *Newsweek* column called "Belief Watch" that, like the *Time* magazine article, endeavored to acknowledge "both sides" while adopting the view that Wright's comments were, indeed, scandalous and required an explanation for the audience who was likely offended. Obama's "place of worship" was characterized as "a church of contradictions" that "look[s] so different to different people."[32] Author Lisa Miller, a senior editor at *Newsweek* who "oversees all of its religion coverage" ostensibly endeavored to mull over the significance of those perspective differences, but in an essay filed under the category "On Faith" and posted on-line, Miller instead reaffirmed the idea that "the Wright controversy" compromised Obama's judgment.

> More to the point, how is it that presidential hopeful Barack Obama, a member of that church for two decades, could fail to anticipate how terrifying Wright would look to the rest of the world? Trinity Church, like so many places of worship, is a place of contradictions. From the inside, it's a place of comfort and solace, a place where the most heated conversations are about what kind of music the choir should sing on Sundays: hip hop or gospel. From the outside, it looks like a hotbed of radical, anti-establishment talk.

The writer's affinity with that "outside" view was evident in her use of pronouns: As we learned after September 11, Americans pay scant attention to the religious practices of the minorities among us. When the spotlight does shine on adherents of an unfamiliar religion or religious movement, we do a bad job trying to understand them and they, in turn, do a bad job trying to explain themselves.

The Americans categorized as "we" and "familiar" versus those that designated the "unfamiliar" were not only clearly demarcated, the phrase "minorities among us" also indicated assumptions about the reader's ostensible point of view about which styles should be regarded as representative of the citizen collective. Miller's language also conveyed expectations about who would be expected to explain what "they" do as they participate with language and seek to be heard. Her grammatical choices implied that the explanations from those aligned with the group of "they" remained inadequate to those waiting to be convinced that an explanation was offered to appease. "Last Friday, in an effort to gauge just how 'out there' Wright's sermons are in the context of the African-American tradition, *Newsweek* phoned at least two dozen of the country's most prominent and thoughtful African-American scholars and pastors, representing a wide range of denominations and points of view. Not one person would say that Wright had crossed any kind of significant line." This apparent omission was treated as if it justified the reaction of those who remained skeptical and sought further input from candidate Obama, "the person with the most explaining to do."

To not consider how cultural and personal differences infiltrate conceptions of which modes of representation are credible is to effectively safeguard the practice of invoking dominant cultural norms as the standard and genuinely ethical point of reference for assessing who is doing what with language. This default position does not read identity categories such as "race" within intertextual frameworks. Instead, it takes recourse in the narratives of evaluation that privilege neutrality and disinterest as ideal goals for representations that should apply equally to everyone. As Michael Warner notes, abstract pronouns, such as the "we" in "We the People," appear to mark the collective because no single body is referenced with any particularity, while the mechanisms that structure each person's engagement with symbols that demarcate "the collective stance" appear to be universalizable (Mass 379). That generalizing stance may be challenged when the word "public" is conceived intertextually via a "framework for understanding texts against an organized background of the circulation of other texts, all interwoven not just by citational references but by the incorporation of a reflexive circulatory field in the mode of address and consumption" (Warner Public 16). Were we to acknowledge this intertextual complexity, we would also acknowledge that the meanings of terms can only be understood in connection with whatever narratives are already circulating at a given historical moment. We may only speculate on whether there is a rational order beyond narrative organizing ways of making connections between representations and judgments, and our various enculturated perspectives. And as Susan Miller observes, no singular act of reference will compel all audiences to retrieve the same elements within that "background" when determining what a given signifier represents. This is particularly significant when considering how to contend with those signifiers that aim to represent the idea of "race" and its connection to judgments of ethos.

STYLE, RACE, NATIONALISM

The mounting negative publicity given to "the Pastor Problem" began to take a toll and threaten Obama's lead in national opinion polls. The prolonged discussion about those sermons seemed to put pressure on the candidate to act in some way to reestablish trust with audiences who questioned whether his association with Reverend Wright implicated his ability to become the nation's representative. The force of this exigency appeared to be real, as if constituted by a bona fide crisis rather than by, for example, a ginned up media event. One might have wondered about whether "the nation" truly was up in arms about Obama's relationship with Wright or whether the whole event was another controversy fabricated by the press to promote spectator interest. Regardless, Obama decided to respond to calls for an explanation of his relationship to his minister, and did so in an impressive way—by creating an occasion for a speech that restored perceptions of his good character.

On March 18, 2008, Obama took to the stage in Philadelphia, laying claim to the symbolic birthplace of the nation. He called upon citizens to trust his candidacy and recognize his right to seek the office of the president.

> I chose to run for the presidency at this moment in history because I believe deeply that we cannot solve the challenges of our time unless we solve them together—unless we perfect our union by understanding that we may have different stories, but we hold common hopes; that we may not look the same and we may not have come from the same place, but we all want to move in the same direction—towards a better future for our children and our grandchildren. This belief comes from my unyielding faith in the decency and generosity of the American people. But it also comes from my own American story.[33]

Obama described his mixed heritage as "the son of a black man from Kenya and a white woman from Kansas." He delineated his educational experiences that included his having "gone to some of the best schools in America and lived in one of the world's poorest nations." And he noted his wife's legacy as "a black American who carries within her the blood of slaves and slave owners—an inheritance we pass on to our two precious daughters." But his overarching theme was that of unity. "It's a story that hasn't made me the most conventional candidate. But it is a story that has seared into my genetic makeup the idea that this nation is more than the sum of its parts—that out of many, we are truly one."

Media coverage of Wright issued a provocation that asked of Obama, just what do you have to say about your private judgments, your private religion, indeed your private *person*, to indicate that you "belong" in the public sphere? Obama responded to that provocation by delivering a measured and yet intense response that not only invoked commonplaces that would wrap the discussion of race into agreeable promises about "building coalitions," but also by referencing his private person and physical body. In offering this narrative to the nation, Obama gave permission to citizens to read his private story (and his body) as a material marker that registered just how far the nation has progressed past that history in which expulsions were more than symbolic. Meanwhile, the rhetorical situation confronting Obama indicated how designators of that "private publicity" are marked differently depending on whose body is put on display for public review. Whereas presidential candidates who are "unmarked" by race typically navigate the public-private domain by discussing, for example, how long they have been married (with marriage being an unspoken requirement for the office of the president), or what food they like to eat, Obama was put in the position of having to call attention to the "color" of his body. "Some commentators," he noted, "have deemed me either 'too black' or 'not black enough,'" a sentence that gave an indication of the anomalous context surrounding this speech. How many political candidates have stood before a national audience and made a decision to reiterate such claims? And how many could do so without communicating annoyance about having to make that decision? As with his response to Biden, instead of showing irritation at being put in this position, Obama delivered a speech on race that acknowledged that while perceptions of embodied racial differences may continue to create divisions between some citizens, it is also possible to see signs of reconciliation triumphing over struggle.

The speech was hailed as a stupendous success and earned high praise. "Mr. Obama's Profile in Courage" ran the headline of an editorial in the *New York Times*. "BAM Shows Amazing Grace—Race Speech was One for the Ages" headlined a story in the *New York Daily News*.

"Obama may have wished to avoid this moment, but when he found he could not, he handled it with courage and candor and grace," wrote Cynthia Tucker in *The Atlanta Journal-Constitution*. The candidate spoke openly and compellingly "with a pander-free hour, at a difficult moment in his campaign. It doesn't happen often."

"Obama's speech will go down in history as one of the best modern speeches about America's on-going racial divide . . . He handled the controversy over Rev. Wright's remarks with agility and deftness," wrote Tod Robberson in *The Dallas Morning News*.

"Obama Urges U.S. to Grapple with Race Issue" ran another headline in the *New York Times*. According to author Jeff Zeleny,

> Mr. Obama again condemned the more incendiary remarks of the pastor, the Rev. Jeremiah A. Wright Jr. By drawing on his experiences as the son of a white mother and a black father, Mr. Obama went on to try to explain to white voters the anger and frustration behind Mr. Wright's words and to urge blacks to understand the sources of the racial fears and resentments among whites . . . His language reached at times for the inspiration and idealism of the civil rights movement, but for the most part addressed the politics of race in straightforward terms that seemed intended to keep the discussion grounded it the realities of the moment.[34]

Journalists effectively incorporated a positivistic logic to praise the speech and then Obama, and to explain why the speech mattered and was memorable. In the process they exemplified the ways in which normative views that link authenticity to integrity oversee ways of judging who is credible and powerful. Most crucially, Obama's use of both intimate examples and generalizations about "all people" was regarded not as a rhetorical tactic but as the antithesis of political calculation. Presumably, if one chooses to speak in this way about *this* difficult issue, then one must be speaking genuinely and honestly. And that sense of honesty was part of what, for many commentators, gave Obama's speech integrity and solidified a sense of his noble character.

"Under Fire, Obama Tackles Race Relations Head-On" noted a headline from an editorial in *USA Today*. Walter Rubel's view (Las Cruces Sun-News, New Mexico) was similar. "I tuned in Tuesday expecting the same kind of shallow platitudes politicians typically turn to when forced to confront this issue. . . . Instead the speech was the most honest and forthright examination of this issue that I've heard from a public official." Editors at the Monterey County Herald (CA) declared that "the true genius of the Obama speech was both its frankness about the nation's racial problems and its insistence that America is not defined by the evil of its past, but rather by its ability to repent and to be redeemed by our efforts to renew the bright promises of our nation's founding."[35]

Obama's speech seemed to move audiences to a new context that not only looked straight at the "pastor problem" but also aimed at something beyond—transcendence itself: "Obama on Race: A Visionary Speech Reminds This Nation of Its Better Self" (*Salt Lake Tribune*); "Beyond Racism: Obama Strives to Build Bridge" (*San Jose Mercury*). According to the *Arkansas Democratic Gazette*, "In a stroke this young man lifted us out of ourselves. He rose above the usual, petty political calculations and resultant doldrums, sought to rekindle a national faith in the possibility of shared interests and community and by most reports, he succeeded." In a *Washington Post* commentary, "Invited to Wrestle in a Racial Mud Pit, Obama Soars Above It," Courtland Milloy recounted his interpretive process that included an initial desire to reiterate commonplace complaints about "how slimy the presidential campaign had become" and "about those whites who want Obama to 'transcend race' while they get to hold on to their racist ways." All of that changed after listening to Obama's speech. "Then Obama spoke and I had a mind-altering experience. After hearing him deliver what was essentially a treatise on faith, hope, and charity, I no longer wanted to risk getting stuck in a racial tar pit . . . I just wanted to hop on that Obama bandwagon and head for a new America"[36] For those who were impressed, the speech had character and so did the speaker. By directly addressing a thorny and difficult issue, Obama provided audiences not only with evidence of his personal integrity but also of his sincere desire to foster acts of communication and mutuality.

But given that these responses occurred within a context that also wrangled with the question of whether and how to represent categories of race, it is also important to note that part of what made Obama's race speech seem remarkable was that his rhetorical style/ethos seemed to differ dramatically from Wright's. Obama commanded attention by delivering an eloquent response in a style that echoed those old Belletristic lessons in civility. Indeed, he effectively said, "Let us be civilized" and called upon everyone to identify with that "us." From this perspective, Obama mesmerized by deploying discursive practices that seemed to channel persuasive power towards satisfactory impulses rather than unsavory ones.

This stance was conveyed stylistically and via content that delivered a familiar message: Be in accord. In offering a speech that reconciled angst with hope, he managed to both deliver a thematic message about conciliation through a style that enacted a structural unity that merged emotion with reason, private with public, the prosaic with the spiritual. For theorists like Marshall W. Alcorn, this kind of harmonious strategizing constitutes the very character of a modern ethos. "If the modern self is highly divided, and if reconciling the self's inner voices of opposition is the task of both rhetoric and self-building, then texts that activate and direct these oppositions and reconciliations embody the key principles of modern ethos" (28).

Obama's speech could also be read as exemplifying the architectonic structure that appears to represent and produce the requisite rhetorical action for instigating shared acts of identification and communal dwelling. Obama constructed a persona that appeared to be trustworthy by exhibiting language choices that aimed to participate coherently with that existent text-based interpretive order. Because of this apparent alignment, it was possible to ascribe to his speech the power that presumably engineers the transactional dynamic that uniformly constitutes social identities by invoking undeviating interpretive procedures. Accordingly, all were implicated by the idea that a theme of commonality can unite us and get us to look past perceived differences. By proclaiming this version of equity in a speech that appeared to be stylistically and emotionally "balanced," Obama simultaneously delivered a message of unity that also produced a felt sense of balance. If the power of his speech could then be attributed to an internal representational dynamic intrinsic to language, then the act of identifying his "good character" would seem to merge with the act of aligning his specific locutions with a timeless, apolitical, transcendent, and equitable force that generally oversees communication.

It is important to note that while this framework underwrote the praise given to Obama, it also appeared to explain and justify the criticism of Wright, whose sermons were instead read as a troublesome deviation from a discursive aim to both advocate and represent linguistic harmony. Arguably, the word *race* was invoked in mainstream media reports to reaffirm the validity of the idea that, to be ethical, citizens should internalize the cultural imposition of disciplinary power. Because this message is also embedded within dominant interpretive practices, the socio-political relations between the use of particular discursive practices and the acquisition of cultural authority tend to go unnoticed. Once a premium is placed upon a limited set of stylized formal patterns, then citizens will be expected to look for them and ascribe to them automatic significance. One's good will seems to be manifested when one uses language in a way that communicates a commitment to the idea that situations recur and call for familiar, habituated, discursive formulations packaged in styles that provoke acceptable emotional responses. Meanwhile, those utterances/texts that fail to exhibit expected patterns may be justifiably dismissed.

Ethos and Cultural Hegemony

By conflating the display of a culturally sanctioned representational order with a generalized "good will," theories of ethos simultaneously engender an interpretive technology that validates the act of ignoring the "cultural zones and social spaces of mediation" (Jackson 261) relevant to citizens who are marginalized within culturally dominant interpretive locations. A less charitable response to Obama's speech might point out that what garnered audience identification was Obama's willingness to police his speech—that in an interpretive context that denigrated his minister's ardent fight for social justice, what Obama's speech generated was a comforting reassurance about his relationship to an interpretive space of mediation that includes a history of fears about angry black men.[37] Arguably, Obama's style of speech conveyed a promise to use language in ways that did not challenge the legitimacy of that specific historical narrative. His ability to captivate audiences was due in part to a mode of delivery that expressed a disciplined (prudent? domesticated?) discernment, textually realized through a style that seemed to command attention by displaying a measured yet potent incisiveness that produced powerful but culturally sanctioned affective responses.

For theorists who analyze the reproduction of cultural hegemony, this kind of validation provides one of the most effective means of naturalizing discourses of power that contribute to making it possible to invalidate "deviant" representational practices. Here we can note Gayatri Spivak's explorations of the ways in which dominant discourses reproduce systems of power by privileging their own methods for drawing categorical differences, including those that would identify differences between the "normative" and the "marginal." This privileging demands that all speakers imitate the "dominant cultural voice" to garner an authorized and legitimated ethos. When Robert Con Davis and David S. Gross apply Spivak's work to theories of ethos, the terms change for evaluating representational aims that depend upon the act of identifying "the discourse of the 'other'" (68) via an act of marginalization. Theories of ethos have historically not addressed how conceptualized exclusions establish the very mechanisms that seem to enable "good discursive character" to make an appearance. Hence, according to Davis and Gross, "the difficulty of representing the other is the problem of defining the concept of ethos in a manner responsive to the critique of colonial, neo-colonial and postcolonial practices" (68).

When charting conceptions of how an exclusionary interpretive dynamic can appear to be inclusive, a doubled perspective may be adopted—one that simultaneously works with and challenges prevailing visions of how language acts to constitute knowledge about the quality and character of identity categories (such as race or citizen or nation). Here, it is possible to take a cue from scholars affiliated with the study of African American rhetoric and communication, who trace the ways in which cultural narratives that conflate "neutrality" with morality effectively erase a lived history of conflict that has not disappeared for speakers whose styles are read as noticeable rather than unobtrusive. Such speakers may neither valorize nor read benevolent aims in those stylistic markers that get treated within dominant cultures as automatic agents of moral interpretive action. And they may find that disaffiliating with prevailing cultural scripts about how to linguistically constitute "good character" can add an element of emotional dissonance to the endeavor to craft an ethos that will be read as an acceptable and respected aspect of discourse.

For example, in an article that examines the rhetorical strategies of nineteenth century African American rhetoric, Victoria Cliett challenges the narratives of universalism embedded within discourses conventionally regarded as inclusive and inherently democratic. Cliett's argument is congenial with Michael Warner's and traces how the word *we*, when used within public and legal documents as if automatically representative of everyone, instead invokes "a code of social relations" that marginalize discursive styles associated with African American speech by labeling those stylistic practices as "merely dialect" (171). The discriminatory part of the code of relations may be ignored when the idea of neutrality is summoned to veil the power dynamic that underwrites the ability to label language practices identified with race (and ethnicity) as "abnormal," potentially deviant, and in need of surveillance. According to Cliett, the ostensibly neutral term "democracy" is implicated by this dynamic. "The idea of democracy assumes a natural relationship between a subject/citizen and a community in which the subject/citizen is represented within the community and is also a representative of the community" (171). In practice, however, to be recognized as belonging to "the" community, African American writers were required to "perform within the formalized frame of Standard English and its ideologies" (171–2) by mimicking the prescribed styles that also signified their cultural subordination. One potential result: rather than finding unity between narrative and selfhood, speakers experienced psychic and somatic ruptures and then a "structure of double consciousness" (180). The discursive histories that excluded blacks from full membership in public life and structures double consciousness "elicits dual readings in American society that necessitate the African American subject to see himself or herself simultaneously in the detached gaze of White America and the frustration of Black" (180).

Indeed, the interpretive mechanism that would seem to solidify everyone's potential to get harmoniously positioned within an ethics of representation instead can enact feelings of alienation, particularly when an invisible motive like "has concern for others" is ascribed to a limited and exclusionary set of discursive practices that get treated as if they are infused with a moral teleology that carries an inherently recognizable force. Ronald L. Jackson II not only explores how a sense of estrangement has accompanied the communication practices for African Americans historically, he also notes its damaging effects on African American Communication scholars who are expected to adopt sanctioned academic styles when discussing how racial identity and language use intersects with the rhetorical acts of identification that presumably build communities. "Essentially, many African American Communicologists are being forced to negotiate their identities on a daily basis in academe . . . We tend to function with a Du Boisian 'double consciousness' . . . It is extremely difficult to maintain complete alliances to African American epistemologies and ontologies; hence identity negotiation ensues" (250).

Scholars of African American rhetoric and communication have long argued that language practices are not universal but instead reflect differing cultural perspectives on what part of an interpretive dynamic has significance. In *The Voice of Black Rhetoric*, Arthur Smith and Stephen Robb consider how differing cultural perspectives will influence perceptions of what aspect of language use generates persuasive power. The authors note: "It is a cardinal mistake in our society to operate on the basis that language functions of whites are everywhere reproducible in black societies in terms of influences and ends" (qtd. in Gilyard 12).

Eric King Watts examines the relationship between cultural identity and rhetorical style with reference to the work of Alain Locke's *The New Negro*, tracing how Locke reinvented the very meaning of the word *race* by rejecting the conventional wisdom that envisions race to be biological, proposing instead that the category of "race" be "conceived as an idiom or a style" (75). Accordingly, "'race' is derived from cultural practices that can reasonably be grouped together" (75). Watts notes that Locke recognized the value of cultural difference and maintained that discursive practices must be understood in terms of the demands of the cultural contexts in which they arise. Similarly, Michael L. Hecht, Sidney Ribeau, and J. K. Alberts argue, "Cultural distinctiveness, and its attendant differences, may be most notably expressed in communication rules and style" (105). "Contrary to the assumption that Afro-Americans and whites share identical speech and cultural conventions, [there are] differing norms and social styles, pointing to divergent patterns of intonation, expressive intensity, spontaneity, aggressiveness and argument" (106). Any refusal to acknowledge that audiences may not share visions of which language practices should be valued imposes, as Davis and Gross observe, a "colonial, neocolonial, and postcolonial" framework on the interpretive dynamic that formulates a culturally dominant ethos, encoding the violence of expulsion within that framework's very conception. "Civilized groups rationalize the imposition of their identities on others," notes Watts, by "erasing the other's cultural distinctiveness. Such an imposition does not constitute an invitation to dwell in a common place; rather, it signifies the maintenance of abstract categorical schemes of rightness" (78).

Once we consider how race describes a rhetorical style, we will find an iteration of the idea that style signifies ways of participating with language that will be read according to the precepts of variously constituted cultural scripts. Those scripts teach audiences how to make connections between apprehensions of stylistic features and judgments of valuable discursive aims. When we acknowledge the ways in which race has functioned as a culturally stigmatized language practice, then we must question the legitimacy of elaborating a rhetoric of ethos that conflates discursive responsibility with representations of textuality inherited from an Enlightenment tradition that claimed an ability to discursively render "the unmarked"/morally superior representational form. This is precisely the tradition that, as Molefi Kete Asanti observes, purposefully enacted exclusions against blacks and rendered their experiences insignificant and effectively invisible and in the process, established the interpretive framework that regard the possibility of difference from a putative norm as a threat to cultural stability (16).

Rhetorical studies of ethos conflate the ethos of a text with an "antecedent ethos" (See Short 369) of the presupposed structural order. This conflation creeps into representations of the transactional apparatus audiences are expected to reference when evaluating the rhetor's language choices. A prior idea of how ethos connects to style will already be in mind, influencing ways of seeing who is doing what with words, and influencing narratives that depict how judgments are authorized and rendered legitimate. Given that the discursive history that has marginalized marked speech remains entrenched, it is possible to question whether Obama had much choice when determining how to respond to "the" public's "shocked" responses to Wright's sermons other than try to ameliorate that response. The racialized dynamics inhabiting this assemblage of terms may go unremarked when ethos is treated as an aspect of a discursive system that organizes how to make connections between speakers, audiences, and the representational expectations that precede an audience's discursive encounters. A general faith in the legitimacy of a dominant antecedent ethos, along with a trust in the mechanisms of a specific kind of textual reproduction, would almost compel a speaker on the national scene to obey discursive protocol if he seeks audience acceptance. To be identified as "good," that speaker will be expected categorically to put forth "normative" discourses aligned with an antecedent ethos as a way of showing that he or she is a trusted language user. Audiences will be expected to approve of the speaker's putative act of "going back" to reference known and familiar speech acts *as* a fulfillment of the social obligation to appear to be trustworthy.

Calling upon rhetors to reference a history of sayings effectively regularizes the transactional work of inference while the ruling paideia will offer support and affirmation by training citizens to be satisfied with representations of that regularity. Obama's apparent willingness to stay neutral garnered him praise. The narratives of acclaim for a speech that offered the possibility of transcendence seemed to simultaneously reenact its power, as if laying claim to a "real" interpretive result. Such responses reaffirmed the ruling paideia that marginalizes in predictable and socially sanctioned ways. When conflating the speech that transcends with a manifestation of good character, narratives of acclaim simultaneously allow for adversarial discourses to be constructed *as* unethical, their persuasive power rendered an obstruction to the "good work" of crafting community. When prescribing modes of participation, narratives championing transcendence offer an especially virulent technology for reproducing power and masking its reproduction.

Given that rhetorical studies emphasize that all judgments are negotiations influenced by time, context, and personal predilections, Wright's example shows how only some acts of negotiation will get read as being emblematic of a national interpretive experience capable of producing dwelling places that others should want to occupy. Further, a generic conception of rhetorical action will fail to consider how any occupation will also enact dislocations maintained, at least in part, by the social bonds of emotional satisfaction drawn around a presumed ability to ethically and regularly exclude the language practice that is not welcome. When the "problem" of race is hurled into a national conversation about who a candidate is that then implicates who "we" are as we respond to a perceived problem, then any response to that putative "problem" requires more careful consideration of how audiences are expected to convert the "convenient fictions" that accompany interactions with language into seemingly stable points of reference for enacting those sound and morally responsible judgments that seem to characterize our own good sense.

Critical analysis can begin with a look at the presupposed inevitability of emotional responses to discursive power and a willingness to question whose emotional experiences with narratives seem to speak for the collective and why. Subjects adopt multiple identities when participating in the power structures that regulate conceptions of how language practices become authoritative. This attention to cultural positionality promotes a "new" conception of ethos "constituted by race and ethnicity as these signs function as markers within late capitalist society and culture" (Con Davis and Gross 67) to reveal not a neutral and equitable economy of interpretive exchange, but a tangled, irregular, thorny dynamic that can act to position ethos "at the site of social oppression" (Con Davis and Gross 67). Rather than prioritize a conflation between a textually-inflected representational order and moral virtue, the study of ethos might include the act of excavating the ruling paideia and the emotional attachments citizens are expected to have to epistemological presuppositions that organize conceptions of rhetorical action. Ethos would mark a site of interpretive fracturing that accompanies any suturing between reception and a representation's production. Hence style would be read not as a resource for assessing whether speakers show good will towards their audiences, but as a site for considering how cultural ideologies affect ways of judging who to credit and believe.

Indeed, the moment that we feel or recognize the emotionally satisfying representation, we signal a point of contact between our personal predilections and the "complex of apparatuses, practices . . . and assemblages" (Rose qtd. in Greene 50) that have been culturally deployed to organize a ruling paideia that shapes perspectives of which modes of linguistic participation have value. Rather than revel in the satisfaction produced by an given set of assemblages and read a correspondence between an enactment and an ideal as ethical, we may question how we have been trained to feel satisfied when particular kinds of rhetorical styles make an appearance and authorize us to ascribe and withhold judgments of who and what is credible.

On the other hand, it is equally important to not attribute the positive responses to Obama's speech only to the coercive forces of dominant ideologies, as if doing so could fully explain power's appeal. That attribution reinstalls a logic of hierarchies. It replaces the nebulous space of judgment with an explanatory narrative that seems to fully describe how judgments are rendered. And it positions that narrative at the site of what is specifically rhetorical—the performative and lived part of our interactions with linguistic productions that cannot be contained within statements that would describe what happens as we judge. The "lived" experiences of our encounters with texts (oral and written) affect receptivity but in ways that exceed narrative depiction. In attempting to describe why Obama's speech was effective we might note, for example, that its power did not emerge solely because he was able to construct a palatable persona that soothed anxious voters, but also because he showed compassion and a heartening kindness when addressing an issue that might otherwise have provoked ire. As with that early 2007 response to Biden's bungled comment, Obama implicitly said, "I get it. I get that race is a big deal for some people and that, unlike any other candidate, I will have to talk intimately about my personhood, even thought that demand is itself a racist one. Rather than scoff or respond with sarcasm at the buffoonery of this false 'urgency,' I will ask people to be their better selves." In showing compassion, Obama also showed wisdom, fighting his critics by reaffirming his right to lay claim to the narrative of "America," a claim he had already begun when he delivered his remarkable keynote speech at the 2004 Democratic convention. Obama presented himself as an embodied rhetorical subject authorizing himself to call upon citizens to have faith in an ideal, trusting his audience to read him and his story sympathetically while simultaneously referencing his person as proof of the ideal's achievable reality. From this perspective, his speech bore witness to that razor's edge locus in which positive change remains imaginable, and where we can hope that potential progress may be converted into a reality.

I make this point because when discussing why words galvanize, it is important to consider how our relationship with linguistic power is erratic, especially within speculations about ideology's role in the training of affect. To say that speech is ideology is to reduce the significance of inexplicable powers that may be categorized under the term *aesthetic*. Any explanation of why certain texts galvanize will fail to contend with the radical potential within Aristotle's advice to only *seem to be* a particular way. This premise restores the centrality of what Kathleen McHugh calls "the enigma of the aesthetic" (244), an enigma that, arguably, implicates our conceptions of a rhetor's character. Acknowledging the role of the aesthetic within political thought reminds us to preserve a humble skepticism about the legitimacy of our interpretive technologies, particularly those that are authorized by historical precedent. At most, our methods of interpretation allow us to tentatively explain why any text might move our intellect and passions. More importantly, how we think we should respond to aesthetic/fictional enigmas inherent to our use of narrative will influence how we think we should evaluate the credibility of political candidates. Indeed, we may encounter "epistemic antagonisms" (McPhail 32) in response to the question of which part of any explanatory narrative or conceptual framework is authoritative and representative of a dependable ethics of interpretation, and that antagonism need not be definitively resolved.

The power of the aesthetic may be found within its capacity to disrupt our ways of affiliating with ruling conventions that influence how texts are received. Rhetorical studies of ethos erect a language of foundations when configuring dwelling places exactly at that point where ephemeral and ambiguous elements of persuasion emerge to affect audience receptivity to styles and ideas. While Obama's race speech provides an occasion for thinking about the ways in which textuality is positioned as a point of reference for judgments of what appears to be the good man speaking well, the inability to totally explain its power also provides an occasion for raising questions about what gets referenced within judgments that appear to demonstrate an ethics of interpretation. When an order of narrative is positioned as a legitimizing resource for enfranchisement, the unruly "event" of reception gets subordinated. As put by Bryan C. Short, "the ethics of . . . ethos . . . resides in an 'authentic' (the term is even theological) temporality related to the possibility of resistance to ideology . . . of momentary discourse questioning, destabilizing, and redefining the determining structures of language" (377). From this perspective, the ethical act of interpretation will remain alert to the doubled dynamic in which a need to craft conceptual order coexists with the potentiality of aesthetic power that exceeds that order and whatever explanations it promises to provide. And this was so in 2008. The power of change was simultaneously present and contained. Even as the citizens of the United States engaged in a historically momentous decision to elect a man of color to be the nation's representative, public discussions about race relied upon inherited conceptions of ethos and style to reproduce "an exclusionary form of nationalism."[38]

4 Inhabiting the Call to Change

If speakers garner cultural authority by displaying stylistic competence, then it should be possible to delineate how competency is discursively represented. Another iteration of this idea can be found within rhetorical studies of genre. Genres are styles writ large. They invoke the recognizable representational form to mark an absence: an order of thinking; an identifiable methodology to organize participation with symbolic constructs. Like other branches of rhetorical inquiry, genre studies organize conceptions of persuasive power while acknowledging that representational processes are malleable. Rhetoricians regard genres as elastic categories that become meaningful when situated contextually and with reference to an order of textuality. The gap between meaning's unrestricted potentiality and the representation that may be generically identified is bridged by consulting discursive histories that have also established the means for distinguishing responsible language uses from disreputable ones. Genres facilitate collective understanding of who is doing what with words.

To accept genres as valid signposts aiding acts of reception, we must forget what interpretive steps must be taken to enable the categorical type to be not only recognizable, but also relevant to the occasion of its use. When acting as a place-holder for a process of mediation, genres will displace other conceptions of discursive interaction by retaining a conserving (and hence conservative) framework that affirms the idea that unbridled expressive possibilities should be controlled. Genre studies suggest that part of rhetoric's purpose is to convince audiences to internalize a preference for the repetition of forms that appear to have been used in orderly ways on prior interpretive occasions. In effect, genre studies teach subjects to associate the act of retrieving a sanctioned form with the enactment of representational virtue.

This chapter situates this premise at the center of further analysis of media representations of candidate Barack Obama and the Reverend Jeremiah Wright, who continued to be hammered by negative publicity during the spring of 2008. Of interest is a key statement from Obama's race speech, as well as a series of public appearances made by Wright in April as he attempted to reclaim his good name. Wright's attempt to speak publicly and restore his reputation failed. Not only was he subjected to another round of negative publicity, his mode of delivery provoked controversy and prompted an official expulsion from Obama. This move was generally applauded and deemed necessary to the survival of Obama's campaign.

In this chapter, I turn to genre studies to consider how it was possible for the press to heap negative publicity on Wright as if such publicity was not only warranted but also apolitically motivated. I aim to show a connection between the media's treatment of Wright and dominant interpretive frameworks, like those advanced by genre studies, that endorse some of the same premises that have been explored throughout book: difference remains subordinated to identity, reduced to a principle of negativity, rendered an obstacle to achieving interpretive unity. The very idea of difference—including discursive difference—is effectively expelled from authorizing technologies of evaluation. Perspectival unity is proposed as an inherently ethical representational goal and audiences are trained to look for representational similitude as key to community formation. By failing to contend with interpretive negotiation's uneven processes, genre studies minimize the ways in which audiences may feel differently about whether a given style manifests a trustworthy, inspirational, recognizable, and valuable act of representation. In effect, genre studies sustain the interpretive hierarchy that prioritizes the cultural reproduction of dominant styles over those that, in refusing to follow "generic" codes, get rebuked as "renegade."[1]

Genre's Reflexive Action

Genre offers one way of understanding why the "good man" who speaks well may be trusted when he puts forth acts of representation that follow a "strong narrative rule." That phrase comes courtesy of an article by Gerard Hauser and Chantal Benoit-Barne that defines the parameters of discursive trust. Trust, they argue, emerges in rhetorical situations when rhetors reference familiar representational forms as a way of indicating a desire to be communal. The familiar form will feature language uses that are recognizable, culturally sanctioned, and stylistic competent. Indeed, competency is key when facilitating the give and take that inheres within the interpretive labor undertaken by solicitous rhetors and skeptical audiences. When stylistic competency overcomes suspicions and inspires trust, it effectively advances the very essence of democratic action.

Because trust emerges through a dynamic of negotiation, it is situated within the realm of the social, acting not as an objective entity but as an intangible phenomenon that functions rhetorically to both designate and enact interpretation as a communal endeavor rather than a solitary one. Rhetorical trust dispenses with the isolated preferences and personal sentiments possessed by individual selves, marking instead a site of reflexive mediation, a potentiality that requires conscious deliberation and then active consent from audiences who make choices when determining which acts of representation seem to be trustworthy. Hence, rhetorical trust is depicted as "social capital" (270) that serves a social purpose.

When situated within the realm of the social, then certain conditions must be delineated so that everyone will know what to do when speaking with the purpose of earning trust. These conditions form the basis of a social contract overseeing acts of communication in which all agree to adhere to a "normative dimension" that "makes trust self-sustaining" (Hauser and Benoit-Barne 270). Accordingly, "to trust, one must rely on the familiar to anticipate the unfamiliar in the sense that one uses the available repertoire of experiences to form expectations" (269) about who is doing what with language. Speakers should be willing to use languages in familiar ways to inspire trust, especially when "dealing with circumstances of strangeness" (269). By assenting to a social contract that promotes trust, citizens can actively devise a framework for interpretation that generates and sustains participatory communicative exchanges.

We can extrapolate from this argument and posit genre as a representative example of a trustworthy representational form. Genres earn our trust because once identified, they give advance notice of how a text or utterance should be read. Through genre, the unknown speech act is converted into something familiar and situated within an identifiable and orderly rubric overseeing the interpretive transaction. Genres might be said to be trustworthy because they seem to guarantee that control may be exerted over language's performative possibilities, anchoring language use to a promise to satisfy expectations to fulfill contractual obligations.

While rhetorical theories of genre do not discuss trust explicitly, the social benefits of genre studies are certified with a similar logic. Sonja K. Foss, for example, explains how "generic criticism is rooted in the assumption that certain types of situations provoke similar needs and expectations in audiences and thus call for particular kinds of rhetoric" (134). Significantly, those expectations give genres their performative power as they intersect with three elements that exist in all speech situations and could be called elemental. These include the audience's perception of conditions affecting the interpretive moment, the invocation of proper styles, and the internal dynamic of a constellating process through which the apprehension of a rhetorical situation is "fused" to an exercise of judgment.[2]

Here, we can note how this narrative of fusing promotes a conception of anonymity as an endorsed source of representational power for generating familiar and then trustworthy representations. Conceptions of that fusing dynamic are worth reviewing for what they seem to tell us about the dynamic of interpretive conversions that transform the apprehension of form into a judgment of its value and trustworthiness. Because genre studies seem to offer a flexible rubric when charting how audiences connect the apprehension of generic signs to judgments of moral action, they appear themselves to be trustworthy and aligned with the expansive and inclusive aims of democratic inquiry. The "constellating process" premise reiterates a generalizing narrative about rhetorical action but it also acknowledges the significance of specific and changeable rhetorical events. By accommodating the general and the specific, the rhetorical study of genre is rendered a supple tool in any analysis of how persuasive power works. It reiterates the rhetorical idea that any rhetorical intervention will involve the interplay between what is enduring and what is changeable.

This commodious approach to the study of genre can be traced back to a seminal essay published in the 1970s by Karlyn Kohrs Campbell and Kathleen Hall Jamieson, who invigorated genre studies by calling for a rhetorical understanding of genre that challenged the prevailing conception of genre as an objective form that may be empirically identified. Rather, they define genre as rhetorical form that is "recurrent" and "reflexive" (444).

> In a number of cases, critics have assumed, *a priori*, that a genre already exists and is known and defined—e.g., the sermon, the presidential inaugural, the apology, among others—and an in-

ductive procedure, content analysis in some cases, applied to parse its elements. Such studies are suspect because the *a priori* definition of a genre and identification of its members generates a circular argument: an essential and preliminary procedure defining the generic characteristics has been omitted. Generic critics need to recognize explicitly the assumptions they are making and the procedures required to establish their claims. (455)

Campbell and Jamieson introduced the phrase "constellation of [fused] elements" in order to "emphasize the interrelationships among generic elements. Genres often exist in dynamic responsiveness to situational demands" (456). They illustrate what they mean through analogy.

The stars forming a constellation are individuals but they are influenced by each other and by external elements; consequently they move together and remain in a similar relation to each other despite their varying positions over time. Like genres, constellations are perceived patterns with significance and usefulness—they enable us to see the movements of a group of individual stars and they enable us to understand the interrelated forces in celestial space. . . . Approaching [rhetorical] acts generically gives the critic an unusual opportunity to penetrate their internal workings and to appreciate the interacting forces that create them. (456-57)

The study of genre promises to provide a methodology for accounting for rhetorical success if it is possible to take stock of how we evaluate texts by delineating those "internal" elements of rhetorical action and how they interrelate within specific moments of judgment. Genre theories seem to challenge positivistic logics by incorporating a narrative that characterizes interpretive processes as active, variable, and yet influenced by well-established social practices. Genre studies suggest that the dynamic of persuasion occurs in typical ways because situations recur and demand standard (conventional) responses. Ethics is implicated because the good rhetor is the person able to grasp how a present occasion of speech connects to and is informed by past occasions, and in understanding those relationships, determines how to stylize words that will prompt audience adherence.

Here it is possible to see connections between genre study and that of ethos and propriety. Genres might be characterized as modes of speech that allow the rhetor to create familiar "dwelling places" that listeners may inhabit as they evaluate whether a rhetor's words will earn their regard and approval. A favorable ethos would seem to be one result of a confluence that involves putting prudence and exigency in action by formulating discursive styles that winningly convey the attributes of generic discursive models and hence promote trust over estrangement. From this perspective, genres can be characterized as ethical resources within explanatory narratives of how the constellating fusion within persuasive power works. This is especially so once their mediating work is conflated with a neutral linguistic force that supersedes the personal biases and cultural conditioning that inevitably affects judgments of what has significance and value. Because our judgments of genre seem to follow identifiable procedures within situations that "recur," then, as put by Carolyn R. Miller, their very invocation can be regarded as being representative of "typified rhetorical action" (151). It is that aspect of "the typical" that enables rhetorical scholars to look to genre to "*account* for the way we encounter, interpret, react to and create particular texts" (151—my emphasis). Genres chart patterns of identification and presumably the motives that people have for identifying with a given pattern, motives that would seem to be knowable, explainable, and redeemable.

Arguably, responses to Barack Obama's speech on race in 2008 exemplified this dynamic. The unfamiliar and "new" presidential candidate put forth a redeemable pattern of signs when he reiterated the customary idea that a representational ethics can be achieved through interpretive acts of transcendence. Obama's particular strength upon that occasion of speech could be described as an ability to take a conventional narrative about democratic unity and make it seem both fresh and achievable.

The idea that rhetorical action can be "typified" presumes to describe what cannot be observed, including the act of conversion itself, the act in which apprehension moves to comprehension and then judgment of whether a given representation has effectively convinced audiences to accept that a recurrent motif continues to have significance and value. Such theorizing raises questions about how and where to locate both the element of "the typical" and "the energized" response to its exhibition. The attempt to describe transactional components of interpretive experiences may appear to be flexible but it nonetheless will arrest conceptions of how transactions occur and effectively portray those actions as inevitable and predictable. This dynamic plays out in conventional discussions that envision persuasive power in the shape of a rhetorical triangle. Typically, rhetoricians depict persuasion flowing within a triad comprised of rhetor, text, and audience positioned within changeable contexts. This model expresses a cause and effect logic in which one element within the triad can be counted on to affect the others via a regularizing flow of constituting influences (i.e., my purpose will influence my word choices and then my intended audience). But as Drew Loewe observes, the languages that we use to characterize what occurs as a result of discursive interactions impose a "possessory vocabulary to describe what is really a relational judgment" (245). That vocabulary takes hold through the repetition of narratives that would explain the contours of interpretive processes by describing the mechanisms that drive and compel persuasion's force. So, for example, student writers are instructed to consider questions such as, "Have I established the purpose of my text, and have I utilized the most effective genre?" The unspoken implication is that an affirmative answer will help the student engage the persuasive power that activates how rhetor, text, and audiences "move together and remain in a similar relation to each other."Once genres are deemed to be trustworthy, their ethical character seems to be mobilized through their very invocation. The rhetor who decides to use the recognizable genre seems to do his or her job of responsibly enacting persuasive power to provoke audience adherence.

But it is also the case that any narrative that would describe interpretation as a transaction to account for what happens as we engage with symbols will also structure expectations and then experiences of how rhetorical power enacts identification. The conception of interpretation within genre studies that combines "typical and recurrent" with "renewable action" effectively imposes a prefabricated way of seeing interrelationships within rhetorical situations. Such formulations ostensibly champion the idea of a changeable dynamic but then incorporate a principle of stability without fully accounting for how that move is made possible. To the extent that genres appear to be identifiable, any theorizing about their role in aiding communicative processes will correlate ethics with being conventional. The invocation of the conventional will act as a kind of criteria, a silent point of reference preceding any local judgment about how to evaluate what is typical in relation to what seems to be new. Genres support the idea that discursive practices should be orderly and that orderly acts of representation will be expressed via specific styles that aim to reproduce what is already recognizable.

Generic Hope

Campbell and Jamieson illustrate how the dynamic of generic fusion played out in a remarkable speech delivered by Congresswoman Barbara

Jordan at the 1976 Democratic Convention. Jordan was elected to the State Senate in Texas in 1966, the first African American state senator since 1883 and the first black woman to serve at all. She won a seat in the U.S. Congress in 1972, where she served until 1979, when she retired from politics. Jordan was reportedly considered to be a possible running mate for incumbent President Jimmy Carter but was not chosen. Instead she was tapped to give the 1976 keynote address speech. That speech is listed as the fifth most important speech in Top 100 American Speeches of the 20th century, compiled in 1999 by researchers at the University of Wisconsin-Madison and Texas A & M University.

Campbell and Jamieson note that when Jordan spoke, her words electrified the audience and earned her a standing ovation (444). "There is something different about tonight," Jordan said by way of introduction. "There is something special about tonight. What is different? What is special? I, Barbara Jordan, am a keynote speaker" (qtd. in Campbell and Jamieson 444). The thunderous applause that followed those introductory remarks also followed her next galvanizing statement: "And I feel that, notwithstanding the past, my presence here is one additional piece of evidence that the American dream need not forever be deferred" (qtd. on 444).

The power enacted by this speech, argue Campbell and Jamieson, had more to do with Jordan's position as keynote speaker and less to do with what she said. Accordingly "an 'enactment'" is a speech event in which the speaker "incarnates the argument" and simultaneously offers "the proof of the truth of what has been said" (444), and in this case, Jordan's speech succeeded because *she* represented what she described. Jordan's speech galvanized audiences because as she stood at the podium, she called attention to her embodied presence and conveyed a willingness to highlight the uniqueness of that positioning in order to deliver a communal message about national pride and a promising future for all citizens. As a black woman, Jordan was unlike the typical speaker at political conventions and her difference from that norm added to the audience's sense that they were witnessing a remarkable moment. She may have given many speeches throughout her career, but most memorable was this speech, one that disrupted expectations about who could deliver a mesmerizing message at a conventional political event.

But for Campbell and Jamieson, the electricity sparked by Jordan's speech began and ended with her introductory comments and the fact of her presence on the stage. The rest of her speech, they argue, was a rather generic and regularized keynote that refashioned old tropes and made common claims. Campbell and Jamieson write an alternative speech that they say might have been delivered to further enthrall audiences, one that would call even more attention to what was unconventional about Jordan's presence on the stage:

> Imagine Congresswoman Jordan saying these words next: They did not make keynote addresses, nor indeed addresses of any sort, the Barbara Jordans of those days. They were not welcomed into this, or any other, political party. Surely some of them, some of those blacks, some of those women, were as able as I, and undoubtedly were far more gifted . . . It is for that other Barbara Jordan, for all the blacks and women and minorities and poor people of yesterday and tomorrow, that I ask your support. (445)

The critique of Jordan's speech conveys unspoken assumptions about the very function of rhetoric and what should be its motives and aims.[3] The proposed alternative suggests that Jordan should have used the occasion to do more than replicate the standard political speech. She instead should have delivered a statement that would be memorable for being atypical. When Campbell and Jamieson assess Jordan's speech as generic, they effectively enact the conversion described by Loewe; they invoke the language of possession as a placeholder for a particular way of drawing connections between elements within a rhetorical scene. Presumably, had Jordan made other choices, her speech would have accomplished more than reiterating generic platitudes. A way of situating and then seeing Jordan's speech within a context of prior political speeches was expressed as an assessment of what her speech lacked, which, in this case was a noticeable difference from a putative norm.

The paradox here is that the expectation of "going beyond the norm" is itself generic in political contexts and does not address the question of specifically how such an expectation might be fulfilled in stimulating ways. We might agree, for example, that their proposed alternative was compelling or not, but beyond that local assessment, we should note that the idea that the political speaker should inspire with innovative rhetoric treats such rhetoric as an identifiable phenomenon and as such, a phenomenon that audiences might legitimately expect to encounter when assessing the value and effectiveness of any given speech. Presumably, an inspiring-because-innovative speech may act as a valid point of reference when explaining why someone galvanized an audience or failed to. In this regard, Jimmy Carter could be said to be a failure. When speaking realistically to citizens about the energy crisis during the 1970s, asking homeowners to curtail the use of energy at home, he did not even try to meet the "be inspiring" expectation in any familiar way. President Ronald Reagan, who in 1980 defeated incumbent President Carter, is memorialized as the man of inspiration *par excellence*, one who Obama invoked favorably in 2008 in an interview in which he praised Reagan's capacity to invigorate audiences and then put the nation "on a fundamentally different path because the country was ready for it."[4]

The language of possession drives such assessments in that the effect of "being inspirational" in ways that maintain sociability may be attributed to the speaker as she decides which language to use to provoke audience responses. Implicitly, the constituting action of those choices originates in the speech *performance* rather than with the linkages audiences make between elements within a rhetorical scene. So that even as Campbell and Jamieson theorize genre as action rather than a textual object, the speech act remains the focal point of attention to be evaluated in terms of the effects it might produce. And when that evaluation is placed under the rubric of genre, it is possible to see how assessments encode a desire to see rhetorical action aiming in a putatively identifiable and valued direction.

It is also possible to locate the possessive logic underwriting the idea that a given speech fails to galvanize because of a lapse on the part of the individual performance rather than, for example, in the circumstances that placed Jordan on that stage. Obviously, there are other ways of reading what Jordan's speech communicated besides an ordinary reiteration of a keynote address. While her presence on the stage may have signified "progress," it also signified containment—that she was, precisely, *not* selected as the candidate for Vice President because she would not have been regarded as a serious candidate. (It is even questionable whether any African American woman running for office today would be seriously considered a bona fide contender for the White House.) Jordan's speech in 1976 stands as much as a signifier of alienation as well as enfranchisement and offers a classic example of the discursive contradictions faced by suborned speakers who are compelled to use dominant modes of representation to demonstrate a willingness to "get along" when addressing a national audience. Whether she took the advice of Campbell and Jamieson and explicitly referenced the history of alienation that preceded her appearance. Jordan was generally expected to follow protocol and show satisfaction with being tasked to act as the keynote speaker, and to use the occasion to deliver precisely some sort of uplifting statement about progress over racial inequities. What kind of response would have emerged had Jordan communicated a fierce protest about being passed over for the position of Second in Command?

At this point, then, we might take note of the ways in which genre protocols not only register what is possible to say to achieve the presumed goal of enacting social bonds, they also register representational limits. The act of establishing expectations and limits in a rhetorical context that seeks to "balance" innovations with conventions can influence the linkages drawn within judgments of what any statement might mean. Indeed, at that 1976 political event, what did Jordan go on to say? In addition to calling attention to her embodied self in her opening statements, Jordan delivered a speech that stressed the importance of national unity:

> There is no executive order; there is no law that can require the American people to form a national community. This we must do as individuals, and if we do it as individuals, there is no President of the United States who can veto that decision. As a first step, we must restore our belief in ourselves. We are a generous people so why can't we be generous with each other? We need to take to heart the words spoken by Thomas Jefferson: "Let us restore to social intercourse that harmony and that affection without which liberty and even life are but dreary things." A nation is formed by the willingness of each of us to share in the responsibility for upholding the common good. A government is invigorated when each of us is willing to participate in shaping the future of this nation.[5]

Interestingly, much of what Campbell and Jamieson describe as generic in 1976 resonates with Obama's race speech of 2008. Jordan and Obama made similar claims about America, about what their presence on the national scene promises, and about their sense of civic responsibility when occupying center stage at a political event that had national significance. And they each positioned their bodies as material referents that offered proof that the dream of equity could be made real. Was there a qualitative difference between their speeches that might explain how one version of the same ideas could be described as generic and another as galvanizing and fresh? Did Obama's speech emerge differently from the context preceding its delivery?

That these two speeches arose in different historical contexts and yet offer similar messages gives us an opportunity to look more closely at the idea that suggests that a repetition of "the typical" enables us to draw upon genres and offer an account of how we "encounter, interpret, react to, and create particular texts" (C. Miller 151). How the identification of innovation versus conformity emerges will be determined ambiguously and contextually, but the study of genre presupposes the existence of a general structure supporting the collective assessment of which quality has made an appearance. Genres appear to enact mediation by calling forth a neutral force of textuality that directs audience recognition of which representations are recognizable and yet galvanizing. But to offer this account of interpretive practices, descriptions of recurrent encounters with texts must be themselves representative of a neutral dynamic (purely information, unaffected by ideology), and then able to truly index how processes of mediation work.

Susan Miller's study of the intertextual dynamics that influence how audiences learn to "trust in texts" offers a counterpoint to the idea that anonymous rhetorical action may be referenced to systematize assessments of whether any given act of persuasion is valuable and significant. "Framed language," she writes, "is trusted in proportion to a perceptible fit between its conventions and the locally intelligible charisma of its sources. Those sources share metadiscursive teachings . . . Such lessons also differ historically in accommodations to available resources and altered ends that characterize their temporal, always material settings" (107).

Genres and genre study offer a framed language, one that has become trustworthy because it seems to get outside of any local act of judgment when explaining how perspectives are constellated by multiple elements within a rhetorical scene. But the language of possession infiltrates such accounts of interpretive mediation and it is most noticeable when (following Lyotard) we mull over the properties of designation. The narratives that would "take account" of how subjects "mediat[e] private intentions and social exigence" (C. Miller 163) are treated as if they do offer a verifiable account of a generalizable rhetorical action, and this helps to propagate perceptions of how genre categories designate an organizing and fair-minded interpretive process. Because we've learned to trust in precisely this kind of explanatory narrative, we typically do not consider the "locally intelligible charisma of its sources." Instead, we regularly reference the explanatory narrative and incorporate it into our daily conversations, rendering the explanation of how interpretations get processed as familiar and eventually a taken-for-granted given. The habitual repetition of the explanatory narrative (of genre) gets institutionalized, cognitively recognized, experientially felt to be familiar, and then anticipated. Once we learn to trust textual representations, once they seem to satisfy institutionalized expectations of what should happen, then they begin to function as if they carry an inherent designating power that bolsters narratives of accountability.

Genre studies also affirm a trust in texts by designating which stylistic conventions are dependably available to negotiate the social exigency of evaluating a speaker's private intentions. By appearing to rely on a generic and anonymous order of textuality, the act of referencing convention in such evaluations seems to be neutral rather than saturated by ideologies that can influence conceptions of how public signs connect to private responses and shape assessments of whether a given statement (text) is innovative, familiar, comforting, or menacing. The invocation of the normative style will be characterized as both a sign and a source of "responsible stability" within representational acts that also carry the potential to produce change—to transform perspectives, inspire feelings of connection or perhaps estrangement.

An examination of how Obama's race speech mediated typical and atypical exigence offers an occasion for considering how that training may have affected ways of identifying the qualities of innovation versus conformity. When thinking about how we have been trained to look to style when identifying innovations and repetitions, then we can also consider how our acts of differentiating "the normal" and "trustworthy" from the "alienating" and "strange" will be ideologically inflected. More crucially, Obama's speech provides an occasion for thinking about how genre's conserving framework contributes to naturalizing the reproduction of power within politicized contexts that perpetuate stereotypes and interpretive struggles when contending with socially constructed categories of race.

The rhetorical situation that Obama faced, once criticism of Wright became regularized, was both typical and unusual. As a politician defending himself, Obama was put in a conventional position. But as a presidential candidate having to publicly broach the troubled topic of racial prejudice to demonstrate his political viability, Obama faced unique circumstances. Deciding to speak at all was one act that was simultaneously familiar and atypical. He could have said nothing and waited for the controversy to die down. But if he chose to speak, he also had to weigh how to address a doubled and paradoxical demand: show that he was like any good politician and able to handle controversy in a non-threatening way, but also demonstrate an ability to exceed expectations and offer something new given the particular constellation of negative narratives about race that threatened his campaign. To navigate the specific disparity between a call for a "regular" locution and one that was also "atypical," Obama made a brilliant decision: he got personal and recounted his unique—and yet familiar—story about his experiences with racism. Obama combined innovation with convention by personalizing the generic commonplaces that Jordan used in her speech as she celebrated her historic presence on the national scene. Obama's well-received speech offered a glimpse of the "locally intelligible charisma" that continues to be ascribed to language uses that enact trusted versions of representational order.

More specifically, Obama invoked the authorizing language of emotion when explaining why he continued to associate with Wright and Trinity church. He spoke of his affection for Wright, and compared those feelings to the fondness he had for his Caucasian grandmother, who had uttered objectionable statements about race but nonetheless has a tender place in his heart.

> I can no more disown him than I can my white grandmother—a woman who helped raise me, a woman who sacrificed again and again for me, a woman who loves me as much as she loves anything in this world, but a woman who once confessed her fear of black men who passed by her on the street, and who on more than one occasion has uttered racial or ethnic stereotypes that made me cringe.[6]

This was, perhaps, one of the more difficult utterances he had to make. Few public figures make confessions about having heard that kind of statement, let alone reference it in so personal a way while campaigning for public office. Stylistically, Obama combined this anecdote with a general observation about shared misunderstandings and suspicions, and held both races equally responsible for perpetuating stereotypes and misconceptions. Arguably, it was that depiction of shared culpability along with statements about his faith in the human spirit to be able to do better that made his speech both unique and recognizable in ways that electrified audiences. While the circumstances preceding his speech offered the familiar scene of a political candidate having to explain himself in the face of public ridicule, Obama's confession about his grandmother's shameful attitude altered the well-worn commonplace about how his presence on the stage represented democratic possibilities. His troubling anecdote was likely familiar to many—part of an ongoing national story about racial discord. Obama's willingness to "go there" in a respectful way demonstrated an awareness of audience as well as an ability to refashion genre as an enabling discourse capable of forming community among listeners.

Accordingly, Obama accomplished the difficult goal of enacting a "clarifying affinity" (Northrop Frye qtd. in Campbell and Jamieson 457) that gave everyone a better perspective on this strange rhetorical event. His response to public critique was not defensive; it was generous and heartening. Indeed, a benevolent reading of genre and its implicit connection to ethos might include the following observations: When Obama referenced his specific person and his history to revise the standard identity of the individual who reaches for the American dream, he added the atypical category of mixed race, and used it to address how the pursuit of that dream can generate conflicts and misunderstandings between people who are otherwise principled. But then he resolved that emotional quandary by finally affirming the validity of the dream narrative and the promise it offers to everyone. Presumably, no one would interfere with another's right to pursue the dream of self-improvement and aspiration. Because the dream of bettering one's circumstances is shared, Obama's eloquent invocation of it helped make his story about where he worshipped recognizable to a potentially skeptical audience.

Similarly, Obama created an unconventional space of "public intimacy" (Lauren Berlant's phrase) by calling attention to contentious feelings of racial prejudice but in a way that simultaneously made room for a kind of deliberation that went "beyond" the intimate and looked at "the big" national picture. He dug into specifics, got personal, but then pulled back to an overarching space of neutrality that allowed him to place Wright, his grandmother, and the people of the United States on an equal level. Further, his tone was measured. Obama responded magnanimously at a time when the old and indeed regularized narratives of racial prejudice were being unloaded by media personalities who have devised their own generic conventions when using language to foment rancor and divisiveness. In response to rancor, Obama got neither angry nor disgusted and instead offered a modulated self-representation that, given the overwhelming positive responses, did manage to enact community. Many conservative commentators were impressed by Obama's willingness to issue an appeal that suggested that all of us equally share the burden of righting past wrongs. "Obama thinks the defects are only part of the story and that a unity transcending ancient racial distrusts is achievable," noted conservative columnist Steve Chapman approvingly.[7] Indeed, it was precisely Obama's ability to speak about the difficult topic of racial discord and nonetheless formulate a national "we" that helped to solidify his candidacy. The positive response to his speech seemed to be propelled by a moralizing force engendered by his trustworthy delivery.

Calling to Order

The idea that Obama found the right words to mediate a peculiar/normal exigence not only informed media assessments of how Obama got past his "pastor problem," it also appeared within scholarly analyses of Obama's language practices and character. Robert C. Rowland and John M. Jones, for example, characterize Obama's race speech as a contemporary iteration of The American Dream—itself a generic construct but one that was reinvigorated by Obama's candor about race. They write, "Obama incorporated an honest discussion of race" (145) within the story of seeking to perfect the union. By engaging honestly with this topic while invoking the prevailing mythos about "the United States as a place of opportunity," Obama "'stitched together' a compelling narrative that . . . 'might actually lead somewhere,' in which black and white Americans (and Americans of other groups) had been denied access to the opportunity implicit in the American Dream, but could rectify that problem and move toward perfecting the union by working together" (145).

In effect, Obama's use of the familiar and unfamiliar narrative codes enabled him to bend genre to effectively suit his purposes. More broadly, Rowland and Jones incorporate a rhetorical analysis that ascribes rhetorical power to the anonymous elements of textual order that seems to both represent and enact interpretive resolutions and in the process, convince audiences of the wisdom of the orator who knows how to harness power effectively. The speech on race, they conclude, "persuaded many that Obama had the values and judgment to serve as president and that he might be able to lead us down the road to a society in which what would matter would be the content of our character" (145).

Marilyn Cooper's reading of Obama's race speech challenges the logic of cause and effect that is often ascribed to rhetorical power and instead invokes the category of genre to delineate a rhetorically based conception of agency as "emergent." It makes little sense, she argues, to question "how Obama caused people to believe that a politics that heeds divisiveness is bad for the country" (438). Instead, she proposes a notion of rhetorical agency as "emergent and enacted," working to situate agency within complexity theory that "understands causation as a circular process in which an agent's action perturbs another agent who responds" (437).

When the phrase "perturbation and response" replaces "cause and effect," it revises linear (or top down) conceptions of the genesis of rhetorical action. "Cause" is not depicted as a genuine antecedent of such action while the speaker's rhetorical choices are not read as provocations for specific outcomes and consequences. Cooper's use of the word *perturb* offers another flexible descriptor of how linguistic productions interact with audience reception. Nonetheless, her analysis of Obama's race speech reiterates the common view that suggests that politicized speech should act responsibly—as if we know what that means.

Words may perturb but we generally believe that they should do so in conscientious ways. When that happens, we may trust the rhetor's agency. "Conceiving of agency in this way enables writers to recognize their rhetorical acts, whether conscious or non-conscious, as acts that make them who they are, that affect others and that can contribute to the common good" (Cooper 420). Here, the idea of "the common good" functions in a generic way to demarcate trustworthy rhetorical action that presumably may be identified. So that while Cooper's turn to complexity theory situates agency within a field of flexible and shifting relations, she nonetheless positions that complexity within a framework that prioritizes specific (and familiar) kinds of language uses—those that are recognized as aiming towards "the good." Obama's race speech offers a representative example. Cooper credits Obama for delivering a speech that enacted a choice for listeners. Rather than admonishing audiences with a forceful and explicit exhortation detailing how they should react to the problem of racial divisions, Obama crafted a "perturbation, an invitation to change beliefs" (439). Obama's decision to perturb rather than exhort illustrated that he is "'skilled at deliberative rhetoric'" and *therefore* has "good judgment" (432). By offering listeners a choice (his very words: "we have a choice in this country"), Obama "emerges as a responsible agent. He strongly argues for the choice he would make, but ... he is open to other possibilities. He knows he might be wrong" (443).

This analysis makes use of the language of possession. Because Obama used particular modes of expression, it seems fair to conclude that he conducted himself in a responsible way and is deserving of audience trust. Cooper's vision of Obama's speech as an invitation to change echoes Amy DeVitt's conception of genre conventions as neutral instigators of possible enactments. DeVitt would dispense with the idea that conforming to conventions necessarily carries negative overtones. "That there are generic conventions to which reader's expect conformity is not negative; that those conventions identify members and nonmembers is not negative. Like other standards, genre is used by society to accomplish its ends. A benevolent society may use those standards, including genre, benevolently; a fascist society may use those standards fascistically. . . . [I]t is not genre that has agency, not genre that creates a social agenda" (87).

This statement is credible so long as audiences may trust the representational order that enables advantageous acts of conformity/invocations of standards to be differentiated from those that constrain and disempower. If the narrative of hope and change that helps to constitute shared perspectives is, indeed, able to provide a formal site for shared affiliations, then any conception of hope and any message of equity embedded within the proposition that all should share in the responsibility of enacting change, will indeed offer a benevolent discursive enactment. Presumably this version of hope and change offers a welcoming dwelling place for all to occupy.

But given that genres are ways of seeing interrelations between elements within a rhetorical scene, then we have to pause to consider how precisely one element gets fused to another and, more specifically, how we have been emotionally trained to regard some conventional agents of fusing as more salient than others. Indeed, if, as Campbell and Jamieson suggest, genre is a "recurrent form" (446) that is "intensely historical" (459), then we might ask about ideology's influence on perceptions of which statements generate the "clarifying affinities" that direct ways of distinguishing platitudes from innovations, and that influence judgments about which innovations are trustworthy. At what point does the invocation of "the recognizable" *act* to inspire us to see our better selves versus merely re-present the generic and conventional? When is *the normative* read as a winning formula versus formulaic?

Any act of identification that resolves interpretive ambiguities will do so by doing *something* to contend with those discursive histories that fulfill the kairotic moment of trust. What that something is, however, will remain ambiguous. We lose sight of that perpetual tenuousness when we look to the formal features of a text to explain how persuasion enacts identification. Once the perpetually ambiguous elements of discursive interaction are replaced with orderly explanations of how we negotiate meaning, then we are given permission to overlook the ways in which we have learned to "trust crafted language insofar as it acknowledges its mediation of specific immediate circumstances and what they do not reveal" (S. Miller 107).

Here we will find that spirited dynamic of inference once again mediating the gap between representations and methods for converting apprehensions of narrative into judgments of meaning and significance. We are, per genre's logic, expected to infer discursive histories to help fill the gaps between the said and unsaid as we consign meaning and value to signs put up for review. The history part of genre's typified action refers not only to ways of reading propositional content but also to histories of forging connections between what is present and what is inferred to enable a speech to communicate and compel. We look for presences when crafting relationships between the elements within a rhetorical scene that presumably produce discernible interpretive results. We do not conventionally attend to any lingering ambiguities intrinsic to questions about what makes a given representation possible. But those ambiguities are significant in that they demarcate doubled and indeed troubled locations within conceptions of how we should regard our emotional receptivity to prevailing discursive codes. The idea that "available repertoires" of style build trust functions to enfranchise not only a history of sayings but also an entire landscape for organizing how those sayings will be linked to other sayings to establish significance and value—or a way of seeing which utterances deserve what kind of attention. Those linkages will stand as valid so long as their relationship to ruling ideologies goes unmarked.

Among the "repertoires" available to Obama were the discourses of sentimentality that, as noted by Lauren Berlant, are now commonly invoked in public discourse to accomplish political ends. Berlant argues that the priority placed on the communicative exchange of feelings alters the ways in which citizens are expected to connect to the domain of politics. Accordingly, one connects not by weighing reasons and then assenting to proposed policies but by engaging in mutual acts of listening to the "noise" of discourses in an "intimate" public sphere—a space that emerges via *"the affect of feeling political together"* (Berlant, "Affect, Noise, Silence, Protest"; See also Cruel).

The intimate public sphere allows citizens to form loose connections to a social world and then to register political action in terms of, for example, passive listening or having an emotional response, especially when the felt emotion affirms the sentimental idea that publics are formed *through* a spontaneous sharing of sentiment. Arguably, those narratives that declared Obama's race speech to be stunningly successful at creating community can also be read as a representative example of the politics of public intimacy, where what was applauded was that which provoked exactly "the affect of feeling political together," indicating not just shared sentiment but also the broadly conceived emotional training that citizens receive about the virtues of linguistic practices that provoke this anticipated response and the resulting approval granted to the sanctioned power of charisma. Obama's speech succeeded in part because it conformed to the demand for a public representation of intimacy that enabled audiences to feel politically connected by fusing a sentimental narrative about shared triumphs and responsibilities to judgments of Obama's prudent yet potent and temperate character. Sentimental narratives depict integrity as a kind of interpretive wholesomeness. Audiences come to expect to be emotionally satisfied after encountering an inspirational message about the possibility of transcendence overcoming dissonance. That training seems to manifest a structural logic when directing readers to overlook the "ideological sleights of hand" (J. Kelleher 77) that enable the repeated representation of the familiar to appear as a responsible and ethical act indicative of a speaker who understands and lives up to his "obligations" rather than as, for example, a case of pandering or of mercenary calculation.

The public's appreciation of Obama's candor when addressing the question of how to mediate a history of racism positions rhetorical power within the speaker's language choices rather than as a result of an interpretive transaction that involves the audience's ideology-inflected consent to a way of seeing what has significance and value. So that while the decision to use language to help everyone adopt a shared perspective about a need to overcome racial division may be regarded as admirable and a trustworthy choice, the accolades directed to Obama for making that choice do not acknowledge the hierarchy of values embedded within the governing technology of evaluation. Nor do those accolades address the ways in which a generic turn to a narrative of transcendence and equity reinstalls a conception of mediation that, presumably, actually takes us out of the interiority of emotions into a "public" space of anonymity, as if that conversion truly happens and is itself deserving of trust, and as if that conversion truly creates a rhetorical space that all may occupy and experience in the same way.

That act of conversion will be regarded as ethical so long as other features within that interpretive scene are rendered insignificant, including, for example, how Obama depicted his grandmother as an object of shame that he then had to negotiate as he came to his own enlightened state of consciousness. Accounting for the specific role the figure of his grandmother played in clarifying affinities can prompt further questions about what precisely is being invoked as a resource to aid the act of community formation. If we agree that Obama crafted a statement that could be characterized as a representation of "public intimacy" in Berlant's sense of the word, then we might also agree that the statement that conjoined Wright's discourses on racial oppression to Obama's grandmother's attitudes about "blacks" acted in a familiar way to diminish conceptions of Wright's stature and significance. That particular rhetorical connection effectively trivialized decades of work that Wright accomplished on behalf of his community and the nation. It also invoked the familiar narrative that diminishes conceptions of grandmothers by positioning them as foolish seniors whose ideas may understandably be ignored. The traces of a gender hierarchy that contributed to making intelligible this attempt to diffuse racial discord was even more significant given that at the time of Obama's race speech, his formidable opponent was Hillary Clinton.

Other significant contextual features included the comparison audiences would have made between Obama's "measured" delivery and the "blistering" expressions about Wright that circulated on cable television. Those stylistic differences were notable because it was through that comparison—both to Wright's mode of delivery as well as the incendiary commentary reiterated on *Fox News*—that Obama's discourse seemed to enact a soothing and responsible corrective. By making his multi-layered experience with racism available for an imaginary act of identification, Obama seemed to take hold of the controversy and put it in its proper perspective, one that stood "outside" and got an "overview" of what was being said either by the preacher, the grandmother or the hyperbolic talking heads on cable TV, all presumably similarly situated as obstacles to be overcome on the way to transcendence. By confessing to this embarrassing personal history, Obama indicated that he understood how to manage personal disclosures for the sake of "the public good." In so doing, he apparently presented himself as the preferred rhetorical subject whose perspective was aligned with that of neutrality and equity itself. And by choosing words that identified him to be reason's emissary, Obama's measured delivery seemed to offer a representational space in which citizens could "fuse" his utterances to trustworthy representational standards that teach citizens to be emotionally receptive to the rhetorical presentation of unperturbed affect.

Arguably, Obama invoked a normative standard of validity when he rendered a "super power moment of (racial) injustice"[8] as a moment that "we" all recognized as distressing and wrong but also available for remediation. That Obama ascended in stature *as* Wright was rebuked can be made to seem like a mere byproduct of a ruling order, less significant than the "larger" result of inspiring audiences to think of their better selves. This kind of conclusion helps to illustrate how narratives that depict interpretive acts in generalized terms get naturalized and then referenced to account for power's representation and effects.

An ethical dilemma "brews"[9] when we are called upon to decide whether and how the familiar and conventional should guide our judgments in a "new" rhetorical situation. It is also possible to argue that Obama's "regularizing" of Wright via the grandmother comparison left intact standing narratives that would authorize a hegemonic version of reality. And the "reality" he helped to affirm demanded an old story: the public humiliation of a charismatic and powerful African American man. Obama's campaign ultimately benefited from the story of that humiliation. To become "normalized," Obama chose not to challenge the status quo and did not express outrage over the treatment of Reverend Wright, and for that reason, at least according to the narrative trajectory circulating within news reports, he prevailed. That this outcome may have contributed to the emotional satisfaction presumably felt by those who praised Obama's speech illustrates how genres, like explanatory narratives associated with ethos, signify an act of "positioning within culture and always in relation to power" (Con Davis and Gross 66).

The Reverend Speaks

At the end of April 2008, approximately one month after Obama delivered that historic speech, the Reverend Jeremiah Wright resurfaced in a series of speaking events that gave him a chance to respond to his critics. On April 25, Wright appeared in a PBS interview with Bill Moyers.[10] Two days later, he gave a keynote address at the NAACP's 53rd Annual Fight for Freedom Fund Dinner in Detroit. The following day, Wright spoke to the National Press Club.

Anyone who might have hoped that Wright would issue an apology or renounce his earlier statements condemning the United States for perpetuating atrocities would have been disappointed. Instead of distancing himself from his earlier observations about U.S. politics, he renewed them. Upon each occasion of speech, Wright made a similar point: Perceived differences between people often get conflated with the pejorative label of *deficiency*. This point was made in several ways while speaking to members of the NAACP.

> In the past, we were taught to see others who are different as being deficient. We established arbitrary norms and then determined that anybody not like us was abnormal. But a change is coming because we no longer see others who are different as being deficient. We just see them as different. Over the past 50 years, thanks to the scholarship of dozens of experts in many different disciplines, we have come to see just how skewed, prejudiced and dangerous our miseducation has been.[11]

Using historical examples and referencing academic research, Wright delivered a series of speeches that repeated a refrain familiar to Obama's supporters: "Believe that a change is going to come." He emphasized inclusiveness and the need for the unified support of "the Jewish community, the Muslim community, the Christian community, Protestant and Catholic" to share in the burden of enacting change to overcome historical oppression.

> Many of us are committed to changing how we see others who are different. Number one, many of us are committed to changing how we see ourselves, not stepchildren, number two, but God's children. Many of us are committed to changing, number three, the way we treat each other. The way black men treat black women. The way black parents treat black children. The way black youth treat black elders and the way black elders treat black youth. We are committed to changing the way we treat each other.

At the National Press Club appearance the next day, Wright continued to make the point that difference is not the same as deficiency, and he explored how that premise can be applied to perceptions of "liberation theology," the religious tradition informing Wright's own and one that, Wright noted, was rendered invisible within mainstream press depictions of his person. He outlined the history of "the prophetic tradition of the Black church," noting that "black worship is different from European and European American worship" as is "black" preaching. "It is not bombastic; it is not controversial. It's different."[12]

Wright also offered concrete examples of the social justice work conducted by his congregation, noting that

> liberation and transformation have . . . been at the very core of the congregation of Trinity United Church since it was founded in 1961. . . . Our congregation has had an HIV—AIDS ministry for over two decades. Our congregation has awarded over $1 million to graduating high school seniors going into college and an additional $500,000 to the United Negro College Fund, and the six HBCUs related to the United Church of Christ, while advocating for health care for the uninsured, workers' rights for those forbidden to form unions, and fighting the unjust sentencing system which has sent black men and women to prison for longer terms for possession of crack cocaine than white men and women have to serve for the possession of powder cocaine.

He also noted his membership in the community of those able to claim that the U.S. is "a country . . . some of us has served." And he called for reconciliation while refusing to simplify what that might mean and how it might be accomplished. Arguably, the propositional content of Wright's speech was congenial with the "hope and change" slogan advanced by Obama's campaign. Wright's call for equity, fairness, progress, and mutual tolerance was precisely in keeping with Obama's agenda.

None of this, however, impressed media commentators, who mostly expressed another round of serious disapproval and shock. One report described Wright as "combative," his stance as "confrontational and rancorous."[13] The significance of his public appearances was read in connection with Obama's campaign and characterized as "providing colorful commentary and feeding the story Obama had hoped was dying down."[14] Explicit critiques characterized Wright's very appearance in public as "a shockingly timed betrayal"[15]; an act of "war"[16]—an egregious act of showmanship that forced the already "strained . . . bond" between Wright and Obama to "finally snap."[17]

Significantly, Wright was criticized for a style that seemed to indicate that he had selfish motives and was indifferent to helping Obama's standing among the electorate. According to *New York Times* columnist Bob Herbert, "the Rev. Jeremiah Wright went to Washington on Monday not to praise Barack Obama, but to bury him. Smiling, cracking corny jokes, mugging it up for the big-time news media—this Reverend is never going away. He's found himself a national platform, and he's loving it."[18]

According to a widely disseminated AP article, Wright made "a defiant appearance" and "seemed to relish the chance to speak out after weeks of being derided in the press. He reveled in his retorts, high-fiving an audience member, pointing and winking at his supporters, and mocking descriptions of him as Obama's spiritual mentor."[19]

The *New York Times* also printed a front page "review" of Wright's public appearances by television critic Alessandra Stanley, whose work is typically filed in sections devoted to style or art. Stanley also took issue with the style of Wright's speech, describing it as "a rich, stemwinding brew of black history, scripture, hallelujahs and hermeneutics," speech acts that, she maintained, called into question Wright's motives for speaking, and proved that his purpose was ultimately self-serving. As put by Stanley, "Mr. Wright's monomania over the last three days has helped prove the point Mr. Obama made about his former pastor . . . Mr. Wright revealed himself to be the compelling but slightly wacky uncle who unsettles strangers but really just craves attention. . . . Now it turns out that Mr. Wright doesn't hate America, he loves the sound of his own voice."[20]

The typically unflappable David Gergen summed up this reaction in a commentary delivered on CNN in which he called Wright's appearances "the dumbest, most selfish, most narcissistic thing I've seen in 40 years of covering politics."[21]

Such conclusions expressed a way of making connections between utterances and the contexts that shape interpretations of what gets communicated. They illustrate how a textually based representational order can act as an invisible point of reference for judgments of who is credible and authoritative. Given that the propositional content of Wright's 2008 speeches echoed that of the wildly popular Obama, then it becomes that much more important to consider the political consequences of Susan

Miller's point about the ways in which a use of language will be "trusted in proportion to a perceptible fit between its conventions and the locally intelligible charisma of its sources" (107). Wright's style was charismatic and participatory. When, for example, discussing at the NAACP dinner differences between African and European music, he and the audience counted beats, as he called out:

> Listen to this—Blessed assurance. Jesus is mine, two three, four, five, six—Oh! Why are you clapping on the wrong beat? Africans have a different meter and Africans have a different tonality. European music is diatonic, seven tones—do, re, me, fa, so, la, ti, do. That's Italian, Europe. In West Africa and South Africa, it is not diatonic, seven tones, it is pentatonic with five tones.

Here, humor and a direct call to engage the audience was offered to demonstrate that, in Wright's words, a "skewed, prejudiced and dangerous miseducation" has affected the ways in which audiences learn to see differences as deficient—an argument that was propositionally congenial with the one made by Obama about his grandmother. Wright, however, did not deliver this message in the form of a controlled personal confession, but as a poetic and exuberant performance that, to borrow from Victoria Cliett, could be said to "recod[e] meaning, recontextualiz[e] history, and deconstruct the values of dominant culture" (177).

> Please run and tell my stuck-on-stupid friends that Arabic is a *language*, it's not a religion. Barack Hussein Obama. Barack Hussein Obama. Barack Hussein Obama. They are Arabic-speaking Christians, Arabic-speaking Jews and Arabic speaking atheists. Arabic is a language, it's not a religion. Stop trying to scare folks by giving them an Arabic name as if it's some sort of a disease.

Presumably, this was the kind of statement that media critics deemed "over the top" and irresponsible—not cautious and then presumably not thought out in advance, as if the act of repeating Obama's name was indicative of a solipsistic relishing by the speaker of his own voice that audiences could rightly renounce rather than, for example, an expression of impatience with the ridiculous and insulting tacit racism underwriting oppositional responses to Obama's very act of presuming to run for the White House.

Arguably, genre studies assisted the mainstream media's decision to disseminate negative portraits of Wright as if doing so was sensible. Studies in genre affirm the logic that looks for a perceptible fit between a given speech/text and the text-based conventions embedded within dominant European based rhetorics that have come to be trusted within dominant cultures. Accordingly, rhetors are expected to reproduce signs of reason in the form of stylistic clarity to convey both intellectual rigor and authorial integrity. The generically "sound" rhetorical argument, per dominant genre conventions, should exhibit "clear, orderly, convincing arguments which show respect for evidence, build in refutation, and accommodate their audience" (Fahnestock and Secor 235).

These commonplaces express an enculturated perspective that, as Michael Warner observes, "leads people to speak as though there were a moral imperative to clarity, and a moral imperative to political position taking as well" (Publics 144). Wright instead adopted a mode of communication that exhibited eloquence differently and prompted an alternative mode of participation—not composed contemplation but stylized agitation representative of disquieted feelings that might provoke a fight for social justice. Media responses that ridiculed Wright's performances effectively characterized his delivery as a disruption to "The Tradition," as if that tradition stands as a singularly virtuous point of reference for judging whether his speech acts behaved responsibly.

But it is also the case that Wright invoked a rhetorical style that carries its own venerable history and tradition. As discussed in the previous chapter, African American Rhetoric and Communication scholars have studied cultural norms that oversee conceptions of eloquence within African American discourse communities. Like any identity category, these are multiple and potentially contradictory (see Gilyard 1), but scholars have identified generic conventions associated with African American public discourse, especially for leaders of the church. These conventions comprise alternative points of reference for judging whether a given act of speech fulfills a *kairotic* moment of trust. Genre conventions associated with sermonizing, and more specifically with "liberation theology," are available to generate different ways of reading the purposes that appear to motivate a speaker to engage in a particular language practice—motivations that African American scholars suggest can help to reformulate general conceptions of oral and textual communicative purposes.

Lena Ampadu, for example, argues that teachers of writing should look to African American rhetorical traditions as "exemplars of audience-involving texts (that) include highly orally based forms. . . . These texts provide fertile ground for the study of repetition and provide rich examples of a lively, elegant style created in part by sentences that create complexity of thought and ideas through vivid language and balanced, rhythmical sentences filled with anaphora, antithesis, parallelism, and chiasmus" (137–8). Black preachers, she adds, have modeled potent literacy practices able to "move and fascinate audiences" with rhetorical devices (like repetition) that act to "heighten the dramatic appeal of the oral text" (139).

Indeed, rather than affirm the audience's trust in a textual order, at least one strand of African American rhetorical traditions takes its cue from oral traditions that arose in connection with the experiences of Africans abducted from their homeland and forced to adapt to cultural practices in the new world that also limited their freedoms. As Molefi Kete Asante writes, slaves were "forbidden by law . . . to learn" and forced to adhere to "strict anti-literacy laws during slavery" (16). In response to the enforced alienation from dominant culture, and in an attempt to retain distinctive discursive histories, slaves devised their own conceptions of how to incorporate historical and lived experiences into judgments of what speakers should do when participating with language. Most crucially, rather than prioritize locutions that convey representational coherence by communicating singular points in an orderly way, displaced Africans embraced a perspective that sees significance in the "subtleties, pleasures, and potentials" of oral communication (16). Asante locates alternative modes of participation "in the work songs, Ebonics, sermons, and the spirituals" that do not aim to regularize the reproduction of singular points of view but instead convey the idea that verbal productions carry doubled connotations, "one for the body and one for the soul" (17). That sense of doubling is communicated in a way that combines the time of retrospective contemplation with the immediate participatory response engendered by a representation on offer. There is, Asante writes, a belief in a "transforming power of vocal expression." It "is precisely the power of the word, whether in music or speeches, that authentically speaks of an African heritage" (17).

The "almost universal regard for the power of the spoken word" (17) in African American discourse communities is absent from rhetorics that favor text-based reproductions in both speech and writing. The study of African American discursive practices is long-standing and multifaceted, but it has little "intelligible charisma" within the context of national politics, and its invisibility as a widely recognized genre is precisely the issue when assessing what constitutes "innovation" versus a "responsible" reiteration of a history of norms. An audience in search of representations of an embodied/metaphysical duality will have different expectations about how to read (and know) where a given sign aims. Taking these differences seriously means rethinking how styles function as a resource for enacting participation between rhetor and audiences in ways that everyone will trust.

When European-inflected discursive practices are positioned as the unquestioned point of reference for judgments of who is doing what with words, there will be an inevitable subordination of those discursive practices that diverge, especially those that do not necessarily place trust in the idea that one should reproduce dominant discursive norms by adhering to textually influenced stylistic protocol. But it is equally possible to distrust precisely the act of embracing dominant discursive practices as if doing so automatically confers authority. According to Kimmika L. H. Williams, "the rhetoric and the oral tradition" of African American Vernacular English (AAVE) "historically served as a counter hegemonic strategy of resistance" (88) to white privilege embedded within the idea that one language practice is inherently superior to others. "To accommodate this culturally cherished practice" of resisting domineering mandates, "AAVE speakers incorporate a number of 'showy' modes of discourse such as exaggerated speech, signification, call and response, speaking in tongues, circumlocution, and rhythmicality as a way of demonstrating individual verbal acuity" (88). Keith Gilyard also notes that alternative modes of participation prioritize, for example, "the art of the humorous put down" via "verbal indirection," the "tonal semantics" that involve "the conveying of meanings in Black discourse through specifically ethnic kinds of voice rhythms and vocal inflections; and narrative sequencing, the habitual use of stories to explain and/or persuade" (14–15). Indeed, verbal acuity is a highly esteemed way of participating with language. Asante, meanwhile, emphasizes a crucial difference between European and African perspectives on where to locate the authorizing force driving language use. Argument, he maintains, has no intrinsic power itself. Rather, persuasive power arises through acts of "sharing in the same experiential spontaneity [that] relies upon vocal creativity to transform the audience" (16).

It should be said that a general conception of "spontaneous transformation" is familiar to rhetorical traditions influenced by sophists like

Isocrates, a point that I will address more fully in this book's conclusion. At the moment, however, we can note two things: the specific discursive history associated with AAVE is not only *not* invoked as a trustworthy point of reference for maintaining culture within dominant media representations; in 2008 it was explicitly denigrated for appearing to communicate different aims. Such judgments are enabled by the inferences that get made when drawing upon ideologically-inflected perceptions to "fill in" what is left out of any scene of representation. An alternative perspective would read the stylistic markers deployed by Wright not as obstacles to ethical modes of participation but as part of a critical ethical discourse that seeks to disrupt the automatic reproduction of power generated by the unquestioned repetition of dominant discursive practices and the conceptual logic that authorizes their legitimacy.

When an AAVE interpretive lens is applied to Wright's 2008 public appearances, then ways of reading what his delivery signifies are themselves transformed. The presupposed "verbal bombast"—the repetition, rhythmicality, exaggeration (an enculturated context-based word)—instead communicated the verbal acuity that may be valorized for creating a shared sense of urgency aiming to motivate the audience to *do* something and transform hope to action.

Wright put out a rallying call to listeners at the Detroit NAACP meeting who would share a commitment to change by identifying multiple acts of alienation:

> The way the so-called haves and have mores, to use Bush's speech writers' term. Don't you all think he made that up? The way the have and have mores treat the have nots. The way the educated treat the uneducated. The way those with degrees treat those who never made it through high school. The way those of us who never got caught treat those of us who are incarcerated. Making rehabilitation a priority over incarceration. We are committed to changing the way we treat each other.

Arguably, a sense of urgency was built through the repetition of the phrase "the way" as it underscores the many methods we have for disenfranchising each other. Audiences were invited to experience the sense of urgency about a need to change in response to the "showy" (i.e., astute and discriminating) act of identifying how common it is to adopt perspectives that naturalize hierarchies of which categories of people should be valued.

The way we treat the latest immigrants because everybody in here who's not an Indian do be an immigrant. Some of you all came on the decks of a ship and some of us came on the bows and hauls of the ship, but we all are immigrants. The way we treat non—Christians and folks who don't believe what we believe. We're committed to changing the way we treat each other. The way Sunnis treat Shiites, the way Orthodox Jews treat reformed Jews. The way church folk treat other church folk. The way speakers of English treat speakers of Arabic—Maasalam al hal.

The study of African American rhetorical traditions prompts a reconsideration of how to draw upon conventions and typified action when theorizing how to account for ethical and trustworthy modes of discursive participation. Rhetorical theories of genre suggest that, pragmatically, the person who desires to persuade should use signifiers already circulating within a field of address. Rhetors should know their audiences and should also remember that audiences can choose how to evaluate texts put up for review. But when "the conventional" gets characterized as the facilitator of social cooperation, then the presupposed "contract" that regulates the exchange between "the inference" and "the trusted" will naturalize those interpretive frameworks that designate which modes of discursive participation have value. This point would apply to any study of genre, whether derived from the linguistic practices associated with the category of "Standard English" or of "African American Vernacular English."[22] But the prospect of rethinking how to judge Wright's way of participating with language can also prompt a reconsideration of what it means to reference "conventions." The permission presumably granted to journalists to depict Wright as an extremist who deserved another round of public shaming was made possible not only by the ideas that one set of conventions *should* be invoked and that style should act as the unacknowledged marker of a threshold between one's public and private selves. That permission was also granted by the more subtle training audiences receive in how to convert a sense impression about what is represented into a judgment about whether the (invisible) aims (stylistically encoded) are laudatory. As Spencer Schaffner writes, "genre systems, by their very nature of being largely taken-for-granted, can be dangerous propagators of the status quo" ("Review"). They blandly disseminate unquestioned assumptions about how speakers should act and think, and in the process institute a dynamic of pacification as a sign of social responsibility. (See, also, Shapiro on this point.) Genres valorize representational duplication in situations where we might instead question *how* to represent our relationship to discourses of power.

The idea that we should retrieve the normative to craft a space to be inhabited by shared perspectives allows audiences to forget that the idea of retrieval is itself a narrative that promotes a metaphor of interpretive reconciliation rather than actualizing real phenomena. The act of "going back" to discursive histories is not itself representable or necessarily achievable, but we overlook the significance of those absences to conceptions of the inferring labor that those histories presumably describe. Because we must make inferences when judging what words mean, we are inherently dependent upon the languages that precede us; we must use the terms made available in a given culture if we want to be heard. But how we treat that dependency—whether, for example, we regard speech habits as obligations—is open to discussion. When genres are set forth as aids to communication, they incorporate a doubled dynamic of enabling while constraining conceptions of how language uses intersect with human activity.

Ironically, the ability of the mainstream press to denigrate Wright's mode of participation enacted precisely the dynamic that he described. His stylistic differences were rendered as deficiencies and that assessment was put forth as if indisputably valid and as if default methods of representation do not require their own critical scrutiny. While it was common enough to encounter critiques of Wright's style—as if it was intrinsically and recognizably problematic—mainstream journalists failed to notice the hyperbolic exaggeration encoded within the ostensibly neutral reporting on Wright's public appearances.

The AP report on Wright's National Press Club appearance, for example, included the following statement: "Wright said he's told Obama that if he is elected in November and is inaugurated in January, 'I'm coming after you.' He said that's because his differences are not with the American people, but U.S. policies."[23] The article implied that through this apparently obsessive response, Wright really *was* that "wacky uncle" who does not know his place and remains a perpetual embarrassment. What Wright actually said to audience members was: "And I said to Barack Obama, last year, 'If you get elected, November the 5th, I'm coming after you, because you'll be representing a government whose policies grind under people.' All right? It's about policy, not the American people."[24] Wright's interest in social justice and the mission of the presidency was misread, depicted as a personal obsession with Obama and that specific act of conversion authorized the use of pejorative terms within reports about his speech acts.

The most egregious example of this kind of power play was evident in responses to a comment made by Wright that presumably was so outlandish, it prompted Obama to publicly denounce his former pastor and "cut all ties." Obama's decision followed a statement that Wright made at the National Press Club about Louis Farrakhan, the leader of that Nation of Islam known for his own controversial explicitly anti-Semitic stance. Farrakhan's name came up at the behest of the moderator (unnamed in the transcripts) overseeing the question and answer session that followed Wright's speech—one that reissued his call for progressive change that enacts social justice. Wright's speech appeared to generate little interest for the moderator or the journalists who reported on Wright's Press Club appearance. Attention instead was focused on Wright's responses to questions posed by the moderator that referenced the prior controversy about his sermons. The moderator asked for a clarification of Wright's patriotism, and whether Wright thought that he owed the public an apology for uttering a statement "damning America." He asked Wright how he would "purport to fix" misunderstandings "particularly when some of (Wright's) comments (were) found to be offensive to white churches."[25]

Wright's responses were poised and often humorous. He argued for the need for more education about black traditions. He mentioned authors of import to him and frequently referenced a historical record to back his claims. Indeed, what cannot be communicated in any summary of the exchange was the sense of Wright's quick wit. "We're going to end," stated the moderator, "with a joke. Chris Rock joked, 'Of course Reverend Wright's an angry 75-year-old black man. All 75-year-old black men are angry.' Is that funny? Is that true? Is it unfortunate? What do you think?"

Wright's response: "I think it's just like the media. I'm not 75."

It was in this context that the moderator posed a question about Wright's relationship to Farrakhan. Contrary to reporting that implied that Wright spoke to resuscitate and promote Farrakhan's controversial perspectives, the topic was raised because the moderator asked for Wright to comment upon his relationship with Farrakhan. "Do you agree with and respect his views, including his most racially divisive views?"

This is itself of interest because of what it tells us about how it is possible to invoke a presumably neutral context when mobilizing evaluations of which speech acts are honorable. Presumably, the moderator's question could be filed under the genre of "seeking clarification" or "seeking an explanation" and hence it would not be labeled "an inflammatory provocation." Because the question was regarded as a neutral quest for information, expectations arose about how Wright should have responded—primarily by adopting a mode of speech that, in fact, offered the desired clarification. The expectation that his answer should clarify would appear to be a neutral one—one that audiences had every right to expect. In this case, however, the call for an act of clarity—the call placed upon Wright to "clarify affinities"—was also a call for him to deliver a specific mode of expression: denouncement. Only an explicit repudiation of Farrakhan's anti-Semitism would have sanctioned Wright's response and placed it in accord with the invisible set of principles that, presumably, we are obliged to adhere to if we want to *be* ethical. Further, clarifying his distance from Farrakhan's policies presumably would have allowed Wright to speak a language that all would recognize and valorize.

To his credit, Wright refused this demand for verbal conformity and any reproduction of a satisfying sentimentality, and instead offered a lengthy response that addressed the ways in which context affects perceptions:

> As I said on the Bill Moyers' show, one of our news channels keeps playing a news clip from 20 years ago when Louis said 20 years ago that Zionism, not Judaism, was a gutter religion. And he was talking about the same thing the United Nations resolutions say, the same thing now that President Carter is being vilified for, and Bishop Tutu is being vilified for. And everybody wants to paint me as if I'm anti-Semitic because of what Louis Farrakhan said 20 years ago. I believe that people of all faiths have to work together in this country if we're going to build a future for our children, whether those people are—just as Michelle and Barack don't agree on everything, Raymond (ph) and I don't agree on everything, Louis and I don't agree on everything, most of you all don't agree—you get two people in the same room, you've got three opinions. So what I think about him, as I've said on Bill Moyers and it got edited out—how many other African Americans or European Americans do you know that can get one million people together on the Mall? He is one of the most important voices in the 20th and 21st centuries. That's what I think about him. I've said, as I said on Bill Moyers, when Louis Farrakhan speaks, it's like E.F. Hutton

speaks, all black America listens. Whether they agree with him or not, they listen. Now, I am not going to put down Louis Farrakhan any more than Mandela would put down Fidel Castro. Do you remember that Ted Koppel show, where Ted wanted Mandela to put down Castro because Castro was our enemy? And he said, "You don't tell me who my enemies are. You don't tell me who my friends are." Louis Farrakhan is not my enemy. He did not put me in chains. He did not put me in slavery. And he didn't make me this color.

This response could engender any number of interpretations and that multiplicity helps to illustrate how rhetorical theories of genre can offer inadequate models when directing audiences to reference conventional categories when judging where a speech act aims. What Wright meant when he observed that not many individuals can call upon one million to gather, and that when Farrakhan speaks, all listen whether they agree or not, is not immediately clear. Wright's decision to present a response that could be interpreted in multiple ways could be evaluated by an interpretive lens that, as Cliett notes, values the use of language to "make new meanings that surpass those of the original language by reconstituting reality and recoding meaning" (177). But once a generic category (i.e., a question and answer session) is locked into place as legitimate, it will convey expectations about what words should *do*, and those expectations will set up the conditions in which ambiguity and multiplicity of meaning will be read as obfuscation. Wright indicated how the act of recognizing Farrakhan's persuasive power is not the same as endorsing that power, but that difference appeared to be lost on reporters, even though everything else said by Wright was at variance with the idea that any group of people should be disenfranchised.[26] But because he failed to offer a "clarifying affinity" recognizable to audiences trained to look for specific signifiers as concrete representations of one's private perspective, it was permissible to deem Wright's views as untrustworthy. Once mainstream journalists depicted the absence of a vehement denouncement of Farrakhan as a veiled endorsement, they disseminated what appeared to be a "logical" narrative about Wright's extremism.

That depiction had material consequences. Wright's response to the moderator's question was portrayed as a provocation that was so vile, Obama had no choice but to finally end his relationship with his former pastor and to publicly announce his intention to do so. Reportedly, Obama's cool demeanor finally cracked, but it did so at the point that it presumably should have—in response to Wright's publicized reappearance and specifically because of the Farrakhan statement. According to an article on MSNBC.com, Obama's dismay at Wright's message prompted him to issue a vigorous repudiation of Wright and "finally" to officially cut ties. "I am outraged by the comments that were made and saddened by the spectacle that we saw yesterday," Obama said in reference to Wright's appearance at the National Press Club:

> What became clear to me is that he [Wright] was presenting a world view that contradicts who I am and what I stand for. And what I think particularly angered me was his suggestion somehow that my previous denunciation of his remarks were somehow political posturing. Anybody who knows me and anybody who knows what I'm about knows that I am about trying to bridge gaps and I see the commonality in all people.[27]

The presumed value of "authenticity" raised itself once again, underwriting and authorizing Obama's public act of expulsion, which was, obviously, politically driven, but mostly treated as necessary and indicative of a show of strength. The *New York Times* published an editorial applauding Obama's decision to break ties with Wright by characterizing it as a late but proper move to make:

> It took more time than it should have, but on Tuesday, Barack Obama firmly rejected the racism and paranoia of his former pastor . . . and he made it clear that the preacher does not represent him, his politics or his campaign. . . . In the last few days, in a series of shocking appearances, (Wright) embraced the Rev. Louis Farrakhan's anti-Semitism. He said the government manufactured the AIDS virus to kill blacks. He suggested that America was guilty of "terrorism" and so had brought the 9/11 attacks on itself . . . It was the most forthright repudiation of an out-of-control supporter that we can remember.[28]

Newsweek's digital edition drew upon a historical reference: "Obama's Sister Souljah Moment" read a leading headline along with a subheading, "The candidate slams his former pastor . . . for 'divisive and destructive' comments."[29] The headline referenced the 1992 Presidential campaign of Bill Clinton, who endeavored to demonstrate that he was "mainstream" by publicly denouncing hip hop artist and author Sister Souljah. In response to riots in Los Angeles in 1992, Sister Souljah ignited a controversy when she said, "If black people kill black people everyday, why not have a week and kill white people?"[30] Clinton was applauded for a statement delivered during a speech to Jesse Jackson Sr.'s Rainbow Coalition: "If you took the words 'white' and 'black' and you reversed them, you might think David Duke was giving that speech."

Apparently, a "Sister Souljah Moment" is itself recognizable, and references a categorizable genre involving the explicit denouncement by a candidate running for public office against a perceived zealot. The phrase has earned an entry on Wikipedia:

> A Sister Souljah moment is a politician's public repudiation of an extremist person or group, statement, or position perceived to have some association with the politician or the politician's party.... Such an act of repudiation is designed to signal to centrist voters that the politician is not beholden to traditional, and sometimes unpopular, interest groups associated with the party, although such repudiation runs the risk of alienating some of the politician's allies and the party's base voters. The term is named for the political activist Sister Souljah.[31]

The entry is filed under the category of "political terms," and in the process, denuded of the racial overtones that might inform ways of reading categorical identities such as "centrist" versus "extremist." Indeed, the "Sister Souljah moment" is rendered generic and universally applicable—Wikipedia lists other examples including a speech by Gov. George W. Bush in 2000 repudiating the religious right.[32] Of course, this is ironic given subsequent statements by Bush about how he felt himself to be answerable to God, not to public opinion, once voters began to change their minds about the ethics of launching a preemptive strike against a foreign country that did not pose an immediate threat to U.S. security. Meanwhile, the inclusion of this example in the Wikipedia entry speaks to another subtext lurking within the controversy about Obama's pastor—that any Presidential candidate must prove himself to be a "good Christian." Obama has explained that he was raised without religion but converted to Christianity after he began to attend Wright's church. But doubts about the legitimacy of that conversion, especially since it involved Wright's church, continued to haunt his campaign and reemerged during the 2012 election cycle, especially after it was revealed in March of 2012 that fifty-two percent of Republican voters in Mississippi and forty-five percent in Alabama said that they believed Obama to be Muslim, and believed this to be a quality that should discredit him as a presidential candidate.[33]

For those of us who reject the idea that any specific religion should have a prominent role in public discourse, especially in presidential elections, indeed who find the "Are you Christian?" question to express a virulent and insidious form of sentimentalism, Obama's "transcendence" beyond the "problem of Wright" also marked a moment in which he acquiesced and decided to leave alone a disturbing hegemonic norm for the sake of his political career. That conclusion was affirmed after Obama selected the homophobic Reverend Rick Warren to stand with him at his historic inauguration in 2009.

The mainstream coverage of Wright's speeches, however, suggested that Obama's break with his minister was inevitable, indeed "logical" and it is important to note how rhetorical studies of genre (as well as ethos and trust) contribute to substantiating such conclusions. Ideologies influence ways of reading expressions of emotion, and in this case, contributed to depicting Obama's "anger" as proper, a reading that made sense by the act of drawing a comparison to Wright's expressions of "anger," as if the two expressions were equitable, both about personal emotions (rather than in the case of Wright's, about something *else* like a history of social injustice). Both kinds of expression were treated as offering "hard" evidence about the character of the person using an emotional appeal to connect with an audience. That their disparate expressions were categorized as comparable types helps to illustrate that genre is not a benign placeholder for judgments of meaning and significance. Rather, genre categories helped to organize evaluative readings of the category "angry response" and then to deem one expression to be more proper than the other.

Here, rhetoric's traditional call for eloquence as an artistic language able to bridge the gap between self and other takes on renewed importance. A conventional reading of eloquence would suggest that Obama was persuasive because he conveyed a sense of restraint via expressions of "controlled affect" that, to borrow from Joshua Gunn, "allows audiences to walk right up to abject rage or desirous ecstasy alongside the speaker, but without topping completely into . . . uncontrolled affect" (Public 20)—or the place presumably occupied by Wright. The compliments paid to Obama after his speech on race positioned him as presidential because he used language in a way that allowed "us" to go with him to the space of rage enunciated by Wright, to consider its power from a "safe" distance, acknowledge its presence, but then pull back and put it in a "rightful" place of balance. But the idea that rhetorical competence constitutes the audience's sense of whether to trust the speaker to take them elsewhere but then return to a "typical place" betrays the ideological slippage that allows trained emotional and embodied responses of identification to be regarded as morally superior to feelings of strangeness and disorientation. Ideology's influence on emotion will be masked by the idea that feelings are simply and directly provoked by utterances that presumably can be clearly categorized as incendiary. When such substitutions become normalized—when they are referenced and reiterated as if automatically valid—they seem to emerge as an inevitable result of a structurally intact rhetorical action that then can be named and "referenced" to provide cover for race baiting, for the worst motives to create outcasts in order to appear to proclaim concern about the goodness of a "horrified" "us."

Faith in a generic "structural" economy makes it possible for people like conservative radio talk show and television host Sean Hannity to perpetuate his own divisive and rhetorically malignant platitudes while piously expressing shock and anger that anyone would harbor uncharitable and unchristian perspectives. "First of all, I will not let up on this issue," he said after getting a hold of clips of Wright's sermons, positioning himself as a crusader for ethics rather than a zealot. "If his pastor went to Libya, Tripoli with Louis Farrakhan, a virulent, anti-Semitic racist, his church gave a lifetime achievement award to Louis Farrakhan. That's been Barack Obama's pastor for 20 years. And we will continue to expose this until somebody in the mainstream media has the courage to take this on."[34]

While *Fox News* has acted as a mouthpiece for the Republican Party that intentionally pushes perspectival conformity, other news stations can be characterized as doing much of the same, at least in principle. The corporate media generally perpetuate an interpretive dynamic wherein the expression of allegiance to institutions of power is normalized and rendered virtuous. Naturalizing our perceptions of this dynamic contributes to instantiating a sentimentalized discursive context in which the worst prejudices of an electorate can be covered over through pious pronouncements about generic allegiances to whatever signifiers have been promulgated as repositories for cherished regard. The *New York Times* version of this sentimentalism was evident in the editorial that praised Obama's decision to cut ties with Wright and affirmed the need to candidly discuss the history of racial inequities in U.S. culture. "This country needs a healthy and open discussion of race. Mr. Obama's repudiation of Mr. Wright is part of that."[35] One might wonder about the ethics of a dialogue that begins with the explicit silencing of a most charismatic speaker.

Of course, any of Wright's points are debatable. One could also quarrel with what might appear to be a homogenized version of "the black church," as did *The Washington Post*'s columnist Eugene Robinson, who objected to the idea that Wright's perspective was representative of all African American church-goers. According to Robinson,

> The reality of the African American church, of course, is as diverse as the African American community. I grew up in the Methodist church with pastors—often active on the front lines of the civil rights movement—whose sermons were rarely exciting enough to elicit more than a muttered "Amen." They were excitement itself, however, compared with the dry lectures delivered by the priest at the Catholic church around the corner. And what I heard every Sunday was nothing at all like the Bible-thumping, hellfire-and—damnation perorations that filled my Baptist friends with the Holy Ghost—and even less like the spellbinding, singsong, jump-and-shout sermonizing that raised the roofs of Pentecostal sanctuaries across town.[36]

Arguably, this perspective affirms Wright's point about the fact that there are differences in the ways in which people observe their faith and participate in life. Robinson's representations of alternative worship practices do not cancel the larger points that Wright made about the tendency many of us have to disparage those discursive practices that are unfamiliar. And none of the media commentary that disparaged Wright addressed the crucial point he made about the capacity of governments in the United States to officially engage in abominable and unjust acts of cruelty. One need only look at the treatment of prisoners at Guantanamo, the use of military drones in countries populated by people identified as non-Caucasian[37] or at what has become a fairly regularized scandal: pictures of U.S. soldiers taking pleasure in displaying the corpses of "the enemy" in compromised positions. For every statement that charged Wright with paranoia when speculating about the AIDS virus, one need not look far to find real historical precedents, such as the practice of injecting unknowing men of color with syphilis.[38] The outrage that Wright expressed might be measured against a question of significance. These events are significant in and of themselves. The political question is how to read that significance in relation to perceptions of what constitutes a "normal" and typified act undertaken in the name of the citizens of the United States.

THE JEREMIAD AND THE INFERENCE

If the question, "Can I trust you?" haunts our interpretive encounters, then our dependence upon cultural narratives takes on a particular poignancy. Any training in validating "the habitual" act of representation is designed to facilitate the creation of the "abodes" that we inhabit. At the point of giving over our trust, we are at our most vulnerable, and the potential to be moved by the words of another and feel community is, indeed, a basis for "the audacity of hope." Here the ethos of genre studies is implicated, especially when we question the ethics of going back to what is known to assuage any fears we might have about what language can do for and to us.

Interestingly, and significantly, the etymology of ethos speaks to the significance of habits and typified acts of representation. Etymologically, ethos is connected to the word *haunt*, as in "animal lair," "abode" or "dwelling place" wherein people dwell and bond together. According to Margaret D. Zulick, a metaphorical application of the word "haunt"—the habitual territory returned to by wild animals—and ethos as a dwelling was provided by Charles Chamberlin. Ethos as haunt or as lair also suggests "custom" or "habit." She writes, "one can perhaps see how the name has traveled from `lair' to `habit' (via `habitat') to `character' in the sense of the constellation of habits of thought, manners, and reputation that constitutes a rhetorical subject" (20).

The metonymic linkages between these historical terms are, as noted, similar to those that inform Hauser and Benoit-Barne's rhetoric of trust: to craft a trustworthy ethos, a speaker will be expected to put forth the familiar and habitual—hence the generic, or that which may be habitually aligned with rhetorical competence. Trust in one's good character gets aligned with precisely that sense of dependability—that one can be depended on to invoke the comfort of the familiar when participating with language. By calling forth recognizable language uses, we will be able to craft a "home" for listeners to inhabit. Michael Hyde notes the historical precedents informing this chain of concepts. "Does not Aristotle's understanding of artful ethos presuppose that the character that takes place in the orator's specific text is itself contextualized and thereby made possible by past social, political and rhetorical transactions that inform the 'habitats' and 'haunts' (ethea) wherein people dwell and bond together?" (xvi) In this view, the endeavor to be linguistically hospitable calls for "adaptatory" rhetoric that, as Jacqueline Bacon notes, "aims to reduce dissonant messages" (55) by taking into account "the expectations of others [as] the basis of a persuasive situation" (55).

Speech acts that challenge audience expectations will be subordinated to those acts that appear to be accommodating by appealing to an audience's "beliefs and attitudes" (Bacon 56). Accordingly, *making* a return would seem to signify an ethical impulse. The very definition of ethos, and hence of genre as typified action, suggests that ethical participation means going back to the haunt, the habitat (habitual); consulting the recognizable, the familiar and representable, and invoking the history of sayings to signify a (generic) desire to be regarded as having good character. Genres seem to offer an ethical assist and can be construed as building blocks to hospitable dwelling places that allow the rhetor to establish a welcoming terrain.

But we return again to the problem raised in every chapter of this book, in which we are asked to think more carefully about how we think that we are able to identify the action of conversion and its relationship to stylized forms of representation. When it comes to genre studies, this question might be expressed as one that asks about how to read the elusive act of "adaptability" when it is formulated as an act of "making a return." Any attempt to "go back" to "the familiar" will be implicated by whatever patterns of inferences are deemed to be customary. Meanwhile, acknowledging the customary only underscores how the "dwelling place" metaphor inscribed into the etymology of ethos that welcomes listeners also constructs exclusions. To cultivate a place to dwell means to establish a boundary and then a demarcation of where the welcome mat ends. This is not only a metaphorical premise. Those exclusions will have material effects that become evident when particular modes of expression uttered by particular bodies get designated as expendable to enable the formation of a center, a place "within" which some may dwell. The pragmatic expectation that rhetors adapt and choose rhetorics that feature familiar discursive patterns creates the conditions that make it possible to renounce the rhetor who, like Wright, appears to refuse the mandate to *be accommodating.*

We mark territories of affiliation by adopting attitudes about which rhetorical styles seem to be welcoming. The effects of this kind of territoriality haunted public discussions of how to read Wright's character, and in so doing, created an opening in which to consider another connotation of the word *haunt*. A "haunt" is not only a noun but also a verb, *to haunt* and *to be haunted by*, to engage in "a repetitive practice" that, as Joshua Gunn notes, connotes a compulsion that seems mandatory (Mourning 177) but is indicative of a perspective that is aggrieved and ill at ease. Both connotations of the action of haunt—a return to a welcoming abode, an obsessive repetition—are implicated within our attempts to establish standards of legitimacy within rhetorics that encourage adaptability.

Studies of African American communication practices make it clear that Wright *was* returning to a habitual dwelling place, a terrain recognizable to members of a dwelling community that he inhabits and that, per AAVE scholars, privileges the "interacting, spontaneous process" of "call and response" or "talking" as a form of ethical linguistic participation. (See Daniel and Smitherman.) Not only is this style different from European discursive traditions, so is its authorizing power, one that recalls the social, experiential, and lived components of interpretive action. AAVE scholars explore how the privileging of the lived elements of communicative power grew out of a historical context of necessity, when "talking back" referenced not just a style but as a means of survival for people who were by law disenfranchised. The failure to accommodate a prevailing discursive tradition was both culturally imposed and then adopted as a political necessity. The intricate knot of interpretive entanglements in that cultural positioning establishes a rhetorical context that is at variance with the one that is presumably standard and then a neutral source for identifying an ethics of participation. Recognizing those variations might prompt us to modify conceptions about how to link language practices to narratives of discursive ethics. Rather than depict "adversarial discourse" as an enemy to reconciliation, it may be regarded as its own distinctive ethical practice that interferes with the putatively smooth reproduction of hegemonic power relations embedded within interpretive methodologies. Rhetorical styles can, in this framework, contribute to exposing power differentials.[39]

This use of style has been deployed historically by African American speakers to condemn unjust social practices and hence presents an alternative "background context" that audiences may draw upon when determining which acts of speech are trustworthy. Indeed members of Wright's church community would have expected him to reference this discursive history and renew a call for justice, according to ministers who spoke in Wright's defense. "The role of pastors to speak about what's going on in the community—that's a very historic role," said the Reverend Myron Cloyd in an article published on the front page of *The Houston Chronicle*[40] just after Obama delivered his speech on race. The article noted that Cloyd characterized Wright as "one of the nation's most eloquent preachers," speaking in a tradition that acknowledges "pain" and that "provides a voice for the voiceless" by telling parishioners "it's not all in your head." The Reverend Robert Scott offered a similar description in an article from the *St. Louis Post-Dispatch*. "We are called to be prophetic. The pastor of an African-American church is perhaps the freest voice in that community."[41]

More specifically, the call to conscience that is regarded as fundamental to a Reverend's ethical obligations is filed under its own genre: "the jeremiad"—an "honored tradition in black church life" named after "the Old Testament prophet Jeremiah," a biblical truth teller who "regularly warned the government that divine destruction was imminent if the nation continued to oppress the powerless" (Melissa Harris-Lacewell).[42] "The African American jeremiad," notes Gilyard, "consists of statements of or references to the popular doctrine of America's divine promise" along with "chastisement because of a present moral decline" (15).

From this perspective, Wright's style and delivery performed the work of memory as it called upon audiences to participate and enact a civic-religious ritual to provoke communal acts of recollection that acknowledged a history of expulsions. The "angry" style deployed within Wright's call to consciousness aimed in a different direction than the call put out by Obama in his speech on race. Listeners were called upon by Wright not to take a "reasonable look" at a history that can be transcended by an act of forgetting, but to a confrontation with the legacy of incalculable traumatic crimes that involved cycles of domination and humiliation—the legacy of which, given Wright's public shaming—have not disappeared. The interpretive framework overseeing his way of being with language as a public speaker obligated him to call out the perpetuation of that cycle, and that expectation was enfolded into judgments of whether he is trustworthy. As his defenders made clear, Wright's sermons served a specific purpose, not only to inspire but also to validate the reality of past experiences and the ways in which the past can intrude on the present. The idea that this purpose was significant to only a subset of the national audience indicates again how racial identities are woven into those seemingly generic narratives that would appear to explain how representational action occurs. If we can generalize about representational action, then we need not bother with the question of which specific stories should be regarded as representative of the nation. Nor need we consider the question of how (in what mode) they should be told.

The doubled connotations of the "haunted" as a dwelling place and a psychic obsession became enfolded within the media spectacle that pitted Obama against his pastor, destroying their public relationship while rendering the story of that specific act of destruction to be less significant than the construction of a grand narrative about a nation progressing towards equity for all. The abstract big story was depicted as an ethically better narrative than any story about personal affiliations between two remarkable men. Meanwhile, this turn to the big story gave audiences permission to overlook the specificity of how Wright's language choices called for a different kind of participation. Wright's words were haunted by a history of oppression and the question put to the nation was whether his invocation of that history—whether the repetition of a style that calls audiences to remember exclusions—should be trusted itself or rendered a sign of obsession. Is it time to move past the old hurts, to get over a history of exclusions especially now that a man of color has been twice voted into the office of the President?

This question not only haunts our national politics it also implicates the technologies of evaluation that we are expected to invoke when settling into communities by sharing responses to interpretive controversies. Discourses of intimacy inhabit those technologies, where interlocutors put forth and "take in" language as they establish communal habitations. But, again, "taking in" also means "leaving out." Within an interpretive context that designates a specific mode of textual order as the trustworthy mediator between private feelings and public disclosures, what will be left out is precisely the dynamic of expulsion that accompanies the act of locating the trustworthy text. The question, "Can I trust you to hear me?" means, "Can I trust you to infer what I infer when I ask you to take my words to heart?" as well as "Can I trust you to deem irrelevant what I abandon?"

Any technology of evaluation will be haunted by what it excludes. If a dwelling place involves referencing norms to invent artistic judgments (rather than to deploy language accurately to re-present truth), those judgments will be haunted by the exclusions that make their quality of normalcy seem to be possible, desirable, and valid. The binary that presumed to distinguish Obama's "reasonable" call to move the country forward rendered that call as being dramatically different from the anger expressed by Wright—anger that appeared to be mired in the past, stuck in a dead zone that should be left behind. Obama calling upon all citizens to look beyond racial discord towards a new future of harmony was rendered as more ethical than Wright's seemingly "fixated" return to a history haunted by a legacy of trauma. Obama's call to reason seemed to differ from Wright's provocations of outrage, even though both men urged audiences to journey to a place of hope and community. Obama called us to remember an ability to transcend history. Wright called us to history—*to* remember it in all its real, bloody, messed up specificity. A call "forward" versus a call "back," one read as benevolent and ideologically neutral, the other as ideologically suspect. But clearly, with every public appearance Wright was also issuing a "call to Being." Wright called upon audiences to occupy a different habitat, one that would force us to sit with the discomfort of haunted memories. Wright delivered a stalwart push towards an embodied recollection of a painful past that continues to haunt our present, one that would call upon all of us, from our varying contexts, to look more closely at how we think we ought to negotiate the gap between remembering and forgetting. And that would ask us to consider which symbolic forms and narratives prompt us to look forward by forgetting which narrativized pasts.

When we are judging who to trust by determining who seems to have good will, who is aspiring for transcendence and using language to call us to be better selves, we will look at any number of indicators, including those that might be associated with "spontaneous" and ephemeral qualities that cannot be textually represented—the act of wrenching us out of our habituated perspectives, the act of sensing that someone means well even if unpolished and clumsy, or as in the case of Wright, the act of creating an artful persona who summons the power of the lament that both encodes a familiar form without reproducing those enculturated genres that, as put by Michael Shapiro, "reinforce the already-in-place ideological discourses vindicating entrenched systems of power and authority" (126).

When discursive histories clash, the rhetoric of trust that valorizes a normative narrative order authorizes the dismissal of speech acts that seem to be "out of order" and helps to establish an interpretive context in which *bringing order* seems to enact an ethics. We might, instead, consider how the call to order can institutionalize forms of racism by redefining racism not only as the tendency to harbor racist thoughts but also as a kind of language use that would promote and regularize a pattern of inferences about how to represent a moral order of thought. Wright's fierce yet controlled style offers an alternative model for judging the meaning and significance of any display, and can prompt us to ask about our responsibilities in relation to those habits/dwelling places already validated by social institutions. That question was precisely not posed within the sentimentalized approval of Obama's race speech.

The rhetorical labor of excluding the prophetic tradition was accompanied by a way of framing "The Wright Controversy" as if it were a problem that Obama could resolve by reassuring non-African American audiences that racial division was precisely not significant to his campaign. That this reassurance took shape through the persistent denigration of Wright seemed to be offset by the generic repetition of platitudinous commonplaces about having hope for the nation's post-racial future. This dynamic allowed the decision to expel Wright and repeatedly shame him to be characterized *as* ethical, *as* community driven. And it created a context in which the repeated shaming of Wright could be characterized as being "out of our hands,"[43] not reliant upon our consent to a particular assemblage of fabricated narratives, but to general (generic) common sense.

5 Conclusion: Passionate Linkages

Persuasion is a matter of consent. This premise has not been given its due, especially in the domain of politics. We choose when to be moved, inspired, accepting or not of another's point of view. We decide when and how to allow foreign perspectives to enter our worlds. And with that, we decide how to manage the terms of our emotional receptivity. Consent reformulates whatever calculus we might deploy when conceiving of linguistic participation.

This is not to say that we have control over acts of reception. But if belief involves choice, then the question of how we judge, and indeed what we judge when assigning credibility, cannot be definitively anchored to either a discernible object of inquiry or interpretive process. Rather than embrace the responsibilities implied by the act of choosing while grappling with the enigma of the aesthetic, we are encouraged to look elsewhere when explaining and authorizing our interpretive habits—either to a putatively neutral organizing structure embedded within language's properties or to a history of practices that seem to foreground citations commended for having character. Audience consent seems to be activated when citizens invoke interpretive methodologies that have been deemed to be trustworthy. With procedural neutrality in place, we may characterize any given act of exclusion as unmotivated or inevitable, logical, and sensible. We need not trouble ourselves with the question of how to contend with a dynamic of expulsion that accompanies the endeavor to advance democratic ideals in significant ways that can be measured in concrete terms. But because meaning is not brought to presence via stable linguistic practices, whatever meanings emerge will reflect choices that have been made about what to notice and then what to ignore at any moment of judging.

The endeavor to rethink participation can build upon the insights of postmodern and feminist theories that acknowledge this coupling within acts of interpretation and explore how it emerges in response to a principle of negativity inhering within meaning-making processes. The possibility that we will fail to persuade, as Shoshona Felman points out, is intrinsic to the endeavor to succeed. But determining what the act of failure means may be detached from those narratives that depict failure as an absence of success. Our judgments of these qualities bespeak the training that would teach us to reference the binary that differentiates substance from mereness and to assign these qualities opposing values while teaching us to recognize an associative link between weight, substance, and importance, and then the corresponding lack of import in the "opposing" qualities: the lightweight, the trivial, the dismissible. When accepting the validity of that binary, we accept a way of framing what matters to judgment and what does not—reality over fabrication, facts over opinions, substance over style, coherence over disorder—the persuasiveness of each of these constructions depending upon the perpetual exclusion of the subordinated term. But as Felman observes, "the act of failing is not a simple negation, a simple absence of presence (of substance), nor even a simple act" (84). "Failing" demarcates an imaginary space of "referentiality," the place at which we observe a linguistic practice and reference a narrative to explain what happened. Failure does not demarcate an absence of success once we discover that something is missing. Rather, failure signifies a discursive site in which "something else is done or . . . something else is said" (84). When characterizing speech failures, we tend to select narratives of negativity as if they automatically apply and sum up what happened in an interpretive encounter that missed the mark of persuasion. Such depictions are just that: aesthetic constructs that stand in for a complex event of judging that cannot be fully represented.

In this book, I have tried to demonstrate how we learn to accommodate ourselves to this binary, to feel its effects viscerally and to reference it while overlooking the intertextual contexts that inform assessments of style's influence on judgments of credibility. The choice to overlook style's significance has been cultivated over time, at least to the writings of Immanuel Kant. Chaim Perelman traces a cultural antipathy for the act of consent in judgment, and for rhetoric itself, within Kantian philosophy that endeavored to "rid philosophy of opinions altogether" (438-39). In Kant's conceptual framework, the Aristotelian interest in "the probable" was no longer "recommended either for the law courts or for the pulpit," neither of which, in his view, should be subjected to language practices that would muddy distinctions between *being* and *seeming to be*. Kant's rejection of rhetoric, which he aligned with discursive deception, was propelled by a corresponding taxonomy of discursive situations and purposes that demand different orders of thought.

> For if we are dealing with civil law, with the rights of individual persons, or with lasting instruction and determination of people's minds to an accurate knowledge and a conscientious observance of their duty, it is unworthy of so important a business to allow a trace of any luxuriance of wit and imagination to appear, and still less any trace of the art of talking people over and of captivating them for the advantage of any chance person. (Kant qtd. in Bender and Wellbery 18)

Accordingly, the luxury of wit and imagination belong to the domain of aesthetics, not politics, and not the law. Kant maintained that the language practices associated with rhetoric (and specifically, rhetorical imitatio) must be considered "the very opposite of genius" (qtd. in Potolsky 67) that gets expressed via aesthetic forms (chiefly poetry) that do not follow rules or mimic established models. This binary sets the stage for a critical slippage that has affected how we go about authorizing discursive practices in political culture. Most importantly, as we refuse rhetoric we are also expected to refuse the acts of invention and consent that accompany the judgments we make about civil laws and the rights of individual persons, ascribing these laws to nature even as they become topics for debate.

Kant maintained that rhetorical eloquence traps judgment by seducing audiences to be mesmerized by beautiful but deceptive language practices that enact verbal trickery. Rhetorical style "borrows from the art of poetry only as much as is necessary to win minds over to the advantage of the speaker before they can judge and to rob them of their freedom" (Kant qtd. in Abbot 275). Here, freedom demarcates freedom *from* some other encroaching entity, and in Kant's version that subordinated other can be characterized as the rhetorical style that incites adherence by crafting bonds of affiliations between rhetors and audiences. "Freedom" in this sense signifies a desire to be rid of language's interpellative hail, to be free of the influence of prior interpretive contexts on visions of meaning and value. Accordingly, one's consent to a given political proposition must seem to have emerged from a domain of thought that is unconstrained by time, situation, and material life. This kind of premise helps to formulate the conceptual framework that valorizes stylistic transparency and the discursive practices that seem to make it happen.

The postmodern/rhetorical rejoinder reminds us of our inherent dependency on the cultural narratives that circulate and delineate conceptual horizons. Our very being is tied to our "fundamental dependency on the address of the other" (Butler Excitable 5), making it impossible for us to achieve a state of contemplation that is unencumbered by cultural and linguistic influences. Meanwhile, our fundamental dependency on the address of the other will be perceived as a problem only if freedom from dependency is promulgated as thought's highest achievement. If we question the legitimacy of *that* premise, then the Kantian conflation of freedom and autonomy may be reformulated. When we acknowledge that we depend upon language then the act of freedom can be reconfigured: "freedom of speech" means freedom *to* engage in creation and reception, freedom *to* be exposed to the linguistic acts of others. Acknowledging this kind of freedom in political discourse opens a space in which to reformulate conceptions of how to constitute a discursive ethics by considering what exposure to another's discursive practices means. An ethics that acknowledges dependencies and exposures can reorient the narratives of legitimation that influence evaluations of language choices.

Given that the choices we make about what to overlook or notice within a scene of representation can be disconnected from "supporting conventions" (Butler Excitable 20), our freedom is comprised of the ability to reconceive how to make a return to the narratives that we must rely upon to be heard. While we are dependent in general on cultural narratives, and while we are interpellated into recognizing specific linguistic rituals that will shape our responses, that dynamic of dependency is not absolute. We are free to challenge it, to not repeat it, to not consent to its automatic continuity. From this perspective, freedom is not expressed by transcending narrative or by denuding style of its material histories but by reshaping perceptions of how to participate with language in order to constitute representational fairness. Judgment is, to borrow a phrase from Bill Readings, "a network of obligation" (University 158) that includes deciding who is obligated to do what stylistically to meet whatever needs have been identified as requiring a response. Rethinking style offers a way to concretize what a new conception of participation might mean and to revise our visions of obligatory networks and what they seem to mandate. The narratives that have been historically attached to rhetorical style, that have shaped embodied preferences for representational forms that fit and cohere, are only placeholders for a dynamic action that exceeds our ability to domesticate it. We may, in each event of judging, consider *how* to factor in contingencies, illusions, and the tacit acceptance of style's contribution to instigating fabricated meanings.

Aesthetic References

In spite of his dim view of rhetoric, Kant offers a theory of judgment that acknowledges the importance of ambiguity within judgments and hence can assist a rhetorical endeavor to rethink participation. Accordingly, there is a difference between determinate judgments that draw conclusions from objective evidence, and judgments described as reflective or aesthetic. These judgments take up the question of how to determine value—or in rhetorical terms, significance. Reflective/aesthetic judgments do not aspire to accuracy or truth or disclosures of authenticity. Rather, reflective judgment considers how thought is implicated by the cognitive ambiguity of the aesthetic (Osborne 33), a quality that is not recognizable, absolute, and repeatable. We cannot definitively identify which representational forms are sublime and in good taste. We may try to do this (i.e., Good Books or best practices), and indeed we may embark on national missions to civilize citizens by teaching them to recognize quality, eloquence, signs of genius, etc. But those lessons will reflect cultural preferences, not universal givens. Kant sought to characterize a kind of judgment that registers an experience that is decidedly different from the endeavor to quantify and concretize which forms of representation should be expected to produce recognition of esteemed values.

Kant's turn to aesthetics carries two important implications: It makes the somatic, sensuous experience of pleasure and pain relevant to social judgment and it posits that judgments of pleasure and pain are not beholden to procedural norms. Further, it destabilizes narratives of method. No identifiable method can predetermine which cultural forms re-present beauty's essential qualities. Instead, reflective judgment addresses the critical problem of how to theorize something more elusive: how to imagine external signifiers, or "sign-vehicles" (Osborne's word), connecting to inner sensibilities of what those sign-vehicles signify. This is precisely the dynamic that we cannot see and validate with recourse to empirical evidence. But clearly, connections between sign vehicles and inner sensibilities get made. The question, then, is how to imagine and regard the acts through which signifiers induce embodied responses.

Rather than offer a definitive answer, Kant draws out the implications of the enigmatic: the gap between a public sign vehicle and a private response is bridged when we experience the pleasurable sense that subjective encounters harmonize with the qualities of objective artifacts (Osborne 33). Kant left open the question of what harmony *is* or how it might be achieved, emphasizing instead an oscillating action that *gestures* towards conjoining narratives and experiences without fully synthesizing their differences. The dynamic never finally converts perceptions into facts or final explanations of what perceptions mean or why they might be significant. Rather, aesthetic pleasure might be characterized as a perpetual action involving a continuous presenting/dismantling of appearances. Aesthetic judgments do not seek final meanings by a method of interpretation that secures "relations between signifiers" but "by a constant fracturing of their formation" (Osborne 31). This vacillating dynamic—or "trembling" as put by Osborne—"underlies and sustains the indeterminacy of any particular interpretation" (Osborne 31) of how signs get attached to meanings. Because neither the act of signifying nor the act of attaching meaning to what gets signified can be fully described, descriptions of interpretive processes and our experiences with acts of interpretation do not get conflated. Rather, aesthetic judgment highlights their intrinsic separation. Judgment is described as aesthetic to underscore what can only be an indirect vision that demarcates not a full explanation but "an experience of an endless *process* of signification as production and immanent destruction of signifiers or sign vehicles in the interpretive apprehension of material form" (Osborne 31—original emphasis).

Interestingly, while tending to the significance of that which eludes representation, Kant retained that hierarchy that would distinguish poetic sign vehicles from rhetorical ones, as if it is possible to isolate their respective stylistic purposes and the kinds of judgment each would provoke. Presumably, rhetorical style is repetitive and formulaic, promoting predictable modes of linguistic participation, merely imitating rather than shaking audiences out of interpretive complacencies. But given that all acts of signification are implicated by the vagaries of how attachments are made between embodiment and narrative, then the element of continuity, the elusive and unknowable thrust of an aesthetic associational force, is always at issue, no matter what kind of sign is being judged. Theorists such as Jean François Lyotard reject the poetic/rhetoric hierarchy, but build upon Kant's conception of reflective judgment and his interest in aesthetics when revising conceptions of political judgment. Lyotard expands Kant's meditations about how signs connect to embodied sensibilities to also consider the significance of the perpetual incommensurability between signs and representational elements that make acts of signification possible. When we acknowledge the significance of *that* gap, then we will notice that there are differences between speculations about how to use language morally and the narratives that prescribe how to represent moral thought.

More specifically, Lyotard takes note of the indeterminacies that permeate the linguistic properties of designation and reference. These are actions that we tend to regard as real, as truly happening when we invoke words associated with what acts of reference *do*. Indeed, we are expected to take the "movement" of referring and designating for granted, as if all we need is our common sense to understand what a phrase such as "there it is" means. The act of reference engages a dynamic of retrospection that seems to truly occur rather than only doing so metaphorically. Presumably, a singular and unidirectional motion comprises that action that facilitates the retrospective dynamic. But Lyotard observes that *reference* is a metaphor for an idea of how we attach language uses to meaning. There is no actual motion triggered by the word *there*. The phrase instead demarcates a sentence—a culturally encoded inscription that would stand in for the idea of referential action. Or as Geoffrey Bennington, writing about Lyotard, explains, "The sentence 'I think' does not entail that I am but that there has been a sentence" (124). This insight is both obvious, once one pauses to consider it, and infinitely complex once we mull over its implications. Sentences do not actually refer to anything, yet we take their referential properties for granted because we are in the habit of doing so and because we have come to agree that certain signs will be deployed to act as designators of actions like pointing to or explaining or clarifying.

Lyotard unpacks the assumptions that must get made to support conceptions of how referential action functions, noting that when we put forth a phrase to signify an idea or an event or even a feeling, we reference not those entities but presuppositions about how sentences should *link*. A commitment to form means being loyal to and then linking one's use of style to a prior narrative that would demarcate how "good form" should appear. Fidelity to prescribed forms means abiding by prescribed formulations of how to draw linkages between the experience of apprehending form and assessments of all that that form represents. But once we acknowledge that we decide how to craft linkages between forms and what they mean, we may also acknowledge the significance of the idea that, as put by Readings, "no judgment is final; there is always another link in the chain. Questions of value are systematically incapable of closure.... The judge at each stage in the process must be called upon to take responsibility for the judgment delivered, rather than hiding behind a ... pretension to objectivity" (University 132).

"Linkage" demarcates an associational dynamic that is not constituted by a natural order of cause and effect but by an order of discursive privilege—preferred modes of communicating through which we seem capable of producing verifiable discursive results—call them conclusions, summaries, final judgments, or explanations. Those results reference standards of evaluation that have themselves been aesthetically/rhetorically created and that signify not true interpretive methods but culturally encoded ways of seeing.

The act of connecting one sentence to another is the site of political struggle because people will have different views of what should be retrieved from that background context to bridge the gap between the visible form and what cannot be seen but is nonetheless "present" to deliberative acts. Any sense of obligation we might feel will not be to a bona fide *rule* delivered to us from "outside," but to a "sentence universe" that has been humanly devised, culturally sanctioned, and politically prized. As Lyotard notes, the phrase "you must" does not emerge from the same sentence universe that makes it possible to say "I know what is right." When that difference goes unnoticed, speculation about what constitutes moral obligation can slide into prescriptions of how to stylize and represent moral thought.

ENTHYMEMES AND KEEPING JUDGMENT OPEN

For Aristotle, the endeavor to persuade is best accomplished with recourse to the enthymeme, the mode of argument that omits a major premise and requires the audience to supply it. The enthymeme specifies a kind of participation that is explicitly concerned with the dynamic of linking. It keeps the question of judgment open by asking audiences to self-consciously consider how they establish linkages between acts of perception and evaluation. Its most significant feature is that it works through a dynamic of presence and absence that complicates any positivistic or mimetic account of language's representational properties. Indeed, the enthymeme poses a challenge to the common regard we are expected to have for representability and its apparent ability to actualize democratic practices.

The enthymeme underscores the ways in which the dynamic of inference—of illusions and inventions—contributes to ways of seeing meaning and significance. And the enthymemic perception cannot be determined in advance. Hence it demarcates judgment as an event involving a "lived" part of interpretive encounters that may not be codified. Enthymemes speak to those elements of mediation that interest Lyotard—actions (signifying, referring, designating, apprehending) that are part of interpretive action but unrepresentable and hence immeasurable with reference to procedural standards; but even though unrepresentable, they remain relevant to conceptions of how to judge. There is a there/not there tension characterizing how interpretive gaps are filled by audiences, and this tension precludes us from knowing in advance whether a given occasion of persuasion will engender shared perspectives or leave us cold for failing to make an impact. It underscores how audience identification involves making a decision about whether to honor or ignore a ritualized call to be heard.

Jeffrey Walker's exploration of the enthymeme as defined in classical rhetorical traditions offers an important starting point for envisioning political judgment *as* an act of interpretive negotiation. Writers of antiquity, he explains, described the enthymeme as a term to name complex interlocking processes involving bodily encounters with texts. Here, the etymology of the enthymeme is of interest. Its root, notes Walker, is "*thymos* or *heart* meaning the seat of emotions and desires, or of motive, or of the sometimes uncontrollable forces of desire that drive human intentionality" (48-9). If the syllogism describes a kind of reasoning in which, per Aristotle, "certain things having been laid down, other things necessarily derive from them," (qtd. in Walker 47), the enthymeme considers how *the heart* factors into whatever conclusions are reached about expressions put up for review. Michael Hyde makes a similar point in his reading of Heidegger, who "recognizes how the primary function of the enthymeme . . . is associated with engaging others in the emotional process of 'taking something to heart' . . . so that they might be moved to thoughtful action. The enthymeme, ethos, and pathos work together:

the moving of the passions . . . is a prerequisite of persuasion; truth alone is not sufficient to guide the thoughtful actions of human beings (xviii).

Linkages between what is present and what is inferred are not discovered or recognized but forged, constructed, invented by way of linking a proposition to a conclusion because it engenders pleasure—what rhetoricians might call an embodied sense of a fit, or what Kant would describe as reflective judgments of elements in harmony. That sense of: yes, *these* words. *This* language, this phrase, this linguistically-produced imagery that gives expression to my memories of happiness and sorrow, and that in recalling my experience allows me to identify with someone else's ways of presenting memory. The enthymeme's attention to inference takes note of audience participation driven not only by what is real but also what is imagined, what is sensed but may not be "proven." Once we sense the fit, we tend to identify with the rhetorical choices put before us.

But ambiguity lingers in the question of what prompts us to reach such conclusions. No formula (or rubric) can guarantee how audiences will fill in the missing premise. Aristotle nonetheless aligned enthymemic processes with a structural logic, what Walkers calls "an underlying rationality" or "intuitive capacity for deriving inferences and forming judgments from relationships between ideas" (54). Walker affirms the *a priori* existence of a ground of rationality that may be referenced to guide how inferences are made and received. Arguably, this affirmation retains vestiges of positivistic logic, given that "the reasonable" may presumably be identified and positioned as the enthymemic "lure" (Walker's word 56).

Other classical rhetoricians were not convinced that rational structures precede and organize audience responses to speech acts. Isocrates, for example, proposed a different model of enthymemic action that noted the centrality of the dynamic of inference in acts of judgment, but did not conflate the "generally accepted" with "the reasonable." Instead, Isocrates envisioned an enthymemic dynamic that features aesthetics as an important aspect of linguistic performances that engage audiences in complex ways—somatically, cognitively and even inexplicably. In her study of differences between Aristotelian and Isocratic rhetorical traditions, Ekaterina V. Haskins notes that for Isocrates, judgment is not driven by the recognition of formal linguistic structures or valid propositional content, but emerges contextually as audiences negotiate and participate with whatever form is put before them. Isocrates emphasizes an "in the moment" aspect of language use that differs from the reflective stance promoted by Aristotle, holding out for the effects of judgment on those fleeting yet vital elements of experience that cannot be conflated with narrative constructs and that prevent any narrative from being wholly deterministic—the "flash of insight" prompted by a well-turned phrase, the effects of timing on audience reception (*kairos*), the stylistic rhythm that can compel a hearing, the sensuous pleasure that can influence the heart's willingness to listen, and, indeed, those fleeting missteps that can seem both endearing and/or a reason for turning away. We cannot know in advance what component part of any ritualistic repetition of familiar forms will engender shared responses of identification, and/or disassociation. But in marking the location at which we will make inferences, enthymemes highlight intertextuality. The enthymeme draws attention to the idea that some styles will be preferred, but it simultaneously reminds us that aesthetic and rhetorical constructs make up the intertextual histories that get referenced to resolve the enthymemic action provoked by political controversies.

To situate style as a site of moral action is to demarcate an ambiguous dynamic in which the act of linking is a poetic act of invention that performs rhetorically to potentially grab the listener's attention anew at every moment of interpretive negotiation. This is what keeps language alive and makes room for the possibility of incorporating the value of the unguarded perspective into conceptions of political debate. Each act of interpretive negotiation will present itself singularly and need not be judged in terms of whether it matches a standing narrative. Instead, the enthymeme attends to discreet acts of linguistic participation that may prompt identification if the rhetorical and aesthetic components of a given text/utterance appear to be pertinent to the time of judging. Meanwhile, decisions about what forms have what purposes remain open and fluid.

In terms of political speech, deciding whether a given "we" "sees" virtuous acts of participation from public speakers and texts will mean a perpetual act of negotiating the conditions of social value. And with this interpretive conception in place, we might think of the enthymeme thusly: the passionate inferences that "feel" right, that seem to justify our conclusions and perhaps motivate our actions and that are driven by the choices we make about how to respond to protocols of style. This is a passion that can be both dangerous and invigorating, but most crucially, it cannot be argued away. Passionate linkages emerge from opinions about what in any representational scene should have significance. The enthymeme demarcates this fleeting site. It might be described as the place at which linguistic interpellation meets individual desire and passion for a particular world view about how language ought to function. The enthymeme demarcates a "space" where opinions about the contours of morality and representability will influence political judgments of who speaks with credibility. If the sense of a speaker's character is manifested by his or her language choices, then the object of evaluation is not a static object but a dynamic that we mull over as we consider whether and how a speaker re-presents the familiar in a new context.

The point of this way of thinking, as noted by Peter Dews, is not to "demonstrate the ultimate illusoriness of any language-independent reality" (41). Rather, it highlights how the significance and value of any cultural form depends on how "it links to a discursive field, as well as how this plane of signification is attached to a conjunctural history made up of different modes of production" (Greene 55). Within the space of representation we make linkages to our sense of a reality, and ambiguously traverse back and forth between the phenomenal, the ephemeral, and the textual, engaging all to get a glimpse of an embodied sense of what we think should *be*. Political fights are waged not over who is speaking the truth but over how to "fill in" that which will inevitably be left out of an utterance in any given case. We fight over how to choose prior contexts to authorize a particular assemblage of propositions. Any sense of reality will be mediated by dominant representations, while the persuasiveness of those representations will be affected by "'our mute contact with things before they have been said'" (Merleau-Ponty qtd. in Dews 43)—a contact that cannot itself be presented and yet is intrinsic to representation's possibility. Feelings of fit and propriety exist in this space of mute contact. They are simultaneously present and illusory, real and imaginary, necessary and constraining to estimations of which words carry persuasive power. They exist in a state that Dews, translating Lyotard, calls "quasi-fictional, quasi-real," a designation that offers a seemingly slight but hugely significant alteration to conceptions of democratic inquiry. Were we to embrace a conception of democracy as quasi-fictional, quasi-real, then we would not need to perceive the "'production and consolidation of reference and meaning'" (Spivak qtd. in de Lauretis 47) in terms of accuracy and truth. Nor would we need to valorize the good work of interpretive resolutions with reference to a putative commonality of interpretive experience. Our very debt to narrative would be reconceived.

Acknowledging that acts of identification and alienation are not automatic but informed by histories that guide how to look back when considering what is occurring at the moment of judging opens a space in which to consider how we are going about fusing conclusions onto embodied responses to sign-vehicles. Those decisions will include not only insight but also responses to the very look of representation. An element of physicality, or materiality, ascribed to both the participating audience as well as to what Lyotard calls "the letter of the line," will affect acts of identification and judgment. Style, then, demarcates not only those techniques that facilitate communicative acts; it also marks the place at which bodies meet texts and subjects decide what in that encounter to value.

Removing ethics from the domain of determinism establishes an alternative demand—that we question what specifically is asked of us as we participate in each event of judging, especially if a perpetual alterity prevents our knowing for sure how to read the aims underwriting a rhetor's choices about which forms to invoke, which sentences to put forth and how to craft a linkage to intertextual histories. By opening a theoretical space that allows for affiliations between ethics and uncertainty, we change the terms organizing conceptions of how to constitute ethical participation with language. Judgments, especially those that apply to political life, involve the creation and maintenance of passionate linkages that tie together sentences and the universes of thought they would aim to represent. Judgment is an aesthetic practice. Ethics resides right there—in our attitudes about how to grapple with language's unpredictable and inexplicable transformative powers.

Notes

Introduction

1. CBS News, advertisement, WBBM Chicago, August 17, 2008, television.
2. Rick Robinson, "The Top Campaign-Ending Political Gaffes in Modern U.S. History," The Daily Caller, August 22, 2012, http://dailycaller.com.
3. Ibid.

Chapter 1

1. Senate, *Impeachment of President William Jefferson Clinton—The Evidentiary Record Pursuant to S. Res. 16—Index to Senate Document 106–3, Vols. I-XXIV*, 106th Cong., 2nd sess., S. Doc. 106–3, Washington: GPO, January 8, 1999, accessed November 10, 2013; "Transcript: House Judiciary Committee," *CNN*, October 5, 1998, http://.cnn.com.
2. House Resolution 611 contained four Articles of Impeachment. Four Republicans opposed all four, five Democrats voted for three articles. One Democrat voted for all four articles.
3. Mitch McConnell, "Closed Door Impeachment Statement," Transcript at *CNN*, February 12, 1999, http://cnn.com.
4. Richard Lugar, "Closed Door Impeachment Statement," Transcript at *CNN*, February 12, 1999, http://cnn.com.
5. Frank Murkowski, "Closed Door Impeachment Statement," Transcript at *CNN*, February 12, 1999, http://cnn.com; Bob Inglis, "Statement at Oct. 5th House Judiciary Committee Meeting. Transcript: House Judiciary Committee," *CNN*, October 5, 1998, http://cnn.com; Robert Aderholt, "Statement from House Final Debate on Impeaching President Clinton. Transcript: House Debates Articles of Impeachment," *CNN*, December 18, 1998, http://cnn.com.
6. Rebekah Metzler, "Straight Talk Wins Wisconsin Votes," *The U.S. News Media Group*, October 8, 2012, http://usnews.com.

7. Straight talk also implies consistency. "There are few people in public life who, through thick and thin, rain or shine, stick to their principles. Ron Paul is one of those few" reads a fan page devoted to the candidacy of Ron Paul that also asks and answers the question, "Who is Ron Paul?" "Ron Paul Revolution," n.d., http://ronpaul.com; "Rare opportunity for speakers at GOP convention," *CNN*, August 15, 2012, http://cnn.com; Sandra Sobieraj Westfall, "Laura Bush Delivers Feisty GOP Straight Talk," *People Magazine*, September 2, 2008, http://people.com.

8. William Kristol, "Impeach, and Convict," *Newsweek*, December 21 1998, 28.

9. Richard Estrada, "Hard To See Payoff In President's Current Strategy," *Sun Sentinel*, August 25, 1998, http://articles.sun-sentinel.com.

10. Joe Gelman, "The Master of Double Speak Engenders Public Debate," *Interstate General Media LLC*, October 8, 1998, http://philly.com.

11. John McCain, "Closed Door Impeachment Statement," Transcript at *CNN*, February 12, 1999, http://cnn.com.

12. Gary C. Jacobson, "Public Opinion and the Impeachment of Bill Clinton," *British Elections & Parties Review* 10, no. 1 (2000): 1–31.

13. Henry Hyde, "Statement at Oct. 5th House Judiciary Committee Meeting, Transcript: House Judiciary Committee," *CNN*, October 5, 1998, http://cnn.com.

14. Tom Delay, "Statement at Oct. 8th Meeting of the House, Transcript: House Debate on Launching Impeachment Inquiry," *CNN*, October 8, 1998, http://cnn.com.

15. Barney Frank, "Statement at Oct. 5th House Judiciary Committee Meeting, Transcript: House Judiciary Committee," *CNN*, October 5, 1998, http://cnn.com.

16. William Delahunt, "Statement at Oct. 8th Meeting of the House, Transcript: House Debate on Launching Impeachment Inquiry," *CNN*, October 8, 1998, http://cnn.com; Henry Hyde, "Statement at Oct. 8th Meeting of the House, Transcript: House Debate on Launching Impeachment Inquiry," *CNN*, October 8, 1998, http://cnn.com.

17. Senate, *Impeachment of President William Jefferson Clinton—The Evidentiary Record Pursuant to S. Res. 16—Index to Senate Docu-*

ment 106–3, Vols. I-XXIV. 106th Cong., 2nd sess., S. Doc. 106–3, Washington: GPO, January 8, 1999, accessed November 10, 2013.

18. Richard Benedetto, "Public Likes Clinton More, GOP Less in Wake of Vote," *USA Today*, sec. 6A, December 21, 1998.

19. Henry Hyde, "An Issue of Principles, Not Politics," *Chicago Tribune*, sec. 1:15, February 18, 1999.

20. Henry Hyde, "Excerpts From Dec. 18 Impeachment Debate," *Washington Post*, December 18, 1998, http://washingtonpost.com.

21. Howard Coble, "Statement at Oct. 5th House Judiciary Committee Meeting, Transcript: House Judiciary Committee," *CNN*, October 5, 1998, http://cnn.com; Charles Canady; Asa Hutchinson; Tom Delay, "Statement at the Oct. 8th Meeting of the House,Transcript: House Debate on Launching Impeachment Inquiry," *CNN*, October 8, 1998, http://cnn.com.

22. Thomas Docherty, *Postmodernism*, 23.

23. Bob Barr, "Opening Statement at the House Impeachment Hearings, Transcript at Dec. 11 Opening Statements," *The Washington Post*, December 11, 1998, http://washingtonpost.com.

24. Lloyd Grove, "Rep. Barr's New Quest: Impeachment," *Washington Post*, sec. E1, February 10, 1998.

25. "Videotaped Testimony of William Jefferson Clinton, President of the United States, 1998," *Jurist: The Law Professor's Network*, September 21, 1998, http://jurist.org.

26. Howard Coble, "Opening Statement at the House Impeachment Hearings, Transcript at Dec. 10 Opening Statements," *The Washington Post*, December 11, 1998, http://washingtonpost.com; Timothy Noah, "Bill Clinton and the Meaning of 'Is,'" *The Slate Group*, September 13, 1998, http://slate.com.

27. "Clinton's Grand Jury Testimony, Part 8, Clinton Accused: Special Report," *The Washington Post Company*, 1999, http://washingtonpost.com.

28. Alternatively, Thomas P. Miller engages a Gramsci-inspired analysis of the hegemonic control executed by social narratives that would dictate the parameters of acceptable linguistic comportment. He would revive the use of "doxa" (public opinion) to counter the legacy of Enlightenment traditions that undermined communal judgments about whether any given representation offers a responsible show of purposes that others should accept. Yet in valorizing doxa, Miller's argument stakes out its own version of stylistic protocol. The idea that

"everybody knew" the impeachment was a bad idea could be read as an example of "doxa" in action. But the functionality encoded with this expression of a rhetorical alternative can instigate its own version of linguistic management. For additional readings on the relationship between narrative, identity, and judgment, see Lois McNay.

29. Andrew Phillips, "Starr Crossed," *MacCleans*, September 21, 1998, 36.

30. Phillips, "Starr Crossed," 40.

31. Ibid.

32. Kenneth Starr, interview by Diane Sawyer, *20/20*, ABC, WLS Chicago, November 25, 1998.

33. John M. Broder and Don Van Natta Jr., "The Testing of a President: The Opponents; Clinton and Starr, a Mutual Admonition Society," *The New York Times Company*, September 20, 1998, http://nytimes.com.

34. Phillips, "Starr Crossed," 38; "What Other News Editorials are Writing," *The Seattle Times Company Network*, September 1998, http://community.seattletimes.nwsource.com; Bob Secter and Lisa Black, "Revelations Shock Many at First Blush," *Chicago Tribune*, sec. 1:15, September 13, 1998; "Clinton's Job Rating Steady, but Public Backs Censure," *Chicago Tribune*, sec. 1:20, September 14, 1998; "Polls: Job Approval Rating Still Strong," *Lubbock Avalanche-Journal*, September 14, 1998, http://lubbock.com.

35. Nancy Gibbs and Michael Duffy, "Is There A Way Out?" *Time*, September 28, 1998, 30.

36. Media commentators who assessed public reactions to the impeachment frequently attributed the outcome to "the people" exercising their common sense. Alexander Cockburn, "Love and Distraction," *The Nation*, Sept. 7/14, 1998, 8; Jonathan Alter, "Bill's Monica Mandate," *Newsweek*, February 22, 1999, 35.

37. Charles Babington, "Democrats Won't Try to Impeach President," *The Washington Post Company*, May 12, 2006, http://washingtonpost.com.

38. Lauren Berlant, *Anatomy*.

Chapter 2

1. Jim Newton, "Kenneth Starr: Open to the Public," *The Tribune Company*, December 30, 2007, http://latimes.com.

2. Bill Clinton, "Public Speech to the Nation," *CNN*, August 17, 1998, http://cnn.com/allpolitics.

3. "Testing of a President: The Editorials; Excerpts from Newspaper Judgments on Clinton." *The New York Times Company*, August 19, 1998, http://nytimes.com; "The 'Unofficial' Bill Clinton on the Web," n.p., n.d, http://zpub.com; "What Papers Elsewhere Have to Say About Clinton." *Tribune News Services*, August 19, 1998, http://articles.chicagotribune.com.; "Many Editors Believe Clinton Should Resign," *Kingman Daily Miner*, August 24, 1998, http://news.google.com; "Mea Not So Culpa," *The Washington Post*, sec. A20, August 19, 1998.

4. Julia Preston, "The Testing of a President: The Governor; After Watching the Testimony Whitman Urges Resignation," *The New York Times Company*, September 22, 1998, http://nytimes.com; Andrew Phillips, "Starr Crossed;" *MacCleans* 21 Sept. 1998: 36; Nancy Gibbs and Michael Duffy, "Is There a Way Out?" *Time*, September 28, 1998, 31; "Sen. Joseph Lieberman Speaks on Clinton," *CNN*, September 3, 1998, http://cnn.com/allpolitics. What Lieberman said: "After much reflection, my feelings of disappointment and anger have not dissipated. Except that now these feelings have gone beyond my personal dismay to a larger, graver sense of loss for our country, a reckoning of the damage that the President's conduct has done to the proud legacy of his presidency, and, ultimately, an accounting of the impact of his actions on our democracy and its moral foundations."; William Neikirk and Michael Tackett, "Three Senate Democrats Tell Clinton to Apologize," *Chicago Tribune*, sec. 1:1, September 4, 1998.

5. See, for example, William Covino; Jasper Neel. James S. Baumlin also discusses *Phaedrus* in an essay about ethos. See "Positioning Ethos."

6. For rhetorical studies of the Belletristic era that promoted this conflation see, for example, Thomas P. Miller; Sharon Crowley; Nan Johnson; Mike Hill; Lois Peters Agnew; Stephen J. McKenna.

7. For other explorations of connections between rhetoric, textuality, emotion and embodiment, see, Laura R. Micciche; Megan Boler; Sara Ahmed; Susan McLeod; Julia A. Stern; Toby Miller; Karen Kopelson; Judith Butler, *Bodies That Matter;* Deborah Hawhee; Kristie Fleckenstein.

8. Jay Leno, "Best of Jay Leno Jokes," *Amray Web hosting*, n.d., http://amray.com; Leno reportedly "stood by his jokes" after speaking

to a news columnist who maintained the jokes were too cruel. See Richard Roeper, "Leno Stands by his Tripp Jokes," *The Ocala Star-Banner*, sec. 7B, July 24, 1998, http://news.google.com; Paul Gray, "Linda Tripp: The Friend from Hell," *Time Inc.*, December 28, 1998, http://time.com; Gary Kamiya, "Mommy Dearest" qtd. in Letter, *Salon Media Group*, February 18, 1999, http://Salon.com; Bill Tammeus, "Sorting Out the Scandal for Future Reporters," *KC Star Publications*, February 6, 1999, LexisNexis Academic.

9. "Poll: Americans Remain Opposed to Clinton Impeachment," *CNN*, October 13, 1998, http://cnn.com/allpolitics.

10. Walter Kirn, "Papa Bill, Mama Linda, Baby Monica: The Dysfunctional Family at the Heart of the Scandal," *Time*, October 5, 1998, 36; "Monica Lewinsky trying to pare down her body and her fame." *CNN*, Janurary 4, 2000, http://cnn.com/allpolitics; "Does Monica's hair make the cut?" *The Detroit News*, March 4, 1999, http://detnews.com; Leonard Pitts Jr., "Hasta la Vista, Baby—Monica Needs to Shed the Weight of Notoriety," *Chicago Tribune*, sec. 1:15, February 15, 2000.

11. Danielle Paquette, "Daniel Tosh Twitter-Apologizes for Rape Joke (Sort of)," *The Tribune Company*, July 11, 2012, http://latimes.com.

12. Sarah Devlin, "Whoopi Goldberg on Daniel Tosh Rape Joke: 'If It Works then It's OK,'" *Mediate LLC*, July 12, 2012, http://mediaite.com; Gilbert Gottfried, "If You Don't Want to Hear an Edgy Joke, Don't Listen," *CNN*, July 16, 2012, http://cnn.com.

13. Piper Weiss, "Daniel Tosh Humor: 9 Funny Women Who DON'T Defend Comic." *Yahoo! Contributor Network*, July 12, 2012, http://shine.yahoo.com.

14. "Understanding the Iran Contra Affairs," *Brown University*, n.d., http://brown.edu/research.

15. "Louis CK addresses Daniel Tosh Twitter Controversy on 'Daily Show,'" *The Huffington Post.com Inc.*, July 17, 2012, http://huffingtonpost.com.

16. "Keeping Score in the Lewinsky Matter," *CNN*, January 31, 1998, http://cnn.com/allpolitics.

17. Keating Holland, "Poll: Most Americans Don't Want to Hear Tripp Tapes," *CNN*, July 9, 1998, http://cnn.com/allpolitics.

18. Karen Heller, "Just Out: Lewinsky, Tripp on Tape. The Voices, Alas, Ordinary," *Philadelphia Enquirer*, sec. A18, November 18,

1998; "Wake Us When It's, Like, Over. The Tripp-Lewinsky Whine-A-thon," *Arkansas Democrat-Gazette, Inc.*, November 22, 1998, LexisNexis Academic; "Monica, Linda, Yada, Yada, Yada," *The New York Daily News*, November 18, 1998, LexisNexis Academic; Richard Roeper, "The Lewinsky-Tripp Tapes were Simply Pathetic," *The Ocala Star-Banner*, sec. 5B, November 21, 1998, http://news.google.com.

19. Anne Gearan, "At Long Last, the Public Will Really Hear from Monica Lewinsky," *The Associated Press*, November 9, 1998, http://apnewsarchive.com; "Monica, Linda, Yada, Yada, Yada."

20. Roeper, "The Lewinsky-Tripp Tapes were Simply Pathetic"; Eric Pooley, "Tripp's Turn to Talk," *Time*, July 6, 1998, 64.

21. Deborah Norville, interview by Larry King, , *Larry King Live*, CNN, November 18, 1998; Marc Fisher, "Tripp Tapes: Listening in On a Betrayal," *The Washington Post*, sec. A1, November 18, 1998, http://washingtonpost.com.

22. Michael Isikoff and Evan Thomas, "Clinton and the Intern," *Newsweek*, February 2, 1998, http://newsweek.washingtonpost.com.

23. James Warren, "After 8 Jury Appearances, Tripp Speaks Out, Casts Herself as Victim," *Chicago Tribune*, sec. 1:9, July 30, 1998.

24. Philip Coughter, "Linda Tripp's Statement after Final Day of Testimony," *CNN*, July 29, 1998, http://cnn.com/allpolitics.

25. Linda Tripp, "Linda Tripp's Statement after Final Day of Testimony,"

26. Rita Braver, "Amnesty for a Wiretapper?" *CBS Interactive Inc.*, December 17, 1999, http://cbs.com; Bill Press, "An Average Mom? Hardly," *The Tribune Company*, July 31, 1998, http://latimes.com.

27. Linda Tripp, interview by Jamie Gangel. *The Today Show*, NBC, WMAQ Chicago, February 12, 1999; Linda Tripp, interview by Larry King, *Larry King Live*, CNN, February 15, 1999.

28. This portion of the tapes was broadcast on *Larry King Live*, "Meltdown in Washington," *CNN*, January 1, 1999.

29. Linda Tripp, interview by Sam Donaldson and Cokie Roberts, *ABC This Week*, WLS Chicago, March 7, 1999.

30. Linda Tripp, excerpts of *The Today Show* Interview by Jamie Gangel. *Dateline*, NBC, WMAQ Chicago, February 12, 1999.

Chapter 3

1. Dan Balz, "Biden Stumbles at the Starting Gate," *The Washington Post*, sec. A06, February 1, 2007, http://washingtonpost.com.

2. Xuan Thai and Ted Barrett, "Biden's Description of Obama Draws Scrutiny," *CNN*, February 9, 2007, http://cnn.com; Jack Tapper, "A Biden Problem: Foot in Mouth," *ABC News Internet Ventures*, January 31, 2007, http://abcnews.go.com; Adam Nagourney, "Biden Unwraps '08 Bid with an Oops!" *The New York Times Company*, February 1, 2007, http://nytimes.com.

3. Fedreka Schouten, "Biden Burned by 'Clean' Language; Description of likely '08 Rival Obama Causes a Stir," *USA Today*, sec. 5A, February 1, 2007, LexisNexis Academic.

4. Saddam Hussein, the enemy Iraqi leader captured in 2003 by U.S. forces, was executed in December, 2006, six months before Obama's announced candidacy in May, 2007.

5. Martin Sieff, "Obama, Dems Win Historic Blowout Victory," *United Press International Inc.*, November 5, 2008, http://upi.com; Kathie Durbin, "Obama in Portland—County Residents Flock to Rally," *The Colombian (Vancouver, WA)*, sec. 1, March 22, 2008, LexisNexis Academic; "Police: More than 100,000 Watch Obama," The Denver Post, October 26, 2008, http://denverpost.com.

6. David Corn, "How Obama Lost the Narrative," *Mother Jones and the Foundation for National Progress*, November/December 2010, http://motherjones.com; Jessica Yellin and Kevin Bohn, "Democrats to President: Get a Clear Message," *CNN*, September 7, 2010, http://politicalticker.blogs.cnn.com; *New York Times* Columnist Maureen Dowd also documented frustration with Obama's rhetoric: "'We just wish he'd be more of a fighter,' said one influential Democrat with a grimace. Another agreed: 'You can't blame him for everything. I just wish he would come across more forceful at times, but that is not the dude's style. Detached hurts you when things are sour.'" Maureen Dowd, "Withholder In Chief," *The New York Times Company*, August 9, 2011, http://nytimes.com.

7. John Hawkins, "The Worst of Barack Obama in Quotes," *Right Wing News*, September 10, 2012, http://rightwingnews.com.

8. "Chris Matthews: 'I Felt This Thrill Going Up My Leg as Obama Spoke,'" *The HuffingtonPost.com Inc.*, February 13, 2008, http://huffingtonpost.com; James Hohmann, "Matthews: Obama's too Cool," *Politico LLC*, October 30, 2011, http://politico.com.

9. Chris Cillizza, "'Big' is Bad, with a capital B," *Washington Post*, sec. A2, April 9, 2012.

10. Zachary A. Goldfarb, "Romney Camp Says Candidate is a Prankster," *Washington Post*, sec. A6, April 29, 2012.

11. Judith Warner, "Tears to Remember," *The New York Times Company*, November 6, 2008, http://nytimes.com; Scott Stump, "Colin Powell Declines to Endorse President Obama," *The Today Show*, NBC, May 22, 2012, http://nbc.com.

12. Michael Powell, "Can We Talk Politics Please?" *The New York Times Company*, September 23, 2007, http://nytimes.com.

13. Perry Bacon Jr., "Why Do So Many Republicans Love Chris Christie?" *Washington Post*, sec. A10, September 29, 2011.

14. Other reporters noted the crowd's enthusiasm as well. When blogging for ABC news, Michael Falcone and Amy Walter described the speaking event as "a remarkable moment. Republicans at the Ronald Reagan Presidential Library last night, pleading, cajoling and begging New Jersey Gov. Chris Christie to run for president." Michael Falcone and Amy Walter, "Chris Christie and 2012's Passion Gap (The Note)," *ABC News Internet Ventures*, September 28, 2011, http://abcnewsgo.com.

15. "Keller @ Large: Likeability a Problem for Romney," *CBS Local Media*, March 28, 2012, http://boston.cbslocal.com; Paul Steinhauser, "CNN Poll: Gender Gap and Likeability Keep Obama Over Romney," *CNN*, April 16, 2012, http://politicalticker.blogs.cnn.com; David Eggen and T.W. Farnam, "March Numbers Show Hefty Cash Advantage for Obama," *Washington Post*, sec. A4, April 21, 2012; And another commonly used word: empathy. In an April, 2012 article, John Sides of the *New York Times* discussed "Romney's Empathy Gap," noting that "Mitt Romney has an empathy problem. A new Washington Post/ABC News poll finds that 49 percent of respondents think that President Obama 'better understands the economic problems people in this country are having.' Only 37 percent believe that Mr. Romney does." John Sides, "Romney's Empathy Gap," *The New York Times Company*, April 11, 2012, http://nytimes.com.

16. Tom Cohen, "Romney's Big Day Marred by Etch-a-Sketch Remark," CNN, March 22, 2012, http://cnn.com; Jonathan Martin, "Election Aftermath: GOP Soul-Searching: 'Too Old, Too White, Too Male'?" *Politico LLC*, November 7, 2012, http://politico.com; Brian Montopoli, "After Romney Loss, GOP Soul-Searching Begins,"

CBS Interactive Inc., November 7, 2012, http://cbsnew.com; "Chuck Todd: the Republican Party 'Has Some Serious Soul-Searching To Do,'" *The HuffingtonPost.com Inc.*, November 6, 2012, http://huffingtonpost.com; Chris Stirewalt, "Republican Soul-Searching Probably Mostly Pointless," *Fox News Network, LLC*, November 9, 2012, http://foxnews.com.

17. Warren Bennis and Andy Zelleke, "Barack Obama and the Case for Charisma," *The Christian Science Monitor*, February 28, 2008, http://csmonitor.com; Kenneth T. Walsh, "Obama's Charisma Doesn't Guarantee a Win," *The U.S. News Media Group*, March 7, 2008, http://usnews.com.

18. Alex Spillius, "Has Obama's Charisma Deserted Him?" *Telegraph Media Group* (blog), November 26, 2009, http://blogs.telegraph.co.uk.com; Seth McLauglin and Stephen Dinan, "Obama Loses His Campaign Charisma," *Washington Times LLC*, November 3, 2010, http://washingtontimes.com.

19. Lydia Saad, "Americans See Different Strengths in Obama and Romney," *Gallup, Inc.*, October 29, 2012, http://gallup.com.

20. Susan Miller, in *Trust in Texts*, also discusses how the idea that textuality should be trusted influenced elocutionary studies in the eighteenth century. The student-orator learned to speak properly by training "the tongue" to mimic standardized forms and eliminate accents associated with regional identities (135).

21. Alex Seitz-Wald, "Poll: 64 percent of Republicans Think that Obama's Hiding Info About His Past," *Salon Media Group, Inc.*, January 17, 2013, http://salon.com.

22. *The Situation Room with Wolf Blitzer*, CNN February 21, 2008.

23. Howard Fineman, "Obama and the Politics of Race," *Newsweek LLC*, May 13, 2008, http://newsweek.com.

24. Katharine Q. Seeyle and Julie Bosman, "Ferraro's Obama Remarks Become Talk of Campaign," *The New York Times Company*, March 12, 2008, http://nytimes.com.

25. Carl Hulse. "Civil Rights Tone Prompts Talk of Endorsement," *The New York Times Company*, January 11, 2008, http://nytimes.com. It might be noted that the sentiment attributed to Bill Clinton is not what he actually said. His comment was made in reference to the contentious issue of who supported the 2003 invasion of Iraq, a decision that, by 2008 had become publicly controversial.

As Senator of New York, Hillary Clinton voted to authorize an invasion and her attempts to contextualize that vote seemed like irrelevant retrospective justifications for a decision that should never have been made. Obama maintained that he had opposed the war since its inception. When campaigning in New Hampshire, Bill Clinton challenged Obama's claims, calling his opposition "a fairy tale," and accusing him of distorting his stance on the war, especially since he was not a member of the U.S. Senate in 2003. Bill Clinton explained all of this in a subsequent call to civil rights leader Al Sharpton's radio show, maintaining that his remark had been taken out of context. "There's nothing fairy tale about (Obama's) campaign. It's real, it's strong and he might win," Clinton said. "I pointed out that he had never been asked about his statement in 2004 that he didn't know how he would have voted on the war resolution." "Bill Clinton Defends 'Fairy Tale' Remark," *Thomson Reuters*, January 11, 2008, http://reuters.com; "Matthews Mischaracterized Bill Clinton 'fairy tale' Quote," *Media Matters for America*, March 4, 2008, http://mediamatters.org/research.

26. John B. Judis, "The Big Race: Obama and the Psychology of the Color Barrier," *The New Republic*, May 28, 2008, 21; Jeffrey Kluger, "Race and the Brain," *Time*, October 9, 2008, 59; Sharon Begley and Daniel Stone, "How Your Brain Looks at Race," *Newsweek*, March 3, 2008, 26.

27. Richard Cohen, "Obama's Pastor Problem," *Washington Post*, sec. A19, March 18, 2008.

28. James Carney and Amy Sullivan, "Why Obama Has a Pastor Problem," *Time*, March 31, 2008, 38.

29. Bill O'Reilly, "Talking Points: Obama Pastor Controversy," *O'Reilly Factor*, Fox News, March 14, 2008; Sean Hannity quoted in Howard Kurtz, "A Complex Speech Boiled Down to Simple Politics," *Washington Post*, sec. A17, March 20, 2008; Joseph Loconte, "The Wrong Reverend," *The Weekly Standard LLC*, March 18, 2008, http://weeklystandard.com.

30. For a discussion of ethos and its connection to disciplinary narratives, see Elizabeth Schüssler Fiorenza; Barbara Warnick; Susan C. Jarratt and Nedra Reynolds.

31. James Carney and Amy Sullivan, "Why Obama Has a Pastor Problem." *Time*, March 31, 2008, 39.

32. Lisa Miller, "Obama's Church of Contradictions," *The Washington Post Company*, March 25, 2008, http://newsweek.washingtonpost.com/onfaith.

33. Barack Obama, "Transcript: Barack Obama's Speech on Race, Philadelphia, PA," *CBS Interactive*, March 18, 2008, http://cbs.news.com.

34. "Mr. Obama's Profile in Courage," *The New York Times Company*, March 19, 2008, http://nytimes.com; Mike Lupica, "BAM Shows Amazing Grace—Race Speech was One for the Ages," *New York Daily News*, March 19, 2008; Cynthia Tucker, "Obama Passes A Leadership Test With Candor and Grace," *Andrews McMeel Universal Co.*, March 19, 2008, http://uexpress.com. (Originally in *Atlanta Journal Constitution*, March 19, 2008.); Tod Robberson, "A Monumental Speech by Obama," *The Dallas Morning News Inc.*, March 18, 2008, http://dallasnews.com; Jeff Zeleny, "Obama Urges U.S. to Grapple with Race Issue," *The New York Times Company*, March 19, 2008, http://nytimes.com.

35. "Under Fire, Obama Tackles Race Relations Issue Head-On," *USA Today*, sec. 10A, March 19, 2008; Walter Rubel, "Frank Discussion of A Sensitive Topic," *Las Cruces Sun-News*, March 23, 2008, LexisNexis Academic; "A Speech that only Obama could Deliver," *The Monterey County Herald*, March 22, 2008, LexisNexis Academic.

36. "Obama on Race: A Visionary Speech Reminds This Nation of Its Better Self," *The Salt Lake Tribune*, March 19, 2008, http://sltrib.com; "Beyond Racism: Obama Strives to Build a Bridge," *San Jose Mercury News*, March 19, 2008, http://mercurynews.com; "To A Higher Level: Barack Obama's Appeal to Reason," *Arkansas Democratic Gazette*, March 22, 2008, LexisNexis Academic; Courtland Milloy, "Invited to Wrestle in a Racial Mud Pit, Obama Soars Above It," *Washington Post*, sec. B01, March 19, 2008.

37. Linda Selzer explores the significance of this fear in an article that praises Obama's "cosmopolitanism." Selzer examines how the "social meanings" of the "raced body" permeated public discussion about the Wright-Obama controversy and she draws connections between the publicity given to Wright and the infamous Willie Horton ad campaign during the 1988 presidential election cycle that contributed to the downfall of Democratic candidate Michael Dukakis. Horton was a convicted felon released by Dukakis, who went on to commit another crime. His images were disseminated to "manipulate white

fears of black rage" (18). For other explorations of Obama, emotional connectivity, and speech, see David A. Frank; Roderick P. Hart and Colene J. Lind.

38. This argument has been influenced by Ali Behdad.

CHAPTER 4

1. For further discussion of this word, see T.R. Johnson's *A Rhetoric of Pleasure*, 4. For other explorations of style, politics, and composing processes, see Min-Zhan Lu; Dion C. Cautrell.

2. Among those elements: "The perception of conditions in a situation that call forth particular kinds of rhetorical responses" including "stylistic characteristics of the rhetoric—features of the rhetoric chosen by the rhetor to respond to the perceived requirements of particular situations" (134). Foss distinguishes "substantive" characteristics that "constitute the content" from stylistic characteristics that "constitute its form" (134). A third element is "an organizing principle" that serves as the label for "the internal dynamic of the constellation that is formed by the substantive, stylistic, and situational features of the genre" (135). Foss's incisive delineation of genre's component parts helps to facilitate ideology critique, but style remains central and undertheorized.

3. See Nan Johnson, "Ethos and Aims of Rhetoric."

4. Obama stated: "I think Ronald Reagan changed the trajectory of America in a way that Richard Nixon did not and in a way that Bill Clinton did not. He put us on a fundamentally different path because the country was ready for it. They felt like with all the excesses of the 60s and the 70s and government had grown and grown but there wasn't much sense of accountability in terms of how it was operating. I think he tapped into what people were already feeling. Which is, we want clarity, we want optimism, we want a return to that sense of dynamism and entrepreneurship that had been missing." Sam Stein, "Obama Compares Himself to Reagan, JFK . . . But Not Bill Clinton," *The HuffingtonPost.com Inc.*, March 28, 2008, http://huffington.post.com.

5. Barbara Jordan, "Keynote Speech at the 1976 Democratic Convention," *American Rhetoric*, http://americanrhetoric.com.

6. Barack Obama, "Transcript: Barack Obama's Speech on Race, Philadelphia, PA," *CBS Interactive*, March 18, 2008, http://cbs.news.com.

7. Steve Chapman, "The Wright-Obama Divide," *Real Clear Politics*, March 23, 2008, http://realclearpolitcs.com; Ryan Chiachiere, "Buchanan on Obama's Race Speech: 'We hear the Grievances. Where is the Gratitude?'" *Media Matters for America*, March 22, 2008, http://mediamatters.org.

8. Lauren Berlant, "The Subject of True Feeling," 58.

9. Judith Butler writes, "The responsibility of the speaker does not consist of remaking language ex nihilo, but . . . of negotiating the legacies of usage that constrain and enable that speaker's speech. To understand this sense of responsibility . . . we understand the speaker as formed in the language that he or she also uses. This paradox intimates an ethical dilemma brewing at the inception of speech" (*Excitable* 27-28).

10. *Bill Moyers Journal*, "Interview with Jeremiah Wright," *Public Broadcasting Service*. April 25, 2008. Transcript at http://pbs.org/moyers/journal.

11. Jeremiah Wright, "*CNN* Live Event/Special: Rev. Jeremiah Wright Speech to Detroit NAACP Dinner," televised April 27, 2008. Transcript posted by *CNN*, April 29, 2008, http://cnn.com.

12. Jeremiah Wright, "Rev. Wright at the National Press Club," *The New York Times Company*, April 28, 2008, http://nytimes.com; For other explorations of Black Theology, see, for example, J. Deotis Roberts; James H. Cone; Larry Murphy.

13. Liz Halloren, "Cutting the Ties of Controversy," *U.S. News and World Reports*, May 12, 2008, 6.

14. "Obama Strongly Denounces Former Pastor," *NBCNews.com*, April 29, 2008, http://nbc.news.com.

15. Liz Halloren, "Obama Cuts the Ties of Controversy," *U.S. News and World Reports*, May 2, 2008, 6.

16. Amy Sullivan, "Jeremiah Wright Goes to War," *Time Inc*, April 28, 2008, http://time.com.

17. Michael Powell and Jodi Kantor, "A Strained Wright-Obama Bond Finally Snaps," *The New York Times Company*, May 1, 2008, http://nytimes.com.

18. Bob Herbert, "The Pastor Casts a Shadow," *The New York Times Company*, April 29, 2012, http://nytimes.com.

19. Nedra Pickler, "Wright: Criticism is Attack on Black Church," *Gannet Company, Inc.*, April 28, 2008, http://usatoday.com.

20. Alessandra Stanley, "Not Speaking for Obama, Pastor Speaks for Himself, at Length," *The New York Times Company*, April 29, 2008, http://nytimes.com.

21. David Gergen, interview by Anderson Cooper, *360 with Anderson Cooper*, CNN, April 29, 2008.

22. Keith Gilyard also takes note of Geneva Smitherman's distinction between vernacular practices (AAVE) and verbal traditions (AAVT) (15).

23. Pickler, "Wright: Criticism is Attack on Black Church"; "Rev. Wright Fights Back," *CBS Interactive Inc.*, April 28, 2008, http://cbsnews.com.

24. "Interview with Jeremiah Wright at National Press Club," *New York Times Company*, April 28, 2008, http://nytimes.com.

25. Ibid.

26. During his NAACP speech, for example, Wright said: "Many of us are committed to changing how we see ourselves. Many of us are committed to changing the way we treat each other. . . . It's going to take people of all faiths including the nation of Islam, but we can do it. It's going to take people of all races, but we can do it. It's going to take Republicans and Democrats, but we can do it. It's going to take the wisdom of the old and the energy of the young, but we can do it." Wright, "*CNN* Live Event/Special: Rev. Jeremiah Wright Speech to Detroit NAACP Dinner."

27. "Obama Strongly Denounces Former Pastor," *NBCNews.com*, April 29, 2008, http://nbc.news.com.

28. "Mr. Obama and Rev. Wright," *The New York Times Company*, April 30, 2008, http://nytimes.com.

29. Richard Wolffe, "Obama's Sister Souljah Moment," *"IBT Media Inc.*, April 28, 2008, http://newsweek.com. (Subsequent title: "Obama Disavows Rev. Wright for Destructive Comments.")

30. David Mills, "Sister Souljah's Call to Arms," *Washington Post*, sec. B1, May 13, 1992.

31. "Sister Souljah Moment," *Wikipedia*, accessed October 19, 2013, http://wikipedia.org.

32. Wikipedia's other examples include George Bush: "As a candidate for the Republican nomination for president in 2000, Texas Gov. George W. Bush, spoke before the conservative Manhattan Institute in October 1999 saying, 'Too often, on social issues, my party has painted an image of America slouching toward Gomorrah,' quoting

the title of a book by conservative jurist Robert Bork. Bush's comments were seen as a repudiation of the religious right and an attempt to appeal to moderate voters; commentator Charles Krauthammer called it 'an ever-so-subtle Sister Souljah on Robert Bork.' Also in the 2000 campaign for the Republican nomination, Arizona Sen. John McCain stated, 'Neither party should be defined by pandering to the outer reaches of American politics and the agents of intolerance, whether they be Louis Farrakhan or Al Sharpton on the left or Pat Robertson or Jerry Falwell on the right.' This was similarly seen as a repudiation of the religious right; columnist Jacob Weisberg called it 'a pungent Sister Souljah moment.'" Ibid.

33. David Meeks, "Poll: Obama's a Muslim to many GOP voters in Alabama, Mississippi," *The Tribune Company*, March 12, 2012, http://latimes.com.

34. *Hannity and Colmes*, "Obama's Pastor's Controversial Remarks," *Fox News*, March 12, 2008. Transcript at http://foxnews.com.

35. "Mr. Obama and Mr. Wright."

36. Eugene Robinson, "Where Wright Goes Wrong," *The Washington Post*, April 29, 2008, http://washingtonpost.com.

37. Greg Miller, "Broader Drone Tactics Sought: Claims to Expand Strikes in Yemen," *Washington Post*, sec. A1, April 19, 2012.

38. The Tuskegee experiments are one infamous example. According to a University of Maryland webpage: "For forty years between 1932 and 1972, the U.S. Public Health Service (PHS) conducted an experiment on 399 black men in the late stages of syphilis. These men, for the most part illiterate sharecroppers from one of the poorest counties in Alabama, were never told what disease they were suffering from or of its seriousness. Informed that they were being treated for 'bad blood,' their doctors had no intention of curing them of syphilis at all. The data for the experiment was to be collected from autopsies of the men, and they were thus deliberately left to degenerate under the ravages of tertiary syphilis—which can include tumors, heart disease, paralysis, blindness, insanity, and death. 'As I see it,' one of the doctors involved explained, "we have no further interest in these patients until they die.'" fyb.umd.edu. First Year Book, Office of Undergraduate Studies, University of Maryland, n.d. Web. 17 Oct. 2013; *The Immortal Life of Henrietta Lacks* presents Rebecca Skloot's study of Henrietta Lacks, a descendent of slaves who was diagnosed with cervical cancer. Researchers at John Hopkins obtained some of

her cancer cells without her knowledge or consent, and those cells were subsequently used in 60,000 research studies. Other experiments inflicted on unsuspecting victims were outlined in a 2010 article published in the *New York Times*: "From 1946 to 1948, American public health doctors deliberately infected nearly 700 Guatemalans—prison inmates, mental patients, and soldiers—with venereal diseases in what was meant as an effort to test the effectiveness of penicillin. American tax dollars, through the National Institutes of Health, even paid for syphilis-infected prostitutes to sleep with prisoners. . . . When the prostitutes did not succeed in infecting the men, some prisoners had the bacteria poured into scrapes made on their penises, faces or arms, and in some it was injected by spinal puncture. If the subjects contracted the disease, they were given antibiotics." Donald G. McNeil Jr., "U.S. Apologizes for Syphilis Tests in Guatemala," *The New York Times Company*, October 1, 2010, http://nytimes.com.

39. Jacqueline Bacon's study of the rhetoric of African American abolitionists takes note of the "emphatic, harshly critical arguments" that "marshall[ed] the dominant culture's texts and myths to condemn them in both overt and subtle ways and to imply radical action—even violent means—to end slavery" (56).

40. Allan Turner, "Black Clergy Explain Obama's Pastor Comments," *The Houston Chronicle*, March 18, 2008, http://chron.com.

41. Tim Townsend, "Black Pastors Here Stress Role as Preacher-Prophet," *St. Louis Post-Dispatch*, sec. A1, March 19, 2008, LexisNexis Academic.

42. Melissa Harris-Lacewell, "Our Jeremiah: Why Obama's Pastor Matters," *The Slate Group LLC*, March 17, 2008, http://theroot.com. See, also, "The Jeremiad: Wright Is Right!" *Wordpress.com*, n.d., http://wrightisright.wordpress.com; Bernard Bell, "Commentaries on the Times: President Obama and Rev. Wright," *Wordpress.com*, n.d., http://commentariesonthetimes.wordpress.com.

43. For discussion of this Toni Morrison phrase, see Judith Butler, *Excitable Speech*, introduction.

Works Cited

Abbott, Don Paul. "Kant, Theremin, and the Morality of Rhetoric." *Philosophy and Rhetoric* 40, no. 3 (2007): 274–92.
Ahmed, Sara. *The Cultural Politics of Emotion*. New York: Routledge Press, 2004.
Alcorn, Marshall. W. "Self-Structure as a Rhetorical Device: Modern Ethos and the Divisiveness of the Self." In *Ethos: New Essays in Rhetorical and Critical Theory*, edited by James S. Baumlin and Tita French Baumlin, 3-35. Dallas: Southern Methodist University Press, 1994.
Althusser, Louis. *Lenin and Philosophy and Other Essays*. New York, NY: Monthly Review Press, 1972.
Ampadu, Lena. "Modeling Orality: African American Rhetorical Practices and the Teaching of Writing." In *African American Rhetoric(s): Interdisciplinary Perspectives*, edited by Elaine B. Richardson and Ronald L. Jackson II, 136-54. Carbondale: Southern Illinois University Press, 2004.
Anderson, Benedict. *Imagined Communities: Reflections on the Origin and Spread of Nationalism*. London and New York: Verso, 1983.
Agnew, Lois Peters. *Outward, Visible Propriety: Stoic Philosophy and Eighteenth-Century British Rhetorics*. Columbia, SC: University of South Carolina Press, 2008.
Asante, Molefi Kete. "The Afrocentric Idea." In *African American Communication and Identities: Essential Readings*, edited by Ronald L. Jackson II, 16-28. Thousand Oaks, CA., London, and New Delhi: Sage, 2004.
Bacon, Jacqueline. "'Do You Understand Your Own Language?' Revolutionary 'Topoi' in the Rhetoric of African-American Abolitionists." *Rhetoric Society Quarterly* 28, no. 2 (1998): 55–75.
Barnes, Elizabeth. *States of Sympathy: Seduction and Democracy in the American Novel*. New York: Columbia University Press, 1997.
Baumlin, James S. "Decorum, *Kairos*, and the 'New' Rhetoric." *PRE/TEXT* 5 (1985): 171–83.
—. "Introduction: Positioning Ethos in Historical and Contemporary Theory." In *Ethos: New Essays in Rhetorical and Critical Theory*, edited by James S. Baumlin and Tita French Baumlin, xi-xxxi. Dallas: Southern Methodist University Press, 1994.
Baudrillard, Jean. *Simulations*. Translated by Paul Foss, Paul Patton, and Philip Beitchman. Los Angeles: Semiotext[e], 1983.
Beasley, Vanessa B. "Democratic Style: An RSVP." *Rhetoric and Public Affairs* 11, no. 3 (2008): 466–70.

Behdad, Ali. "National Identity and Immigration: American Polity, Nativism, and the 'Alien.'" In *Beyond Dichotomies: Histories, Identities, Cultures, and the Challenge of Globalization*, edited by Elisabeth Mudimbe-Boyi, 201-29. Albany, New York: SUNY Press, 2002.

Bender, John, and David E. Wellbery, "Rhetoricality: On the Modernist Return of Rhetoric." In *The The Ends of Rhetoric: History, Theory, Practice*, edited by John Bender and David E. Wellbery, 3-39. Stanford, CA: Stanford University Press, 1990.

Bennington, Geoffrey. *Lyotard: Writing The Event*. Manchester, England: Manchester University Press, 1988.

Bentham, Jeremy. *The Works of Jeremy Bentham*. Vol. 2, edited by Sir John Bowring. London: Adament Media, 2005.

Berlant, Lauren. "Affect, Noise, Silence, Protest: Ambient Citizenship." Presented at the International Communication Association 2009 Mini-Plenary, Chicago, IL, May 22, 2009.

—. *The Anatomy of National Fantasy: Hawthorne, Utopia, and Everyday Life*. Chicago, IL: University of Chicago Press, 1991.

—. *Cruel Optimism*. Durham, NC: Duke University Press, 2011.

—. "The Subject of True Feeling: Pain, Privacy, and Politics." In *Cultural Pluralism, Identity Politics, and the Law*, edited by Austin Sarat and Thomas R. Kearns, 49-84. Ann Arbor, MI: University of Michigan Press, 1999.

Bevilacqua, Vincent. "Adam Smith and Some Philosophical Origins of Eighteenth Century Rhetorical Theory." *Modern Language Review* 63, no. 3 (1968): 559–68.

Biesecker, Barbara A., and John Louis Lucaites. "Introduction." In *Rhetoric, Materiality, and Politics*, edited by Barbara A. Biescker and John Louis Lucaites, 1-16. Bern, Switzerland and New York: Peter Lang, 2009.

Boler, Megan. *Feeling Power: Emotions and Education*. New York: Routledge, 1999.

Burke, Kenneth. *Counter-Statement*. Berkeley and Los Angeles: University of California Press, 1968.

—. *Rhetoric of Motives*. Berkeley and Los Angeles: University of California Press, 1969.

Butler, Paul. *Out of Style: Reanimating Stylistic Study in Composition and Rhetoric*. Logan, UT: Utah State University Press, 2008.

Butler. Judith. *Bodies That Matter: On the Discursive Limits of Sex*. New York: Routledge, 1993.

—. *Excitable Speech: A Politics of the Performance*. New York and London: Routledge, 1997.

Campbell, Karlyn Kohrs and Kathleen Hall Jamieson. "Form and Genre in Rhetorical Criticism: An Introduction." In *Readings in Rhetorical Criticism*. 4th ed., edited by Carl R. Burgchardt, 444-62. State College, PA: Strata, 2010.

Carter, Michael. "The Role of Invention in Belletristic Rhetoric: A Study of the Lectures of Adam Smith." *Rhetoric Society Quarterly* 18, no.1 (1988): 3–13.

Cautrell, Dion C. "Rhetor-Fitting: Defining Ethics through Style." In *Refiguring Prose Style: Possibilities for Writing Pedagogy*, edited by T.R. Johnson and Tom Pace, 228-40. Logan, UT: Utah State University Press.

Cliett, Victoria. "The Rhetoric of Democracy: Contracts, Declarations, and Bills of Sales." In *African American Rhetoric(s): Interdisciplinary Perspectives*, edited by Elaine B. Richardson and Ronald L.Jackson II, 170-86. Carbondale: Southern Illinois University Press, 2004.

Con Davis, Robert and David S. Gross. "Gayatri Chakravorty Spivak and the Ethos of the Subaltern." In *Ethos: New Essays in Rhetorical and Critical Theory*, edited by James S. Baumlin and Tita French Baumlin, 65-89. Dallas: Southern Methodist University Press, 1994.

Cone, James H. *A Black Theology of Liberation*. Maryknoll, New York: Orbis Books, 2010.

Cooper. Marilyn M. "Rhetorical Agency as Emergent and Enacted." *College Composition and Communication* 62, no. 3 (2011): 420–49.

Corbett, Edward P.J. "Teaching Style." In *Style in Rhetoric and Composition: A Critical Sourcebook*, edited by Paul Butler, 209-18. Boston and New York: Bedford St. Martins, 2010.

Covino, William A. *The Art of Wondering: A Revisionist Return to the History of Rhetoric*. Portsmouth, NH: Boynton/Cook, 1988.

Crowley, Sharon. *The Methodical Memory: Invention in Current-Traditional Rhetoric*. Carbondale: Southern Illinois University Press, 1990.

—. *Composition in the University: Historical and Polemical Essays*. Pittsburgh: University of Pittsburgh Press, 1998.

Daniel, Jack L., and Geneva Smitherman. "How I Got Over: Communication Dynamics in the Black Community." In *African American Communication and Identities: Essential Readings*, edited by Ronald L. Jackson II, 3-14. Thousand Oaks, CA, London, and New Delhi: Sage, 2004.

de Lauretis, Teresa. *Technologies of Gender: Essays on Theory, Film, and Fiction*. Bloomington: Indiana University Press, 1987.

Deleuze, Gilles. *The Logic of Sense*. Translated by Mark Lester and Charles Stivale. Edited by Constantin V. Boundas. New York: Columbia University Press, 1990.

Devitt, Amy J. *Writing Genres*. Carbondale: Southern Illinois University Press, 2004.

Dews, Peter. "The Letter and the Line: Discourse and Its Other in Lyotard." *Diacritics* 14, no. 3 (1984): 40–9.

Docherty, Thomas. *Aesthetic Democracy*. Stanford: Stanford University Press, 2006.

—. "Postmodernism: An Introduction." In *Postmodernism: A Reader*, edited by Thomas Docherty, 1-31. New York: Columbia University Press, 1993. Print.

Durham, Scott. *Phantom Communities: The Simulacrum and the Limits of Postmodernism*. Stanford, CA: Stanford University Press, 1998.

Eagleton, Terry. *The Ideology of the Aesthetic*. Oxford: Basil Blackwell, 1990.

Fahnestock, Jeanne and Marie Secor. "Teaching Argument: A Theory of Types." In *The Allyn and Bacon Sourcebook for College Writing Teachers*, edited by James C. McDonald, 235-45. Boston: Allyn and Bacon, 2000.

Felman, Shoshona. *The Scandal of the Speaking Body: Don Juan with J. L. Austin, Or Seduction in Two Languages*. Translated by Catherine Porter. Ithaca, New York: Cornell University Press, 1983.

Fiorenza, Elisabeth Schüssler. *Rhetoric and Ethic: The Politics of Biblical Studies*. Minneapolis: Fortress, 1999.

Flannery, Kathryn. "Style Redux." In *Refiguring Prose Style: Possibilities for Writing Pedagogy*, edited by T.R. Johnson and Tom Pace, 57-75. Logan, UT: Utah State University Press, 2005.

Fleckenstein, Kristie S. "Testifying: Seeing and Saying in World Making." In *Ways of Seeing, Ways of Speaking: The Integration of Rhetoric and Vision in Constructing the Real*, edited by Kristie S. Fleckenstein, Sue Hum and Linda T. Calendrillo, 3-30. West Lafayette, IN: Parlor Press, 2007.

Foss, Sonja K. *Rhetorical Criticism: Exploration and Practice*. 4th ed. Long Grove, IL: Waveland, 2009.

Frank, David A. "The Prophetic Voice and the Face of the Other in Barack Obama's 'A More Perfect Union' Address, March 18, 2008." *Rhetoric and Public Affairs* 12, no. 2 (2009): 167–194.

Frankfurt, Harry G. *On Bullshit*. Princeton: Princeton University Press 2005.

Garver, Eugene. *Aristotle's Rhetoric: An Art of Character*. Chicago: University of Chicago Press, 1994.

Gilyard, Keith. "Introduction: Aspects of African American Rhetoric as a Field." In *African American Rhetoric(s): Interdisciplinary Perspectives*, edited by Elaine B. Richardson and Ronald L. Jackson II, 1-18. Carbondale: Southern Illinois University Press, 2004.

Greene, Ronald Walter. "Rhetorical Materialism: The Rhetorical Subject and the General Intellect." In *Rhetoric, Materiality, and Politics*, edited by Barbara A. Biescker and John Louis Lucaites, 43-65. Bern, Switzerland and New York: Peter Lang, 2009.

Grosz, Elizabeth. "The Future of Space: Towards an Architecture of Invention." Published April 7, 2010. http://dpi.studioxx.org.

Gunn, Joshua. "Mourning Speech: Haunting and the Spectral Voices of Nine-Eleven." In *Readings on Rhetoric and Performance*, edited by Stephen Olbrys Gencarella and Phaedra C. Pezzullo, 176-97. State College, PA: Strata, 2010.

—. "On Speech and Public Release." *Rhetoric and Public Affairs* 13, no. 2 (2010): 1–42.

Habermas, Jurgen. "Discourse Ethics: Notes on a Program of Philosophical Justification." Translated by Shierry Weber Nicholson and Christian Lenhardt. In *The Communicative Ethics Controversy*, edited by Seyla Benhabib and Fred R. Dallmayr, 60-110. Cambridge, MA and London: MIT Press, 1995.

—. *The Structural Transformation of the Public Sphere: An Inquiry into a Category of Bourgeois Society*. Translated by Thomas Burger with Frederick Lawrence. Cambridge, MA: MIT Press, 1991.

Hariman, Robert. *Political Style: The Artistry of Power*. Chicago: University of Chicago Press, 1995.

Harrington, Dana. "Composition, Literature, and the Emergence of Modern Reading Practices." *Rhetoric Review* 15, no. 2 (1997): 249–63.

Hart, Roderick P., and Colene J. Lind. "Words and Their Ways in Campaign '08." *American Behavioral Scientist* 54, no. 4 (2010): 355–381. LexisNexis Academic. Web. 17 Oct. 2013

Haskins, Ekaterina V. *Logos and Power in Isocrates and Aristotle*. Columbia, SC: University of South Carolina Press, 2004.

Hauser, Gerard A. *Introduction to Rhetorical Theory*. 2nd ed. Prospect Heights, IL: Waveland, 2002.

—."Vernacular Dialogue and the Rhetoricality of Public Opinion." In *Readings on Rhetoric and Performance*, edited by Stephen Olbrys Gencarella and Phaedra C. Pezzullo, 294-319. State College, PA: Strata, 2010.

Hauser, Gerard A., and Chantal Benoit-Barne. "Reflections on Rhetoric, Deliberative Democracy, Civil Society, and Trust." *Rhetoric and Public Affairs* 5, no. 2 (2002): 261–75.

Hawhee, Debra. "Language as Sensuous Action: Sir Richard Paget, Kenneth Burke, and Gesture-Speech Theory." *Quarterly Journal of Speech* 92, no. 4 (2006): 331–54.

Hecht, Michael L., Sidney Ribeau, and J. K. Alberts. "An Afro-American Perspective on Interethnic Communication." In *African American Communication and Identities: Essential Readings*, edited by Ronald L. Jackson II, 105-23. Thousand Oaks, CA, London, and New Delhi: Sage, 2004.

Hesford, Wendy S. "*Kairos* and the Geopolitical Rhetorics of Global Sex Work and Video Advocacy." In *Just Advocacy? Women's Human Rights, Transnational Feminisms, and the Politics of Representation*, edited by Wendy S. Hesford and Wendy Kozol, 146-72. New Brunswick, New Jersey and London: Rutgers University Press, 2005.

—. "Reading Rape Stories: Material Rhetoric and the Trauma of Representation." *College English* 62, no. 2 (1999): 192–221.

—. *Spectacular Rhetorics: Human Rights Visions, Recognitions, Feminisms*. Durham, NC: Duke University Press, 2011.

Hill, Mike. "Of Multitudes and Moral Sympathy: E.P. Thompson, Althusser, and Adam Smith." In *Masses, Classes and the Public Sphere*, edited by Mike Hill and Warren Montag, 202-25. London and New York: Verso, 2000.

Huyssen, Andreas. "Mapping the Postmodern." *New German Critique* 33 (1984): 5–52.
Hyde, Michael J. "Introduction: Rhetorically We Dwell." In *The Ethos of Rhetoric*, edited by Michael J. Hyde, xiii-xxviii. Columbia, SC: University of South Carolina Press, 2004.
Ivie, Robert L. "Toward a Humanizing Style of Democratic Dissent." *Rhetoric and Public Affairs* 11, no. 3 (2008): 454–58.
Jackson, Ronald L. "Exploring African American Identity Negotiation in the Academy: Toward a Transformative Vision of African American Communication Scholarship." In *African American Communication and Identities: Essential Readings*, edited by Ronald L. Jackson II, 249-60. Thousand Oaks, CA, London, and New Delhi: Sage, 2004.
Jarratt, Susan C., and Nedra Reynolds. "The Splitting Image: Contemporary Feminisms and the Ethics of êthos." In *Ethos: New Essays in Rhetorical and Critical Theory*, edited by James S. Baumlin and Tita French Baumlin, 37-63. Dallas: Southern Methodist University Press, 1994.
Jay, Martin. *Downcast Eyes: The Denigration of Vision in Twentieth-Century French Thought*. Berkeley and Los Angeles: University of California Press, 1994.
Johnson, Nan. "Ethos and the Aims of Rhetoric." In *Essays on Classical Rhetoric and Modern Discourse*, edited by Robert J. Connors, Lisa S. Ede, and Andrea A. Lunsford, 98-114. Carbondale: Southern Illinois University Press, 1984.
—. *Nineteenth-Century Rhetoric in North America*. Carbondale, IL: Southern Illinois University Press, 1991.
Johnson, T. R. *A Rhetoric of Pleasure: Prose Style and Today's Composition Classroom*. Portsmouth, NH: Boynton/Cook, 2003.
—. "Writing With the Ear." In *Refiguring Prose Style: Possibilities for Writing Pedagogy*, edited by T.R. Johnson and Tom Pace, 267-85. Logan, UT: Utah State University Press, 2005.
Kant, Immanuel. *Critique of Judgment*. Translated by Werner S. Pluhar. Indianapolis: Hackett Press, 1987.
Kelleher, Joe. "Rhetoric, Nation, and the People's Property." In *Mourning Diana: Nation, Culture, and the Performance of Grief*, edited by Adrian Kear and Deborah Lynn Steinberg, 77-97. London and New York: Routledge, 1999.
Kelleher, Tina. "The Uses of Literature." In *Refiguring Prose Style: Possibilities for Writing Pedagogy*, edited by T.R. Johnson and Tom Pace, 78-92. Logan, UT: Utah State University Press, 2005.
Kopelson, Karen. "Dis/Integrating the Gay/Queer Binary: 'Reconstructed Identity Politics' for a Performative Pedagogy." *College English* 65, no. 1 (2002): 17–35.

Lanham, Richard A. *Style: An Anti-Textbook*. 2nd ed. Philadelphia: Paul Dry Books, 2007.

Leff, Michael. "The Habitation of Rhetoric." In *Contemporary Rhetorical Theory: A Reader*, edited by John Louis Lucaites, Celeste Michelle Condit, and Sally Caudill, 52-64. New York: Guilford, 1999.

Loewe, Drew. "Style as a System: Toward a Cybernetic Model of Composition Style." In *Refiguring Prose Style: Possibilities for Writing Pedagogy*, edited by T.R. Johnson and Tom Pace, 241-55. Logan, UT: Utah State University Press, 2005.

Lu, Min-Zhan. "Professing Multiculturalism: the Politics of Style in the Contact Zone." *College, Composition, Communication* 45, no. 4 (1994): 442-58.

Lyotard, Jean-François. *The Differend: Phrases in Dispute*. Translated by Georges Van Den Abbeele. Minnesota: University of Minnesota Press, 1988.

Manolescu, Beth Innocenti. "Formal Propriety as Rhetorical Norm." *Argumentation* 18, no.1 (2004): 113–25.

Mayhew, Leon H. *The New Public: Professional Communication and the Means of Social Influence*. Cambridge and New York: Cambridge University Press, 1997.

McCrimmon, James M. "Writing as a Way of Knowing." In *Rhetoric and Composition: A Sourcebook for Teachers and Writers*, edited by Richard L. Graves, 3-11. Upper Montclair, NJ: Boynton/Cook. 1984.

McKenna, Stephen J. *Adam Smith: the Rhetoric of Propriety*. Albany: State U of New York Press, 2006. Print.

McDaniel, James P. and Bruce E. Gronbeck. "Through the Looking Glass and Back: Democratic Theory, Rhetoric, and Barbiegate." In *The Prettier Doll: Rhetoric, Discourse and Ordinary Democracy*, edited by Karen Tracy, James P. McDaniel and Bruce E. Bronbeck, 22-42. Tuscaloosa, AL: University of Alabama Press, 2007.

McLeod, Susan. "Some Thoughts about Feelings: The Affective Domain and the Writing Process." *College, Composition and Communication* 38, no. 4 (1987): 426–35.

McNay, Lois. "Having It Both Ways: The Incompatibility of Narrative Identity and Communicative Ethics in Feminist Thought." *Theory, Culture & Society* 20, no. 6 (2003): 1–20. Print.

McPhail, Mark Lawrence. "Complicity: The Theory of Negative Difference." In *African American Communication and Identities: Essential Readings*, edited by Ronald L. Jackson II, 29-37. Thousand Oaks, CA, London, and New Delhi: Sage, 2004.

Micciche, Laura R. *Doing Emotion: Rhetoric, Writing, Teaching*. Portsmouth, NH: Boynton/Cook, 2007.

Miller, Carolyn. R. "Genre as Social Action." *Quarterly Journal of Speech* 70 (1984): 151–67.

Miller, Susan. *Textual Carnivals: The Politics of Composition*. Carbondale, IL: Southern Illinois University Press, 1991.

—. *Trust in Texts: A Different History of Rhetoric*. Carbondale, IL: Southern Illinois University Press, 2008.

Miller, Thomas P. *The Formation of College English: Rhetoric and Belles Lettres in the British Cultural Provinces*. Pittsburgh: University of Pittsburgh Press, 1997.

Miller, Toby. *The Well-Tempered Self: Citizenship, Culture, and the Postmodern Subject*. Baltimore: Johns Hopkins University Press, 1993.

Murphy, Larry, ed. *Down by the Riverside: Readings in African American Religion*. New York: New York University Press, 2000.

Neel, Jasper. *Plato, Derrida, and Writing*. Carbondale, IL: Southern University Press, 1988.

O'Gorman, Ned. "Three Cheers for Democratic Style! (Okay, Maybe Just Two)." *Rhetoric and Public Affairs* 11, no. 3 (2008): 450–3.

Osborne, Peter. *Philosophy in Cultural Theory*. London and New York: Routledge, 2000.

Pace, Tom. "Style and the Renaissance of Composition Studies." In *Refiguring Prose Style: Possibilities for Writing Pedagogy*, edited by T.R. Johnson and Tom Pace, 3-22. Logan, UT: Utah State University Press, 2005.

Panagia, Davide. *The Poetics of Political Thinking*. Durham, NC: Duke University Press, 2006.

Perelman, Chaim. "Logic, Dialectic, Philosophy, and Rhetoric." In *Rhetoric: Concepts, Definitions, Boundaries*, edited by William A. Covino and David A. Jolliffe, 436-40. Boston: Allyn and Bacon, 1995.

Plato. *Phaedrus and Letters VII and VIII*. Translated by Walter Hamilton. London: Penguin Books, 1973.

Pollock, Della. "Performing Writing." In *Readings on Rhetoric and Performance*, edited by Stephen Olbrys Gencarella and Phaedra C. Pezzullo, 114-36. State College, PA: Strata, 2010.

Poulakos, John. "From the Depths of Rhetoric: The Emergence of Aesthetics as a Discipline." *Philosophy and Rhetoric* 40, no. 4 (2007): 335–52.

Poovey, Mary. "Feminism and Deconstruction." *Feminist Studies* 14, no. 1 (1988): 51–65.

Potolsky, Matthew. *Mimesis*. New York and London: Routledge, 2006.

Ramage, John D. *Rhetoric: A User's Guide*. New York: Pearson Longman, 2006.

Rankin, Elizabeth D. "Revitalizing Style: Toward a New Theory and Pedagogy." In *Style in Rhetoric and Composition: A Critical Sourcebook*, edited by Paul Butler, 239-49. Boston and New York: Bedford St. Martins, 2010.

Ratcliffe, Krista. *Rhetorical Listening: Identification, Gender, Whiteness*. Carbondale: Southern Illinois University Press, 2005.

Rawls, John. *A Theory of Justice*. Rev. Ed. Cambridge, MA: Belknap Press of Harvard University Press, 1999.
Readings, Bill. *Introducing Lyotard: Art and Politics*. London and New York: Routledge, 1991.
———. *The University in Ruins*. Cambridge, MA: Harvard University Press, 1996.
Redfield Marc. "Imagi-Nation: The Imagined Community and the Aesthetics of Mourning." *Diacritics* 29, no. 4 (1999): 58–83.
Riley, Denise. *Impersonal Passion: Language as Affect*. Durham, NC: Duke University Press, 2005.
Roberts, James Deotis. *Liberation and Contextualization: A Black Theology*. 2nd ed. Louisville: Westminster John Knox Press, 2005.
Rogoff Irit. "Gossip as Testimony: A Postmodern Signature." In *The Feminism and Visual Culture Reader*, edited by Amelia Jones, 268-76. New York and London: Routledge, 2003.
Rosteck, Thomas, and Michael Leff. "Piety, Propriety, and Perspective: An Interpretation and Application of Key Terms in Kenneth Burke's *Permanence and Change*." *Western Journal of Speech Communication* 53, no. 4 (1989): 327–41.
Rowland, Robert C., and John M. Jones. "One Dream: Barack Obama, Race, and the American Dream." *Rhetoric and Public Affairs* 14, no. 1 (2011): 125–54.
Schaffner, Spencer. Review of *Writing Genres*, by Amy J. Devitt. *Enculturation* 5, no. 2 (2004).
Selzer, Linda. F. "Barack Obama, the 2008 Presidential Election, and the New Cosmopolitanism: Figuring the Black Body." *Melus: Multi-Ethnic Literature of the U.S.* 35, no. 4 (2010): 15–37. LexisNexis Academic.
Shapiro, Michael J. *The Politics of Representation: Writing Practices in Biography, Photography, and Political Analysis*. Madison: University of Wisconsin Press, 1988.
Short, Bryan C. "Literary Ethos: Dispersion, Resistance, Mystification." In *Ethos: New Essays in Rhetorical and Critical Theory*, edited by James S. Baumlin and Tita French Baumlin, 367-87. Dallas: Southern Methodist University Press, 1994.
Smith, Craig R. "Ethos Dwells Pervasively: A Hermeneutic Reading of Aristotle on Credibility." In *The Ethos of Rhetoric*, edited by Michael J. Hyde, 1-19. Columbia, SC: University of South Carolina Press, 2004.
Spivak, Gayatri Chakravorty. *In Other Worlds: Essays in Cultural Politics*. New York and London: Routledge, 1988.
Stern, Julia A. *The Plight of Feeling: Sympathy and Dissent in the Early American Novel*. Chicago and London: University of Chicago Press, 1997.
Stob, Paul. "Kenneth Burke, John Dewey, and the Pursuit of the Public." *Philosophy and Rhetoric* 38, no. 3 (2005): 226–47.

Stormer, Nathan. "Encomium of Helen's Body: A Will to Matter." In *Rhetoric, Materiality, and Politics*, edited by Barbara A. Biesecker and John Louis Lucaites, 215-27. Bern, Switzerland and New York: Peter Lang, 2009.

Swearingen, C. Jan. "Ethos: Imitation, Impersonation, and Voice." In *Ethos: New Essays in Rhetorical and Critical Theory*, edited by James S. Baumlin and Tita French Baumlin, 115-48. Dallas: Southern Methodist University Press, 1994.

Thompson, Roger. "'Habit of Heat': Emerson, Belletristic Rhetoric, and the Role of the Imagination." *College English* 69, no. 3 (2007): 260–82.

Walker, Jeffrey. "The Body of Persuasion: A Theory of the Enthymeme." *College English* 56, no. 1 (1994): 46–65.

Warner, Michael. "The Mass Public and the Mass Subject." In *Habermas and The Public Sphere*, edited by Craig Calhoun, 377-401. Cambridge, MA and London: MIT Press, 1993.

—. *Publics and Counterpublics*. New York: Zone Books, 2002.

Warnick, Barbara. "The Ethos of Rhetorical Criticism: Enlarging the Dwelling Place of Critical Praxis." In *The Ethos of Rhetoric*, edited by Michael J. Hyde, 56-74. Columbia, SC: University of South Carolina Press, 2004.

Watts, Eric King. "African American Ethos and Hermeneutical Rhetoric: An Exploration of Alain Locke's *The New Negro*." In *African American Communication and Identities: Essential Readings*, edited by Ronald L. Jackson II, 69-79. Thousand Oaks, CA, London, and New Delhi: Sage, 2004.

Webb, Jen. *Understanding Representation*. Thousand Oaks, CA, London, and New Delhi: Sage, 2009.

White, Hayden. *Figural Realism: Studies in the Mimesis Effect*. Baltimore and London: John Hopkins University Press, 1999.

Williams, Joseph M. *Style: The Basics of Clarity and Grace*. New York: Addison Wesley Longman, 2003.

Williams, Kimmika L. H. "Ties that Bind: A Comparative Analysis of Zora Neal Hurston's and Geneva Smitherman's Work." In *African American Rhetoric(s): Interdisciplinary Perspectives*, edited by Elaine B. Richardson and Ronald L. Jackson II, 86-107. Carbondale: Southern Illinois University Press, 2004.

Worsham, Lynn. "Coming to Terms: Theory, Writing, Politics." In *Rhetoric and Composition as Intellectual Work*, edited by Gary A. Olson, 101-14. Carbondale, IL: Southern Illinois University Press 2002.

—. "Going Postal: Pedagogic Violence and the Schooling of Emotion." *JAC: A Journal of Composition Theory* 18, no. 2 (1998): 213–45.

Zulick, Margaret D. "The Ethos of Invention: The Dialogue of Ethics and Aesthetics in Kenneth Burke and Mikhail Bakhtin." In *The Ethos of Rhetoric*, edited by Michael J. Hyde, 20-33. Columbia, SC: University of South Carolina Press, 2004.

Index

1976 Democratic Convention, 193, 259

accountability, 8, 52, 54, 56, 58–60, 63, 66, 70, 73, 199, 259
actualization, 12, 35–36, 45, 113, 149, 242
adaptatory rhetoric, 228
Aderholt, Rep. Robert, 27, 247
aesthetic, 5, 9, 11, 15, 26, 42, 45–46, 48, 50–51, 74, 131–134, 153, 158, 185, 234–236, 238–239; postmodern, 15
African American Rhetorics, 179–186, 229–231; African American Vernacular English (AAVE), 215–216, 229, 261
agency, 15, 97, 112, 126, 203–204
aims of representation, 29–32, 58–59, 89–93, 152–153, 168, 177–179, 195–197, 205–208
Alberts, J. K., 181
Alcorn, Marshall W., 177
Althusser, Louis, 125
ambiguity in representation, 4, 15, 22, 41, 43, 49, 73, 78, 92, 157, 186, 204–205, 221. 232, 243–244
Ampadu, Lena, 213
Anderson, Benedict, 157
apologies, 6, 17, 77–85, 89–93, 101–103, 110, 128–129, 190, 209, 219
architectonic, 157, 159, 177

architecture, 44, 157
Aristotle, 10, 149, 150, 152, 185, 228, 235, 241–243
Articles of Impeachment, 39, 40, 247
Asanti, Molefi Kete, 182
atonement, 79, 85, 89–92
audience adherence, 5, 56, 96, 138, 191, 193
authenticity, 5–7, 13, 23–31, 37, 42, 50, 57, 71, 82–91, 99, 143–145, 175, 186, 222, 238
authoritative language, 12–14, 95, 139, 169, 183–185, 211
authority, 15, 20–21, 32, 48–49, 67, 78, 107, 108, 111, 132, 138, 153, 157, 178, 187, 215, 232

balance, 83, 105, 177, 197, 225
Barr, Rep. Bob, 54–59, 249
Baudrillard, Jean, 30-2
Baumlin, James, 86, 95–96, 149, 251
Beasley, Vanessa, 52
Belletrism, 153–155, 159, 176, 251
Bennett, Bob, 117
Bentham, Jeremy, 35
Berlant, Lauren, 83–84, 144–145, 201, 205, 207, 250, 260
Biden, Joseph, 72, 136–137, 139, 161, 174, 184, 254
Biesecker, Barbara A., 76

275

Burke, Kenneth, 12, 46–48, 50, 56, 96, 97, 98, 107, 111, 131
Butler, Paul, 11, 52, 126, 237, 251, 260, 263

Campbell, Karlyn Kors, 190–197, 201, 204
Canady, Rep. Charles, 49, 82, 249
categorization, 16, 18, 32, 34, 119, 120, 179–181, 187, 223
choice, 7, 27, 104, 107, 126, 135, 146–147, 182, 203, 206, 222, 234, 235
Christie, Gov. Chris, 28, 145, 255
Cillizza, Chris, 141, 142, 150, 255
civic duty, 17, 51, 118
claims, 3, 23; true and false, 15, 32
clarifying affinity, 201, 220
Cliett, Victoria, 179, 212, 221
Clinton, Bill, 6, 17, 20, 24–28, 39–41, 58–61, 73–75, 81, 105, 161, 223, 247–251, 256, 259
Clinton, Hillary, 136, 160–162, 207, 256
Cloyd, Rev. Myron, 230
Clyburn, Rep. James, 162
Coble, Rep. Howard, 49, 61, 249
coherence, 77, 96–101, 109, 131–133, 159, 214, 235
comedy, 98, 110
competency, 13, 187, 189
Con Davis, Robert, 179, 181, 183, 208
conceptual apparatus, 4, 26, 81, 93, 100, 118, 151, 159, 182
consent, 12, 15, 53, 78, 106, 117, 125, 134, 189, 206, 233–237, 262; as rhetorical choice, 7, 27, 104, 126, 135, 146–147, 182, 201, 206, 222, 234–235
constellating process, 190
constitutive power of language, 15
convention, 9, 17, 38, 47, 56, 63–66, 74, 102, 107, 169, 170, 181, 185, 194–199, 201, 204, 212–213, 217, 237
conversion, dynamic of, 44–46, 50–51, 58, 66–67, 84, 91, 113, 150–153, 207, 232–233, 245–246; as enactment, 183–185
Cooper, Anderson, 4, 260
Cooper, Marilyn, 202
Corbett, Edward P.J., 5, 43, 152
Coughter, Philip, 127, 253
credibility, 4, 7–8, 16, 21, 27, 50, 59, 76, 78, 107, 137, 139, 142, 147, 162, 185, 234–235, 245
cultural attitudes, 17, 107
cultural scripts, 15, 102, 179, 181
culture and interpretation, 12–15, 56–57; cultural conditioning, 16, 125–125, 135, 192; cultural ideologies, 13, 63, 66–67, 91–92, 178; cultural positionality, 183–184; cultural preference, 23, 53, 139, 155, 238; cultural training, 14, 109, 116, 133, 146, 151, 155–156, 181–182, 213–216

debate, 20–22, 29, 85, 139, 144, 236, 244
deception, 7, 85, 152, 236
decorum, 95–98
Delahunt, Rep. William, 36, 37, 38, 248
Delay, Rep. Tom, 34, 49, 248, 249
deliberation, 10, 20, 22, 34–38, 44–46, 72, 96, 146, 189, 201
democratic aesthetic, 5–6, 10, 67–68, 74, 116–117, 125–126, 185–186, 238–239, 243–246
democratic inquiry, 13, 21–22, 40, 48, 73, 190, 245
dependency, 218, 237
Descartes, René, 147
DeVitt, Amy, 204
Dews, Peter, 245
differentiation, 34

Index 277

discursive conditions of existence, 76
discursive networks, 16
discursive protocol, 43, 52, 63
Docherty, Thomas, 5, 6, 249
doublespeak, 29
due deliberation, 37, 38, 72
Durham, Scott, 7, 29, 30, 31; *Phantom Communities*, 7
dynamic of time, 44

eloquence (coherence), 11, 57, 76–77, 97, 115–116, 213, 224, 236–238
empiricism, 34, 35, 57, 75, 238
Enlightenment, 53, 143, 182, 249
enthymeme, 241–244
epistemology, 11, 22, 66, 167, 184
Estrada, Richard, 28, 248
ethos, theories of, 146–153; antecedent, 182; etymology of, 227, 228, 242
explanatory narrative, 58–59, 67–68, 109, 184–185, 192, 198, 208
expulsion, 8, 9, 17, 29, 30, 63, 74, 93, 108, 131–132, 139, 181, 188, 222, 231, 234

Farrakhan, Louis, 219, 220, 221, 222, 225, 262
Fehrnstrom, Eric, 148
Felman, Shoshona, 235
feminism, 14, 18, 21, 99, 118, 122, 235
Ferraro, Geraldine, 161, 256
fittingness, 18, 76–77, 100–101, 107, 131
Fleckenstein, Kristie, 14, 251
Foss, Sonja K., 190, 259
Fox News, 165–166, 207, 225, 256–257, 262
framed language, 198
Frank, Rep. Barney, 35, 248

gaffe, 8, 145, 161
Garner, Eugene, 150
genre, theories of, 190–192, 198–199
Gergen, David, 211, 260
Goldberg, Lucianne, 130
Goldberg, Whoopi, 110, 252
gossip, 104, 105, 117–122, 124, 126, 133
Gottfried, Gilbert, 110, 252
Grand Jury, 59, 65, 75, 79, 103, 249
Gross, David S., 179, 181, 183, 208
Grosz, Elizabeth, 44, 157
Gunn, Joshua, 123, 124, 224, 229

Habermas, Jürgen, 35
Habermasian, 56
habits of interpretation, 14, 92, 199, 215, 227–229
Hall, Fawn, 114
Hall, Stuart, 56
Hannity, Sean, 167, 225, 257, 262
Hauser, Gerard A., 51, 146, 152, 188–189, 227
haunt, haunted by, 227–232
Hecht, Michael L., 181
Heidegger, Martin, 146, 149, 242
Hesford, Wendy, 18, 102, 105, 117, 122, 135
historical past, 24, 42
Hobbes, Thomas, 35
Hollings, Ernest, 72
House Judiciary Committee, 20, 33, 49, 65, 119, 247, 248, 249
House Resolution 611, 40, 247
Hutchinson, Rep. Asa, 49, 249
Hyde, Michael, 146, 156, 159, 228, 242
Hyde, Rep. Henry, 36, 43

identification, 11, 18, 40, 45–46, 57–59, 88–93, 101–102,

116–117, 127–135, 241–246; and paideia, 150–153
imagined communities, 157–158
impeachment, of Bill Clinton, 20–21,23–27, 32–38, 41–42, 49–50, 54–67, 68–74, 78–82, 103–107, 247, 248, 249, 250, 252; Impeachment articles, 50; October meetings, 33–37
inconstancy, 12, 22, 53, 56, 59
indeterminacy, 10, 239
inference, 108–112, 120, 205–206, 217–218, 227, 232; and enthymemes, 242–245; as linkage, 240–241; as reference, 235,
Inglis, Rep. Bob, 27, 247
intention, 34, 47, 54, 198–199, 222, 262
interpellation, 125–126, 245
intertextual dynamic, 9, 14–17, 94–95, 172, 183–186, 198–199, 229, 232–233
intimate public sphere, 201, 205–206
Iran-Contra Affair, 114
Isocrates, 216, 243

Jacobson, Gary, 33
Jamieson, Kathleen Hall, 190–197, 201, 204
jeremiad, 230
Jones, John M., 202
Jordan, Barbara, 193–195, 259
justice, 7, 26, 28, 33, 39, 40, 55, 98, 178, 210, 213, 219, 230

kairos, 105–106, 109, 112, 117, 205, 213, 244
Kant, Immanuel, 50, 235–239, 243
Kendall, David, 71
King, Larry, 121, 129, 253
Kristol, William, 28, 248

Lanham, Richard, 58
law, rule of, 32–33, 49–50
Leff, Michael, 96, 97, 129, 131
legal language, 40, 45
Lewinsky, Monica, media portraits, 104–108, 119–123, 252, 253
Lewinsky-Tripp Tapes, 119–124, 253
Lieberman, Sen. Joseph, 82, 94, 251
linkage, 42, 105, 132–135, 155, 196–197, 205, 227–229, 241, 244–246
Locke, Alain, 181
Loewe, Drew, 135, 193, 195
logocentrism, 63
Lucaites, John Louis, 76
Lugar, Sen. Richard, 25, 247
Lyotard, Jean-François, 5, 198, 240, 241, 242, 245, 246

Magna Carta, 42
Manolescu, Beth Innocenti, 95, 271
materialism, 13–18, 50–51, 133; and judging substance, 42–46, 48–49, 98–99, 113–116; and mattering, 107, 118, 125–126, 131–134, 183–186; as cognitive/somatic response, 116; as fleeting, 126; material effects, 221–222, 228; materiality of the sign, 100–101
McCain, Sen. John, 3, 30, 140, 144, 248, 261
McConnell, Sen. Mitch, 25, 247
McDaniel, James P., 51
McHugh, Kathleen, 185
mediation, 31, 95, 139, 178, 187–189, 198, 205–207, 242
Miller, Susan, 14, 138, 151, 155, 172, 198, 256
mimesis, 24–26, 30–35, 62, 91–92, 242; theory of correspon-

dences, 37; as visual metaphor, 26
mode of delivery, 22, 28, 106, 107, 139, 140, 178, 188, 207
models: analytical, 17
modes of expression, 27, 47, 204, 228
moral character, 9, 155, 159
Moran, James, 72
Moyers, Bill, 209, 220, 260
Moynihan, Sen. Daniel Patrick, 82, 94

NAACP, 209, 212, 216, 260, 261
Nation of Islam, 219
National Press Club, 209– 210, 218–222, 260, 261
nationalism, 4, 74, 155, 186
negotiation, 14, 94, 111–112, 160, 180, 183, 188,–189, 242–244
Noah, Timothy, 61, 249
North, Oliver, 114

Obama, Barack, 7, 18, 28; and ethos, 177–178, 186; and genre, 192, 199–201, 202–204; charisma, 148–149; media portraits, 174–176, speech on race, 173, 200; Wright expulsion, 222–223, 230–233
obstruction of justice, 17, 20–23, 40, 69
omission, 24, 80, 81, 172
On Bullshit (Harry Frankfurt), 3
opposition, 21, 25, 177, 257
order, 56
Osborne, Peter, 238– 239, 272
Owens, Rev. Terri, 169

paideia, 151, 153, 164, 182, 184
Panagia, Davide, 14, 26, 31, 35, 48
participation, 9–10, 59, 77, 101–103, 124–126, 144, 155,

164–165, 168–169, 181–186, 241–246
Paul, Ron, 28, 248
pedagogies of emotion, 99, 151
Perelman, Chaim, 235, 272
perjury, 17, 20–24, 32, 39, 46, 60, 65, 69, 70
Phaedrus (Plato), 85–88, 90–93, 101, 251
piety, 83, 97, 129
Pitts, Leonard Jr., 106, 252
plain speech, 6, 10
Plato, Platonism, 27–31, 62–63, 85–88, 93, 108, 152
political discourse, 3, 5, 21, 42, 98, 108, 237
politics of expulsion, 8– 9, 17, 29– 30, 63, 74, 93, 108, 131–132, 139, 181, 188, 222, 231, 234
positivism, 4, 17, 25–32, 51–59, 77–85, 89–93, 101–103, 242–243; and binary logic, 13, 18, 118; and connective logic, 198; and ethos, 147, 167–168, 175; and genre, 191–192
postmodernism, 7, 15, 22, 32, 51, 73, 95, 235, 237
pragmatism, 10–12, 51–53, 59, 67, 152–153, 228
pretense, 9, 13, 21–22, 31–33, 110
profitability, 53–54
propriety, 18, 40, 76, 77, 83, 94–109, 112–, 116–117, 125–133, 191, 245
purposeful action, 67

Ramage, John D., 147
Rankin, Elizabeth, 11
Rawlsian, 56
Readings, Bill, 9, 237, 241
realism, 22–27, 34
re-cognition, 26
Redfield, Marc, 158
referential action, 6, 240

relativism, 97
remorse, 79, 85, 87–92, 103
representational action, 5, 9, 14, 30, 88, 144, 153, 170, 193, 231; representational indeterminacy, 16, 30; representational normativity, 57
responsible testimony, 62
retrospect, 45
rhetorical competence, 225–227
Ribeau, Sidney, 181
ridicule, 6, 8, 17, 111, 119, 145, 200
Riley, Denise, 93
Robinson, Eugene, 226, 262
Roeper, Richard, 120–122, 252, 253
Rogoff, Irit, 118, 126
Romney, Mitt, 28, 141, 142, 145, 148, 150, 154, 255–256
Rosteck, Thomas, 96–97, 129, 131
Rowland, Robert C., 202

Sawyer, Diane, 69, 70, 104, 250
scopic paradigm, 35, 53
Scott, Rev. Robert, 230
Senate Hearings on the Articles of Impeachment, 25
sexism, 109, 112–116, 123–126
signification, 14, 164, 215, 239, 245
sign-vehicles, 238, 246
simulacra, 7–8, 31–33
Sister Souljah moment, 222–223, 261
Smith, Craig R., 152
sociability, 12, 145, 196
social exigence, 198
social order, 25, 29, 151
Socrates, 85–88, 92, 116, 133
speech failures, 17, 235
spin, 25–26, 41
Spivak, Gayatri, 66, 171, 178, 245
Starr Report, 68–71, 119

Starr, Kenneth, 34, 68–72, 75–79, 104, 119, 130, 250, 251
Stob, Paul, 97
storytelling, 4, 10
straight speech, 3–4, 9, 25–30, 35, 39, 41–42, 78, 176
structural order, 26, 157, 182
style: as attitude, 17, 47–48, 53–54, 107, 113, 122, 167–168, 229; composition studies, 11–12, 51–53, 192–193; and truth, 4–7, 15–18, 22–39, 61–66, 78–79, 243–245; democratic, 48, 51–54, 196–197; emotional receptivity, 10, 14, 16, 82–82, 94–96, 98–101, 112, 133–134, 143, 146–153, 183–185, 242–246; ethics, 96–97; failure, 13, 17, 68, 72, 80–81, 99, 103, 115–117, 128–129, 134, 195, 229, 235; and reason, rationalism, 48, 51–54, 58, 66, 70, 242–244; hierarchical values, 26, 42–43, 53–54, 58–59, 118–119, 188, 205–208, 230–233, 239–240; idiosyncratic, 5, 43–45, 55, 62, 98; judging significance, 6–7, 22, 46–49, 63–64, 66–68, 76, 112–113, 125–125, 131–132, 145–146, 214–215; norms and style, 17–18, 57, 63, 73–74, 170–173, 177–178, 182–185, 205–208, 232–233; racial identity, 19, 162–164, 169–173, 179–181, 213–217; social purpose, 12–13, 51–54, 106–107, 146–148, 179–182, 189–190, 230–231; structural anonymity, 22, 163, 167–168, 177–182, 190–193, 213; vacillating dynamic, 239; Western rhetorical definitions, 4–7, 43, 47–49, 58–59, 234, 236–237; Western

rhetorical traditions, 5, 10–13, 43, 95–98, 154–156, 242–244
stylistic protocol, 6, 9, 59, 138, 154, 164
substitution, logic of, 24–26, 40, 72

techne, 16, 157
textuality, 87–88, 138–139, 155–156, 158, 177–178, 187–188; AAVE alternatives, 214–216; as structural anonymity, 32, 163, 167–168, 177–182, 190–193, 213; as transactional dynamic, 137–138
The New Negro (Locke), 181
Thompson, Roger, 154
Tosh, Daniel, 110–111, 115, 252
translation, 23, 30–31, 36, 40, 43–49, 72, 135
transparency, 3, 50, 56, 58, 118, 237
Trinity Church, 165, 171, 200, 210
Tripp, Linda: "I am You" speech, 127–129; media portraits, 75–76, 104–105, 119–122, 129; will to matter, 130–131

true feeling, 83–85, 90–94, 145
trust: in texts, 138, 155–156, 178, 182–184, 198–199, 208; rhetorical, 188–189, 217, 227–228, 231–233

vagueness, 8, 43, 164
value-neutrality, 17
voice of the occasion, 86, 107

Walker, Jeffrey, 242–243
Warner, Michael, 172, 179, 213
Watts, Eric King, 181
Waxman, Rep. Henry, 82
Whitman, Christine Todd, 82, 251
Wisenberg, Deputy Independent Counsel Sol, 59, 79
Worsham, Lynn, 14, 18, 99, 100, 112, 113, 151
Wright, Rev. Jeremiah, 7, 18, 139; and jeremiad, 230–231; media portraits, 167, 169–172, 210–213, 218–219, 226; Obama expulsion, 222–223; sermons, 165–166; speeches, national press club, NAACP, 210, 212, 216–217, 220–221

About the Author

Eve Wiederhold received her PhD in English (Language, Literacy, and Rhetoric) from the University of Illinois at Chicago. She has taught courses in rhetoric and composition studies, literary theory, and feminist rhetorical theory at George Mason University, University of North Carolina at Greensboro, and East Carolina University. Her articles have appeared in *JAC, Rhetoric Review*, and *The Raymond Carver Review*, as well as several edited collections.

www.ingramcontent.com/pod-product-compliance
Lightning Source LLC
Chambersburg PA
CBHW030528230426
43665CB00010B/808